TAGORE'S THOUGHT ON RURAL RECONSTRUCTION AND ROLE OF VILLAGE DEVELOPMENT SOCIETIES

TAGORE'S THOUGHT ON RURAL RECONSTRUCTION AND ROLE OF VILLAGE DEVELOPMENT SOCIETIES

NITYANANDA ROY

ABHIJEET PUBLICATIONS
DELHI 110094

ABHIJEET PUBLICATIONS
2/46 Tukhmeerpur Extension
Delhi 110094
Phones: 011-22960492, 65698474
e-mail: abhijeetpublication@gmail.com
abhijeet_singh1@indiatimes.com

TAGORE'S THOUGHT ON RURAL RECONSTRUCTION AND ROLE OF VILLAGE DEVELOPMENT SOCIETIES

First Published 2008

ISBN 978-81-89886-64-6

PRINTED IN INDIA

Published by J.K. Singh for Abhijeet Publications, Delhi 110094, Lasertypeset by Gaurav Graphics, Delhi and Printed as Himanshu Printers, Delhi.

Dedicated to

The Villagers

Acknowledgements

I am delighted to express my deepest sense of gratitude and respect to my Supervisor Prof. Sasanka Sekhar Pal, former Head of Palli Charcha Kendra, Sriniketan, for his valuable guidance, supervision, suggestions, constructive criticism, mental support throughout the course of my study and preparation of the book. Without his firm yet friendly pressure I would have never perhaps completed my study.

I must render my grateful thanks and respect also to the Vice-Chancellor, Visva-Bharati and the Principal, Palli Samgathan Vibhaga (PSV), Sriniketan, for their inspiration and encouragement.

I must also hereby record my acknowledgement of debt to the following: Head and the faculty and non-teaching staff of Palli Charcha Kendra for their cooperation and valuable help. Sincerest thanks are also due to the present leading staff and former principal and workers of PSV for their valuable comments and practical help during my investigations.

I owe a very special debt of gratitude to some eminent personalities for their valuable criticism and suggestions. To my profound sorrow I learnt that some of these personalities have passed away. Especially, I must mention the name of one of the most dedicated social workers of our country, the late Pannalal Dasgupta, who often times spared some of his valuable moments for my humble self. May their souls rest in peace. I do not know how to express my gratitude to Prof. Jiban Banerjee, formerly of the English Dept., Viswa Bharati who very kindly had gone through the script, enriched the work by addition, alteration and suggestions.

My indebtedness in not less due to the leaders of villages and to villagers themselves, to the village Development Societies, around Sriniketan for their cooperation during data collection.

My knowledge was much enriched by my talks with the elderly persons of some villages about the past activities of Sriniketan and village organisations.

Library facilities were kindly extended to me by the staff of the various libraries of Visva-Bharati to whom I am thankful.

Lastly, I express my gratitude to my parents, wife, brothers and other well wishers for their psychological support. With out their cooperation, it would not have been possible to complete my work.

NITYANANDA ROY

Contents

1

Introduction

Some humble efforts have been made here to bring home the fact interalia, that it was Rabindranath Tagore in India who set on a crusade against superstitions, conventions and against following self-demeaning methods of running the village administration and self-destructure life, dominated by landlords, money lenders and self-styled leaders belonging to slightly rich farmer class. Above all, it was Tagore who made pioneering work to organise, utilise and exploit village resources and potentials so that villages may become socio-economically self-reliant through societies based on co-operative efforts of the people themselves without caring for meagre governmental aid. From the darkness of ignorance to the lighted world of knowledge, health and education—that was Tagore's vision of a resurgent India. Illiteracy, ill health, poverty-stricken life were eating into the vitals of our rural polity. There were no organisations worth their name, which could provide basic education, elementary medical treatment and hygienic living. In all these aspects, Tagore's contribution is rich. True, he was influenced by Rousseau, Emerson, Gandhi etc. and later on inspired by Russian experiment.[1] Mahatma Gandhi through his lifelong experience wanted to derive self-reliance through self-help process with the utilisation of village resources. Rabindranath also in his early age during the supervision of zamindari of Silaidah gained experience in this regard. Tagore came down from the majesty of poet-laureateship and philosophical heights and desired like Shelley, in a sense, to improve the condition of human existence. Uma Dasgupta and Hiranmoy Banerjee's books (Dasgupta's *Santiniketan and Sriniketan*, Visva-Bharati, Calcutta 1983 and Banerjee's book named *'Experiments in Rural Reconstruction'*, Visva-Bharati, Calcutta 1966) though perceptively analysed the village development schemes of Tagore, interalia, suffer from some shortcomings. They do not take into account the modern developments for comparison. As far as my knowledge goes, there is no comprehensive work on this aspect the think-tank of our social prophet, except a few stray essays and Pulin Behari Sen edited Bengali book, *Palliprakriti* that deals mostly with the love of Tagore for natural charms *sorrows and sufferings of the people* of the countryside, *Rabindranath Tagore on Rural Reconstruction and Community Development in India* by Sudhir Sen (Visva-Bharati, Calcutta 1943 enlarged edition, 1991) which no doubt treat some aspects of my present study ably, but it does not actually touch the poets noble idea in those days in regard to village reconstruction through village development societies on the basis of co-operative efforts of the self-dependent villagers themselves.

As a matter of fact, this is the main thrust of my book as the title itself signifies. During the process of my discussions that would lead to the main proposition, the following aspects have also come under my focus: reviewing of available literature, historical significance of the poet's stay at Silaidah, detailed discussion on the role of Sriniketan, organising village development societies and its contribution as providing experimental grounds for reconstruction and extension programmes analysis of available data with the help of tables. In the end I have drawn a conclusion by pointing out Tagore's role as pioneer in innovating various means through which village development programmes could be carried out. Limitations by the way, have also been pointed out. In fact, the modern Panchayat system should be indebted to Tagore who for the first time perhaps thought of and worked out the process through which the villagers themselves can solve their local problems and petty disputes amicably settled and, also, they can contribute to the all-round development of their village. Indeed, Tagore's idea of forming village development societies* (VDS) are still relevant in modern rural reconstruction programmes.

Now, we have elaborated how Tagore tried to revolutionise the village socio-economic scenario, the means he adopted to make the villages self-reliant, democratic and clean. As Nobel Laureate Amartya Sen stressed: capability is the main spring of progress and that is what Tagore also believed in. Rabindranath's childhood was spent inside the house under the strict vigilance of the family servants. As he could not go outside the young Rabi felt a deep longing for the outside world—the mystery, the wonders, the infinite possibilities of this vast world waiting to be discovered and exploited a romantic yearning in him (reference to the poem ‘Nirjharer Swapna Bhanga') as if through "the magic casement" of his wonderstruck mind he looked for to the fairy lands to roam. The world of nature disturbed him with all its ecstacy and agony. From his *"Jivansmriti"* we came to know that once he accompanied his father, Debendranath Tagore, during his trip to the Himalayas and on another occasion when he got the opportunity to go outside Calcutta. Then he heaved a sigh of relief being far from the madding crowd and the dust and din of city life. He was then and just in his early teens. It was at Panihati when he took shelter for saving him from, a fatal disease Dengu fever which was raging in Calcutta then.

His father, Maharshi Devendranath, was one of the leaders of the Brahma Samaj. He spent most of his times with religious activities. So he could not pay attention to family life and could hardly spare time for supervising his estate. He decided to send one of his sons to look after his estate. He bestowed responsibility on his youngest son Rabindranath, whose childhood was spent inside the four walls of his house. The young romantic was an ardent lover of nature on whose many splendoured appeals he composed hundred of poems. But this was just one of the

---

* Henceforth village development society/societies are called in brief VDS.

aspects of his mental make-up. In his father's estate he got an opportunity to mix with the people of rural Bengal. His sensitive mind immediately felt sympathy for the sorrows and sufferings of the common people and he vowed to solve their problems. A member of a highly aristocratic family, he came down from the height of elitism to the grass root levels. A great poet of international fame, a 'Janma Romantic' (a born-Romantic), as he himself says, came to stay with the backward rural people. His readings of Rousseau and Emerson and his personal knowledge of Russian experiments made him an Indian pioneer in rural reconstruction programmes.

After gaining a thorough knowledge of the problems of the villages, he began to work tirelessly for his tenants in his estate first. His aspiration was to reconstruct the Indian villages through proper utilisation of the neglected village resources and potentials based on co-operative principles. He realised that Indian villages had the unused capabilities to become self-reliant. Standing on their own feet, through the utilisation of the village resource.[2] We all know that there are many village resources as well as human resources which are unutilised due to lack of proper planning. In every villages there are few ponds that should be utilised for fish culture and irrigation side by side rain harvesting should be followed. There are unutilised lands where many crops and plants might be grown by the use of modern science and technology, which Tagore tried to follow at Sriniketan. Emphasis should be laid on the collection of minor forest produce for the improvement of village economy. Skilled, trained and experienced human resources should be utilised for the betterment of the village in all aspects. In this way, Agriculture, Animal Husbandry, Rural Industry would be developed along with Health and Education through the proper utilising of human resources and medical science. With due course it would be changed and villages would almost be self-reliant in economic matters only based on their resources. Indian villagers enjoyed their economic and cultural prosperity in the past. Later on these villages lived in miserable condition, ruthlessly exploited during British period. They were depending on other's charity. He wrote in a mood of frustration (ref. *Swadeshi Samaj*): য়ুরোপের মত আমাদের জনসমূহ নাগরিক নয় - চিরদিনই চীনের মতো ভারতবর্ষ পল্লী প্রধান। নাগরিক চিত্ত বৃত্তি নিয়ে ইংরেজ আমাদের সেই ঘনিষ্ঠ পল্লীজীবনের গ্রন্থি কেটে দিয়েছে[1] (Our people are not urban citizens like those in Europe. Always, India is a village-oriented country like China. With their urban mentality, the British have cut off our intimate ties with rural life). So he endeavoured to bring back self-sufficiency among villagers through utilising their own strength thereby enriching its lifestyle. This can be done by co-operative methods and proper utilisation of village resources. He noted down his ideas in an article, "*Swadeshi Samaj*. He realised it would not be possible to remove the sufferings of the villagers only by government help unless villagers could help themselves. So he emphasised to enrich the quality of a complete human being—a total man. At first he chalked out a plan and implemented that for rural upliftment. This was first practised in his zamindari estate. When most of the political leaders gave emphasis on the struggle for freedom without doing any constructive work in rural areas, Rabindranath emphasised on taking up rural reconstruction programmes. In fact, Tagore with his limited resources earmarked a small area and tried to implement his programmes in such a way that it could become a model to follow by whole India. On this occasion he said:

"আমি যদি কেবল দুটি-তিনটি গ্রামকেও মুক্তি দিতে পারি, অজ্ঞতা অক্ষমতার বন্ধন থেকে, তবে সেখানেই সমগ্র ভারতের একটি আদর্শ তৈরী হবে[2]" (If I can set free only two or three villages from ignorance and incapacity then it will. hold up an ideal symbolic centre for whole of India).

He endeavoured to make self-reliant village in his zamindari estate. He implemented various programmes on health, education and economy to develop the socio-economic structure of the villages. Village potentials should be tapped and that was his main intention. Besides this, he emphasised on village organisation where all village problems would be solved by the villagers themselves. He desired to fulfil the needs of villagers by utilising village resources through the unity of the villagers, specially the rural youth. He also tried to enrich the quality of leadership among the rural youth so that they could organise the available potentials of the villagers. He established 'Brati' organisation in his zamindari estate. Side by side, he had taken different rural reconstruction programmes in the surrounding villages of 'Santiniketan Ashrama' which had been established by his father Maharshi Devendranath Tagore. After a few years with the same objectives he established a separate institution named 'Sriniketan', later on named as Palli Samgathana Vibhaga (PSV)* as a model of rural reconstruction centre for the whole country. Inspired by the successful implementation of his programmes at the surrounding villages of Sriniketan, he sent some of his dedicated trained workers from PSV to his zamindari estate where he first started his work to implement the said programmes. He also established an institution named PSV in that area. It is known to all that during his lifetime the activities of Sriniketan had been successfully carried on in the surrounding villages. The significance of practical idealism was realised with rare earnestness : "এটা খুব করে বুঝেছি, আমাদের সবচেয়ে বড়ো কাজ শ্রীনিকেতনে। সমস্ত দেশকে কী করে বাঁচাতে হবে ঐখানে ছোটো আকারে নিষ্পত্তি করা আমাদের ব্রত"[3] (I have thoroughly realised that our greatest ideal could only be realised at Sriniketan. Our task would therefore be to bring into reality at that very place even if in a small scale, our projects for saving the country).

Some eminent social workers including L.K. Elmhirst and Kalimohan Ghosh dedicated themselves for the successful implementation of Tagore's rural reconstruction programmes at Sriniketan. They devoted themselves to reconstruct the surrounding villages of Sriniketan to make the villagers self-sufficient through proper co-operation and utilisation of village resources. Tagore outlined the objectives of Sriniketan thus : 'To bring back life in its completeness into the villages making them self-reliant and self-respectful, acquainted with the cultural traditions of their own country, and competent to make an efficient use of the modern resources for the improvement of their physical, intellectual and economic conditions."[4] He adopted some strategies at Sriniketan for improving of Sanitation and village health, extension of education, etc. He put emphasis on the

* Henceforth Palli Samgathan Vibhaga referred to in brief as PSV.

development of agriculture and rural industry for a self-reliant economy. Besides this, he gave much importance to the potentialities of future leadership of the village. His workers organised "Brati organisation" to train up young boys and girls for reconstructing the villages at all levels. To enrich the quality of leadership among rural youth, he instructed social workers to help the villagers in such a way that they could help themselves in near future. He directed his followers to establish various organisations through cooperative efforts of the villagers and thus solve some of the village problems. Under his guidance and with the help of social workers various co-operative organisation and Village Development Societies were formed at that time through the united efforts of the villagers. Tagore had a vision that only such type of organisations where villagers would assemble and participate to solve the socio-economic and all other problems of the villagers and thereby reconstruct the stagnant, decaying socio-economy of the village. In his own words: "আমি বলেছি সমাজের ভিতর থেকে সমাজের শক্তিকে জাগাতে হবে, পরস্পর সকলের সমবেত চেষ্টা-দ্বারা শক্তি লাভ করবে। এ সম্বন্ধে চেষ্টাও করেছি পল্লী সমিতি বলে সমিতি গড়ে তুলেছি।[5]" (I have said that strength of the society should be aroused from within the society itself. I have also tried to instil the idea that with mutual co-operation this strength can be gained. I have also founded a village society). As an experiment Tagore had taken various constructive programmes through Village Development Societies so that they could be a model for the whole India.

According to Tagore's idea of rural reconstruction, PSV, Visva-Bharati has implementing various programmes through VDS in the surrounding villages of Sriniketan.

The poet wanted that these reconstructive programmes would create self-confidence among the villagers and they would be able to free themselves from the dependence of the British government. Since then (1922), PSV has been working hard to give a concrete shape to the ideal of Gurudev. During (1995-96) there are thirty-two PSV affiliated VDS in forty-six villages.

Now our country has achieved independence. But due

to long time dependence and servitude our society and economy remained poor and backward. It is not possible for our government to meet all the needs of the villagers. True, different developmental programmes are being formulated and to some extent implemented in villages by our government and Panchayats. But it is observed that neither the villagers participate in these developmental activities nor the human or village resources are properly utilised through co-operative efforts of the villagers for achieving self-reliant economy. This could only be done if there were VDS in every village. Tagore believed that all village problems could be solved through united efforts of the villagers. Modern day economists agree with Tagore's idea that VDS can solve the various village problems through joint efforts of the villagers. The government and non-government organisations (NGOs) etc also realise that only village organisations or societies can motivate the villagers to develop our rural society and economy. In fact, Panchayat system at present owes its inception to Tagore's idea that villagers would sit together and discuss the village problems and would try to solve petty disputes for peace and welfare of the villages. VDS have an active role to play solving all sorts of problems of the village. Villagers are being certainly benefited by such type of organisations. The relevance of Tagore's ideals on rural reconstruction even in this fast changing socio-economic scenario is obvious. If we could truly translate Tagore's rural reconstruction ideas in this small area through these VDS, Sriniketan would be a model for the whole of India. So it will be interesting to examine the role of VDS for solving different rural problems by implementing Tagore's ideas. We know Rabindranath Tagore had established Sriniketan as the ideal centre for rural reconstruction. It is known that Sriniketan activities had been performed in a better manner than those of his zamindari estate. He believed that the Indian villages were to be developed in all its aspects, i.e. its health, culture, education, economy and society. His remarks on education are worth quoting "সকল দেশেই শিক্ষার সঙ্গে দেশের সর্বাঙ্গীন জীবনযাত্রার যোগ আছে। আমাদের দেশে কেবলমাত্র কেরানিগিরি ওকালতি ডাক্তারি ডেপুটিগিরি দারোগাগিরি মুন্সেফি প্রভৃতি ভদ্রসমাজে প্রচলিত কয়েকটি ব্যবসায়ের সঙ্গেই আমাদের আধুনিক শিক্ষার

প্রত্যক্ষ যোগ যেখানে চাষ হইতেছে, কলুর ঘানি ও কুমারের চাক ঘুরিতেছে, সেখানে এ শিক্ষার কোনো স্পর্শও পৌঁছায় নাই। .... ভারতবর্ষে যদি সত্য বিদ্যালয় স্থাপিত হয় তবে গোড়া হইতেই সেই বিদ্যালয় তাহার অর্থশাস্ত্র, তাহার কৃষিতত্ত্ব, তাহার স্বাস্থ্যবিদ্যা, তাহার সমস্ত ব্যবহারিক বিজ্ঞানকে আপন প্রতিষ্ঠা-স্থানের চর্তুদিকবর্তী পল্লীর মধ্যে প্রয়োগ করিয়া দেশের জীবনযাত্রার কেন্দ্রস্থান অধিকার করিবে"[6] (In every nation, education is ultimately associated with the life of the people. But for us modern education is relevant only to turning out clerks, lawyers, doctors, magistrates, munshiffs and policemen - the new favourite professions of the gentlefolk. This education has not reached the farmer, the oil grinder, nor the potters .... if ever a truly Indian school is established it must from the beginning implement its acquired knowledge of economics of agriculture, health, and all other every day sciences in the surrounding villages). He thus established PSV (Institute of rural reconstruction) in 1922 within the broad framework of his educational philosophy. He started his work around Visva-Bharati, which was established in 1918 and registered in 1921. He wanted total improvement of villagers, improving agriculture, education, health and social living and to make them aware of themselves so as to improve the quality of life. After independence, government of India declared Visva-Bharati as a Central University in 1951.

Some selected villages around Sriniketan have come under my study, the role of VDS affiliated to PSV has been discussed. It would be interesting to study: (1) how at present the VDS are playing an important role to solve the socio-economic, education and health problems of the villages. (2) in what way these societies are useful to give leadership and to motivate the villagers so that they can fruitfully utilise the village resources to make themselves self-reliant according to Tagore's idea.

Rabindranath noted that the resources within the village were being neglected and villagers were not able to develop themselves by utilising village resources for the lack of proper organisation and confidence among themselves. So he tried to help them in such a manner that they could help themselves in future. He had endeavoured only to reconstruct the village through the co-operative efforts of villagers by utilising village resources. He hammered the point that outside charity could not help to improve the socio-economic condition of the villagers permanently.

The term 'Reconstruction' is a kind of development process that will revitalise the neglected or unutilised rural resources and potentials. That is why the role of VDS in the surrounding villages of Sriniketan has been emphasised.

Here it may be pointed out that PSV affiliated some village organisations, which are known as VDS (society, in this context means—an organisation of people formed on the basis of common aims, beliefs, interest or occupation). So it is perhaps obvious that these VDS are the organisation of village people formed by themselves. This is an organisation of the village where all classes of village folk can assemble and participate in various activities of common interest unitedly.

The title of my book is : *"Tagore's Thought on Rural Reconstruction and Role of Village Development Societies"*. Objectives of the research work are: (1) in what way VDS take part in rural reconstruction programmes; (2) what are the problems of VDS in implementing Tagore's thought; (3) how Tagore's thoughts on rural reconstruction can be effective to develop our rural society and economy.

METHODS APPLIED

Coverage : The object of my research is to study the role of PSV affiliated VDS in regard to the implementation of Tagore's ideas on rural reconstruction in the contemporary socio-economic condition. His means of making villages Self-reliant through the co-operative efforts of villagers have also been discussed. Various aspects of rural reconstruction programmes as implemented by the PSV affiliated VDS have been highlighted. Eleven VDS have been selected purposely for an in depth study. These eleven VDS have been selected in such a manner that they could represent all the villages affiliated by PSV. The representation of different castes and the socio-economic levels of the villagers living in these villages, have been kept in mind while selecting villages. One representative VDS has been selected through random sampling from those villages where

Sriniketan had the working grounds in the past, but is not now. In all twelve VDS have been selected as my study area. From interviews with leaders of the VDS we have tried to assess their role in rural reconstruction. Discussions were held with the people of Rabindra era and their opinions have been noted down. The opinion of various learned persons have also been taken into account and books and journals consulted.

The Period Covered : From the time of the foundation of Sriniketan upto 1995-96, different steps undertaken by PSV regarding rural reconstruction activities have been discussed and analysed. This analysis is divided into three periods, i.e. from 1922 to 1941; from 1942 to 1950 and 1951 to 1995-96.

a) 1922 to 1941 : At this point of time the freedom movement was reaching its climax. The second world war broke out. Rabindranath in spite of facing many hurdles, planned the programme of self-reliance of the villagers and led the task of rural reconstruction swimming across a sea of troubles.

b) 1942 to 1950 : Rabindranath died in 1941. Due to lack of proper leadership and paucity of funds the activities of Sriniketan had to face a number of difficulties. There was also lack of suitable leaders and workers. No appreciable work was done but some how PSV continued its work.

c) 1951 to (1995-96) : During this period Visva-Bharati was declared a central university. The financial crisis was getting over. Many government development plans were being implemented in most of the villages of India. Although various government programmes, including Community development, were being carried on throughout the country, Panchayat Raj system is implemented. It would be interesting to study how Visva-Bharati has been continuing its rural reconstruction programme according to Tagore's ideology by maintaining its institutional identity.

Tools of data collection

a) Primary data : (1) Data are collected from the leading members of VDS and villagers through suitable structured schedule. Needless to say that observations of Tagore have been incorporated at relevant places. His books, letters, dairies and essays on the related subject have been consulted.

(2) 1 have noted the opinions of some experienced elderly people and have taken the valuable suggestions from various person's well versed in Tagorean ideas.

(3) Also the former staff of the PSV have been consulted.

(4) Different issues have been discussed quite at length with the present staff of PSV.

b) Secondary data : Secondary data like relevant remarks, comments, review, critiques of experts of the subject including those of Tagore quoted by others have been incorporated. The collected data have been analysed with tables and charts and final conclusion has been drawn based not only on various data but also on the basis of my investigation. An attempt has been made to suggest how the activities of development programmes could be more meaningful in order to change the quality of village life. I have laid emphasis on qualitative analysis as well as on databased one.

Limitations

(1) Data from all the VDS could not be collected, but the past activities of the selected VDS have been compared in-depths with the present ones i.e. the programmes during the Rabindra era and during post Tagorean period.

(2) The valuable *Visva-Bharati Annual Reports and Audited Accounts* of several years were not available, nevertheless the data available from some Annual Reports have been analysed.

(3) Many eminent persons who possessed better experience and knowledge on Tagore's rural reconstruction programme could not be consulted either due to their non-availability or over their death. However, conclusions have been drawn and suggestions incorporated based on the discussions

on and analyses of different programmes starting from Rabindranath to the present leadership of Sriniketan (PSV) and different aspects of VDS. It is hoped that an idea regarding the significance of Tagore's idea on rural reconstruction in our present society may be glimpsed from a discussions.

REFERENCES

1. Rabindranath Tagore: Patrabali; 15th November 1934; *Palliprakriti,* Visva-Bharati Granthan Vibhaga, Calcutta, Magh 1368 B.S., p. 196.
2. Rabindranath Tagore : Sriniketaner Itihas O Adharsha (Sriniketaner Karmider Sabhai Kathito), Bhadra 1346 B.S., *PallipmkriH,* Visva Bharati Granthan Vibhaga, Calcutta, Magh 1368 B.S., p. 104.
3. Rabindranath Tagore : A letter to Rathindranath Tagore, 21st November 1930, *Russiar Chithi,* Visva-Bharati Granthan Vibhaga, Calcutta, Vaisakh 1338 B.S., p. 156.
4. *Visva-Bharati Bulletin,* No. 11., 'Sriniketan, The Institute of Rural Reconstruction', December, 1928, p. l.
5. Rabindranath Tagore : Malaria (Antimalaria Societyte Kathito), 23rd February 1924. *Palliprakriti,* Visva Bharati Granthan Vibhaga, Calcutta, Magh 1368 B.S., p. 137.
6. Rabindranath Tagore: Visva-Bharati, (essay), Vaisakh 1326 B.S., *Rabindra Rachcnavali,* (Collected works) Volume 14, Visva-Bharati Granthan Vibhaga, Calcutta, Aswin 1398 B.S., p. 244.

2

Review of Literature

Though it has been stated in the introduction that no comprehensive work has so far been published in regard to Rabindranath's thoughts and efforts on and for the development of village society and on enriching the rural way of life, admittedly there are a few more publications which are worth mentioning for their in-depth presentation of certain basic aspects of Rabindranath's social thoughts.

Following is a brief survey of the literature and persons consulted for reinforcing the present study on Rabindranath's rural reconstruction programmes.

(1) Santiniketan and Sriniketan by Mrs Uma Dasgupta (Visva-Bharati, Calcutta 1983).

Although this book is small in size; we get a comprehensive picture of Rabindranath's idea of rural reconstruction from it. The author has described the process of development of Sriniketan, from the time of its establishment. She has discussed many aspects of rural reconstruction programmes as envisaged by Tagore, including Siksha Satra and Silpa Bhavana. Siksha Satra was established with a particular objective of providing leadership to the village children and this school once played an important part. But as the author has not thrown enough light on this matter, we can hardly know anything about the activities of VDS in the surrounding villages of Sriniketan from her discussion. In this book Mrs Dasgupta has dealt chronologically with the different activities from the time of the inception of Sriniketan. However, she has not discussed the change in perspectives of the activities at Santiniketan and Sriniketan after the death of the poet. However, she has given us an adequate idea about the rural upliftment programmes as implemented in and around Sriniketan.

(2) *Experiments in Rural Reconstruction* by Hiranmoy Banerjee, (Visva-Bharati, Calcutta 1966)

In this book the author has provided us with important information. In the chapter "Experiment of Sriniketan" the author has offered a background discussion on the establishment of Sriniketan after the Silaidah period and on the socio-economic condition of the villages. We have substantive idea about the rural economy from this book. The discussion on the 'Experiment at Sriniketan' may be very short but it supplied a lot of information. The work done in those villages of Sriniketan and names of the villages where Brati organisation was established are mentioned, but what role played by the young men in implementing rural reconstruction programmes have not been touched upon. We can hardly know anything about the role of the VDS either.

Even then one cannot ignore the fact that Hiranmoy Banerjee has discussed at length the chapter under discussion about the 'Experiment at Sriniketan' and socio-economic scenario of the village and also the aims and objectives of Sriniketan, specially during and after Tagore's life time.

(3) *Rabindranath Tagore on Rural Reconstruction and Community Development in India,* by Sudhir Sen, (Visva-Bharati, Calcutta 1943, Revised and enlarged edition 1991.)

Sudhir Sen's *"Rabindranath Tagore on Rural Reconstruction and Community Development of India"* is a very valuable book. Here the author has discussed in detail how Rabindranath's thought on villages first started and his essay *'Swadeshi Samaj'* points out how after his experiments in his estates in Silaidah and Patisar, Rabindranath became interested in rural reconstruction. He has further offered us information about the establishment of Sriniketan and the work done there. He has attributed the phrase 'key role' to the village welfare department, but the author hardly discusses about the various activities of VDS and Brati Organisation in the villages led by PSV.

Nevertheless, it has to be admitted that this particular work of Sudhir Sen is of supreme importance and it provides a lot of information about Rabindranath's idea on rural reconstruction and various aspects of Rural development.

(4) *Sriniketaner Godar Katha* (The early phase of Sriniketan) by Satyadas Chakraborty, (Subarnarekha, Calcutta 1985, 2nd edition 1399 B.S.)

This is an extremely important book in the field of research on Rabindranath as a leader of the thoughts on rural reconstruction. Chakraborty has discussed chronologically the different activities of Sriniketan from its early period. He has informed us about the different programmes, which were implemented in the surrounding villages of Sriniketan. He informed us about nineteen Brati organisations at that time, but he has not mentioned the name of the villages where these activities took place. He has not also referred to the evaluation of the activities of VDS in the surrounding villages of Sriniketan.

The book is small, but it surely at least gives a birds eye view about rural reconstruction activities at Sriniketan.

(5) *Rabindranather Palli Chinta* (Rabindranath's thoughts on Rural Society), by Sukumar Mallick (Nabapotra Prakashan, Calcutta 1989).

Sukumar Mallick has shed light on Rabindranath's ideas and experiments with rural development programmes. He has analysed this particular subject through different poems and songs. At that time Sriniketan played a leading role in conducting activities in the villages. He has also informed us about the activities of Brati Organisation, but we cannot know about the role of VDS from his work. We do not know in detail what kind of village organisations were active in the villages and what problems had been faced by these village organisations.

However in this book Rabindranath's thought on rural reconstruction are analysed earnestly.

(6) *Silaidah O Rabindranath* (Silaidah and Rabindranath) by Sachindranath Adhikary, (Jijnasa, Calcutta 1974)

In this book we get a graphic description of Rabindranath's activities in regard to rural upliftment during his Silaidah days. While working in Silaidah the poet thought of the scheme of Sriniketan. He first developed [4]Brati Organisation at Sriniketan among rural young boys and girls, subsequently, he established Brati Organisation at Silaidah. We also learn that the poet also launched a PSV also in his zamindari estate. But we hardly know anything about the activities of different village organisations. However, had the author make a comparative study of Rabindranath's activities in his zamindari estate and Sriniketan, we would have been got a better evaluations of Rabindranath's activities on rural reconstruction.

This book almost adequately gives an authentic idea about Tagore's rural reconstruction experiments at Silaidah, though it is silent on critical role that VDS had played.

(7) *Social thinking of Rabindranath Tagore,* by Sasadhar Sinha (Bombay (etc.) Asia Publishing House, 1962)

This is rather on in depth study about Tagore's social consciousness. It has covered almost all the aspects of the subject, but the most important chapters are on 'educational trinity' and 'Prospect and Retrospect'. The author has deliberated upon evolution of Santiniketan and Sriniketan. He has described the rural reconstruction activities during Tagore's lifetime, but he did not discuss in useful detail the village organisations, like VDS. He has also not discussed what sort of work these organisations did in the village.

(8) *Rabindranather Samaj Chinta* (Rabindranath's Social thought) by Subodh Chandra Pramanik (Satabdi Grantha Bhavana, Calcutta 1368 BS)

Subodh Chandra Pramanik's 'Rabindranath's Social Thought' is written from the angle of Rabindranath's concentration of different social factors. He has informed us about various problems and their possible solutions related to the establishment of Sriniketan. He has referred to Rabindranath's faith in young people, when he began his work of rural reconstruction. However, no mention is made of the role played by the VDS through the united efforts of the villagers.

True, from this book we can know a lot about Rabindranath's thoughts on social significance of human life.

(9) *Samaj : Pragati: Rabindranath* (Society, Progress and Rabindranath) by Kshudiram Das (Karuna Prakashani, Calcutta 1990).

The author has suggested that he has written this book to bring home to youth the relevance of Rabindranath. The author has informed us about Rabindranath's scheme about rural development and different plans related to it. Das has pointed out Rabindranath's confidence in village organisations in regard to rural reconstruction, though not in detail. Rabindranath wanted to use the youth force of the village as a driving power and for that purpose he built up different village organisations with the young boys and girls of the village. But the author has not elaborated this aspect in detail.

In this book the author has described the various aspects of Rabindranath's rural reconstruction programmes and also referred to some poems and songs that envisaged Tagore's ideas on rural reconstruction.

(10) *Rabindranath Jibon O Sahitya* (Rabindranath Life and Literature) by Sajanikanta Das, (Satabdi Grantha Bhavana, Calcutta 1367 BS)

Sajanikanta Das has thrown light on Rabindranath's literacy endeavours as well as on his missionary zeal in regard to the upliftment programmes in his zamindari estate and the establishment of Sriniketan. However, the author has not referred to what sort of work the different village organisations undertook to carry out Tagore's ideas on rural reconstruction. By reading this book we can more or less be aware of Rabindranath's creative genius as well as thoughts on rural reconstruction.

(11) *Rabindranath: Pallipunargathan* (Rabindranath : Village reconstruction) by Arun Kumar Mukhopadhya. (Dey's Publishing, Calcutta 1997)

Arun Kumar Mukhopadhya in this book has described how Rabindranath monitored his estate and the solutions that the poet found regarding the execution of different plans for social improvement. The writer has also provided statistics of different castes living in his estate. In the final phase, the author has analysed the different programmes of Sriniketan briefly. But he has not discussed the role of VDS which has key significance in regard to the rural reconstruction work.

In the books mentioned above the authors have made valuable contributions to attract our attention towards Rabindranath's rural development schemes and their various aspects. But no information-oriented analytical discussion is their regarding VDS on the basis of collected data from the villages around Sriniketan. So we'have tried to discuss and analyse the role of VDS in Tagore era and their relevance at the present time. Analysis has been made through primary data and other information as to how the VDS are more important in present socio-economic conditions of villages today to solve various problems through the collective efforts of the villagers.

3

Historical Perspective Upto Silaidah

On one hand some eminent national leaders such as Netaji Subhas Chandra Bose, Mahatma Gandhi, were dedicating themselves to achieve Political freedom from the grip of the British government and on the other, our zamindars had been exploiting and torturing the tenants on account of permanent settlement which had been introduced in 1793 by lord Cornawallis. At this moment, Rabindranath had been directed by his father to look after their estates: "এই ক্ষনে তুমি জমিদারির কার্য পর্যবেক্ষন করিবার জন্য প্রস্তুত হও"[1] (Now you get ready to survey the noose which is aching the Zamindar's neck for so long).

Maharshi Devendranath advised and gave him suggestions to prepare him as a suitable zamindar. Rathindranath told us : "Although my grandfather had handed over the management of the estates to father, he himself controlled the expenditure. He was a strict disciplinarian. On the second of every month the accounts had to be brought and read out to him."[2] Rabindranath gradually became a benevolent zamindar. His father directed him to stay at their village 'Kachari' for the supervision of Zamindari estate. Rabindranath did not behave with the tenants like most of the other zamindars of the country. During the supervision of his estate he deeply sympathised with the sorrows and sufferings of his tenants and felt that unless the sorrows and sufferings of those helpless villagers could be removed the freedom of India was a far cry. He realised that it would not be possible to get complete freedom of our country unless the villages were self-reliant with their own power. But, at that time, our national leaders were interested only achieving political freedom of the country. Even Gandhiji himself believed that India lives in her villages' and it is to be found not in its few cities and he tried to launch the self-help movement. Tagore was also a believer, in self-help through which a man could regain his self-confidence, which would give him self-respect and freedom from all kinds of servitude. Tagore not only believed in physical poverty but he also noticed the poverty of mind among his tenants. He naturally grew selfless to find out some way for the freedom from all kinds of bondage of the villagers. Rathindranath Tagore, the son of Rabindranath informed us in this regard : "কেউ যখন কিছু করলেন না তখন তিনি নিজে তাঁর ক্ষমতার মধ্যে যেটুকু করতে পারেন সেই কাজে নেমে গেলেন"[3] (He took up that kind of work on his own which had within his capacity, when he found that nobody came forward to do his bit.).

Rabindranath emphasised to reconstruct the village through the co-operative efforts of villagers themselves and to make proper utilisation of abandoned village resources, which were not utilised for the lack of proper organisation and guidance. At first Rabindranath devoted himself to gain a thorough knowledge about the rural community during the supervision of his estate and tried to solve their problems and remove their sufferings through their united efforts.

Rabindranath put forward various plans and programmes to make the villages self-reliant. He realised that villages are not self-sufficient by its own powers as before and rural life has been totally changed due to the negligence of the British government. He told us: "নাগরিক চিত্তবৃত্তি নিয়ে ইংরেজ আমাদের সেই ঘনিষ্ঠ পল্লীজীবনের গ্রন্থি কেটে দিয়েছে।"[4] (With his urban mentality the British has cut off our intimate ties with rural life). He published his opinion in an article named '*Swadeshi Samaj* in 1904 and wanted to say in this article to bring in new light on dark corners of the Indian villages and release the country from the grip of the British government. He desired to knit together the various loose ends of the village organisations. He also tried to find out methods for utilising village resources for improving their life in all its aspects. The poet thought that gradually the British government would be of no use and they will leave our country when these villages would be self-reliant. Tagore analysed the situation comparatively with the Indian villages in the past and told us : "সেই চিত্ত প্রবাহ চিরকাল বাংলার ছায়াশীতল গ্রামগুলিকে অনাময় ও আনন্দিত করিয়া রাখিয়াছিল, এখন বাংলার সেই পল্লীর ক্রোড় হইতে বাঙালীর চিত্ত ধারা বিক্ষিপ্ত হইয়া গেছে।"[5] (The flowing feelings of heart that maintained the shadowy of our villages full of joy that has been distracted from 'Bengalis' heart and snatched it away from the villages). In this situation he was bound to say about the dependency of the villagers on British government: "কর্তৃপক্ষীয়রা জলবর্ষনের ব্যবস্থা না করিলে তাহার আর গতি নাই।"[6] (Without the merciful arrangement of the authorities, they have no other away out). He realised that villagers were not cooperating with one another for their prosperity. He also indicated the motive of villagers : "দেশের লোকের সঙ্গে দেশ যথার্থভাবে সেবার সম্বন্ধসূত্রে যুক্ত, সেখানেই ঘটেছে মর্মান্তিক বিচ্ছেদ।"[7] (Heart-rending separation has taken place right there where the country is related to people with a spirit of service). Tagore as an universal man wanted to make the villagers self-reliant so that they could become a complete man. He called villagers to take active part unitedly towards the mission of developing their life style. In a Bengali poem 'Ebar Firao Morae' his self-realisation and missionary zeal is expressed with rare earnestness:

এই সব মূঢ় ম্লান মূক মুখে
দিতে হবে ভাষা, এই-সব শ্রান্ত শুষ্ক ভগ্ন বুকে
ধ্বনিয়া তুলিতে হবে আশা ডাকিয়া বলিতে হবে—
মুহূর্ত তুলিয়া শির একত্র দাঁড়াও দেখি সবে।[8]

(We have to render voice to all these
Witless pale and dumb mouths;
We have to raise hopes in the hearts
of all these timid dried up broken
hearted people; we have to call them
near and say 'you fellows instantly
hold your heads high and stand united.')

Rabindranath felt the situation during the supervision of his estate. He further remarked that the inner strength of the villagers was diminished and they have become helpless and due to ignorance they were depended outside charity for the fulfilment of their wants. They lacked the motive for gaining self-sufficiency, Rabindranath reminded the helpless villagers : "পৃথিবীর স্তন যখন শুকিয়ে যায় তখন এরা কেবল কাঁদতে জানে, কোনোমতে একটুখানি ক্ষিদে ভাঙলেই আবার তখনি সমস্ত ভূলে যায়।"[9] (They know only to shed tears when the breast of the earth is dried up. They forget all about their want as soon as their hunger is quenched even a little.) So Rabindranath endeavoured to help produce a complete man and arouse the inner-spirit of the villagers by their own co-operative efforts. This can be done through the implementation of various programmes in his zamindari estate. At first villagers did not respond to these programmes. Rabindranath tried to change the feeling of villagers through the adoption of various policies. He realised with pain and regret : "এই সমস্ত ছেলে পিলে - গোরু লাঙল - ঘরকন্নাওয়ালা সরল হৃদয় চাষাভূষোরা আমাকে কি ভূলই জানে। আমাকে এদের সমজাতি মানুষ বলেই জানে না।"[10] (What a misunderstanding is there between me and all this simple hearted villagers urchins burdened with children cattle and ploughs).

He desired to put an example in front of India and select some villages as model in his zamindari estate. For this reason he employed some young boys. He wrote a letter in 1908 : "হ্লতারা পল্লীর মধ্যে থেকে সেখানকার লোকদের সঙ্গে বাস করে তাদের শিক্ষা, স্বাস্থ্যবিচার প্রভৃতি সকল কাজের ব্যবস্থা তাদের নিজেদের দিয়ে করাবার চেষ্টা করছে।"[11] (They living amongst them, are trying to get their education hygienic habits, etc arranged with their own efforts) and in the same year he made a draft on rural reconstruction in such a manner that villagers could help themselves by relying on their own physical power and soul force. His strategy was, ""শহর গ্রাম কি পল্লীবাসীর অভিপ্রায় মত অনূন্য পাঁচজনের উপর প্রতি পল্লীসমাজের কার্যনির্বাহের ভার থাকিবে। তাহারা পল্লীবাসীদিগের মতামত ও সহায়তা লইয়া পল্লীসমাজের কার্য করিবেন।"[12] The operating means of every village society will depend on minimum five persons who will be guided by the desires of city and village folks) Rabindranath made a kind of constitution in regard to palli samaj for self-reliance. These are mentioned below[13].

(১) বিভিন্ন সম্প্রদায়ের মধ্যে সাম্য ও সদ্ভাব-সংবর্দ্ধন এবং দেশের ও সমাজের অহিতকর বিষয়গুলি নির্ধারন করিয়া তাহার প্রতিকারের চেষ্টা।

(To create unity and fraternity amongst various communities and by finding out harmful social ills to redress them).

(২)সর্ব প্রকার গ্রাম্য বিবাদ-বিসংবাদ সালিশের দ্বারা মিমাংসা।

(To bring compromises all the conflicts among villagers).

(৩) স্বদেশ-শিল্পজাত দ্রব্য প্রচলন এবং তাহা সুলভ ও সহজপ্রাচ্য করিবার জন্য ব্যবস্থা এবং সাধারন ও স্থানীয় শিল্প-উন্নতির চেষ্টা।

(To advocate the uses of home-made cottage industry products and by making them easily available and cheap to improve the quality of the local arts and crafts).

(৪) উপযুক্ত শিক্ষক নির্বাচন করিয়া পল্লী সমাজের অধীনে বিদ্যালয় ও আবশ্যক মত নৈশ্যবিদ্যালয় স্থাপন করিয়া বালক -বালিকা-সাধারনের সুশিক্ষার ব্যবস্থা।

(To arrange good general education for young children by appointing efficient teachers, establishing schools and when necessary, Nights Schools).

(৫) বিজ্ঞান ইতিহাস বা মহাপুরুষদিগের জীবনি ব্যাখ্যা করিয়া সাধারণকে শিক্ষাপ্রদান ও সর্ব ধর্মের সারনীতি সংগ্রহ করিয়া সাধারনের মধ্যে প্রচার ও সর্বোতভাবে সাধারনের মধ্যে সুনীতি ধর্মভাব একতা স্বদেশানুরাগ বৃদ্ধি কবিবার চেষ্টা।

(In order to impart and develop moral values spirituality, unity and by expressing the salient features of science history and the lives of great man).

(৬) প্রতি পল্লীতে একটি চিকিৎসক ও ঔষধালয় স্থাপন করা এবং অপরাগ, অনাথ, অসহায় ব্যক্তিগনের নিমিত্ত ঔষধ, পথ্য, সেবা ও সৎকারের ব্যবস্থা করা।

(To arrange for a doctor and Medicine shop in every village and also to arrange treatment nutritional diet and cremation facilities for incapacitated, orphaned and helpless people).

(৭) পানীয় জল, নদীনালা, পথ, ঘাট, সৎকারস্থান, ব্যায়ামশালা ও ক্রীড়াক্ষেত্র প্রভৃতির ব্যবস্থা করিয়া স্বাস্থ্যের উন্নতির চেষ্টা।

(To improve the quality of health by arranging drinking water, by looking after rivers and canals, roads and bathing ghats, setting up cremation ground gymnasium an sports ground etc.).

(৮) আদর্শ কৃষিক্ষেত্র বা খামার স্থাপন ও তথায় যুবক বা অন্য পল্লীবাসীদিগকে কৃষিকার্য বা গোমহিষাদিপালন-দ্বারা জীবিকা উপার্জনোপযোগী শিক্ষাপ্রদান ও কৃষি কার্যের উন্নতি সাধনের চেষ্টা।

(To establishing ideal tilling fields and farm houses where young men and other village people may be able to cultivate agricultural work, and to impart education and also to improve all this by putting in sincere efforts).

(৯) দুর্ভিক্ষ নিবারর্নাথে ধর্মগোলা-স্থাপন।

(To establish co-operative grain stores for making provisions during famine).

(১০) গৃহস্থ স্ত্রী লোকেরা যাহাতে আপন আপন সংসারের আয় বৃদ্ধি করিতে পারেন এবং অসহায় হইলে সংসারের ভার গ্রহন করিতে পারেন তদনুরূপ শিল্পাদি শিক্ষা দেওয়া ও তদুপযোগী উপকরণ সংগ্রহ করা।

(In order to make the domesticated women capable of adding to family income and when helpless carry on the burden of the family, they have to be given training in arts and crafts and means for collecting the relevant material).

(১১) সুরাপান বা অন্যরূপ মাদকদ্রব্য ব্যবহার হইতে লোককে নিবৃত করা।

(To prevent people from drinking and using drugs.)

(১২) মিলন মন্দির Club-স্থাপন ও তথায় সমবেত হইয়া পল্লীর এবং স্বদেশের হিতার্থে সমস্ত বিষয়ের আলোচনা।

(To establish meeting grounds (clubs or temples) so that villagers can assemble there to discuss issues related to the interests of the rural areas and also of the country as a whole).

(১৩) পল্লীর তথ্য - সংগ্রহ - অর্থাৎ, জনসংখ্যা, স্ত্রী পুরুষ, বালক বালিকার সংখ্যা, বিভিন্ন জাতির সংখ্যা, গৃহ সংখ্যা, জন্ম-মৃত্যুর সংখ্যা, আধিবাসীগনের স্থান ত্যাগ ও নতুন বসতি, বিভিন্ন ফসলের অবস্থা, কৃষির ও বিভিন্ন ব্যবসার উন্নতি অবনতি, বিদ্যালয় পাঠশালা ও ছাত্র ও ছাত্রীর সংখ্যা, ম্যালেরিয়া (জর), উলাউঠা বসন্ত ও অন্যান্য মহামারীতে আক্রান্ত রোগীর ও ঐসব রোগে মৃত্যুর সংখ্যা ও পল্লীর পূরাবৃত্ত ও বর্তমান উন্নতি ও অবনতির বিবরণ ও কারণ ধারাবাহিকরূপে লিপিবদ্ধ করিয়া রাখা।

(To record in a chronological manner the following aspects of the rural problems; (a) Population census, (b) classification of population among men, women, boys and girls, (c) Numerical strength of various Committees (d) Number of houses, records of birth and death, departure and new arrivals of habitats. The condition of various crops. The rise and fall of agricultural products and business projects. The record of numbers of High Schools and Basic Schools and those of students, the patients infected with malaria, cholera, small pox and other fatal diseases, records of deaths due to these ailments, the past history of the villages and the record of its present progress and regression).

(১৪) জেলায় জেলায়, পল্লীতে পল্লীতে, গ্রামে গ্রামে, পরস্পরের মধ্যে সদ্ভাবসংস্থাপন ও ঐক্যসংবর্দ্ধন।

(To create fraternal feelings and sense of unity among the people of villages district and the nation as a whole).

(১৫) জেলা সমিতি, প্রাদেশিক সমিতি ও জাতীয় মহাসমিতির উদ্দেশ্যের ও কার্যের সহায়তা করা।

(To cooperate with district, province and country based societies for fostering various humanitarian aims and objects).

It is obvious from the programmes listed above that Rabindranath possessed thorough knowledge about the rural problems (Ref: *Swadeshi Samaj)* with due respect to our national leader, Mahatma Gandhi, we can not help thinking, desired mainly to achieve only political freedom of the country based on 'truth and non violence' i.e. Satyagraha. He also tried to make villages self-reliant through 'Gram Swaraj'. But this policy too was aimed at achieving political freedom. He emphasised to release the country from the clutches of British Government. Mahatma Gandhi inspired the countrymen by launching different movements based on spirituality and also by introducing 'Charka'. Gandhiji gave opinion regarding this : Khadi (i.e. hand-spun cloth) will cease to have any value in my eyes if it does not usefully employ the million[14] and brings self-confidence among them.

Rabindranath desired to do this through the proper utilisation of not only the village resources but also by using science and technology. Gandhiji tried to develop Indian villages through the traditional system and remarked : "I have no partiality for return to the Primitive methods of grinding and husking for the sake of them. I suggest the return, because there is no other way of giving employment to the millions of villagers who are living in idleness"[15]. Gandhiji wanted to employ the whole countrymen. So he told us regarding the application of machine "What I object to is the craze for machinery, not machinery as such. The craze is for what they call labour-saving machinery. Men go on saving labour' till thousands are without work."[16] In the field of health he emphasised the nature cure methods and suggested giving up modern medicine as far as possible. He opposed chemical fertiliser in the field of cultivation, but, side by side, he advised to weave cloth for Khadi dress in leisure time. During non-coperation movement he asked the people to boycott the western type schools and cottages as well as western cloths. Mahatma Gandhi directed the people not to migrate to the city. Those who had already done so should go back to their villages. Rabindranath also called to the people in Bengali ফিরে চল মাটির টানে।

So it is known from the discussions above that Mahatma Gandhi and Rabindranath though both were interested in removing the sufferings of the villagers, their principles differed. In short Rabindranath like to adopt modern science and technology for the welfare of the villagers and did not want just political freedom. Gandhiji gave opinion in regard to self-sufficient village economy. "Industrialisation on a mass scale will necessarily lead to passive or active exploitation of the villages, as the problems of competition and marketing come in. Therefore, we have to concentrate on the village being self-contained manufacturing mainly for use provided this character of the village industry is maintained, there would be no objection to villages using even modern machines and tools that they can make and can afford to use".[17] Gandhiji attached greater importance to and priority on political freedom. Side by side he also gave emphasis on self-realization. But Tagore thought that only self-realization was the only means to achieve not only political freedom but also freedom from all kinds of servitude and that could be done only through a self-reliant society and economy, which would give the villagers self-confidence and self-respect. In order to create self-confidence among the villagers, Rabindranath took up various projects and implemented them to make a model village before the country. He emphasised the significance of ideal village by reminding the people that

"এক জায়গায় যদি আমরা এরকম আদর্শ পল্লীস্থাপনে কৃতকার্য হতে পারি - তার চেয়ে লাভের আর কিছুই হতে পারে না।"[18] (Nothing can be more beneficial than an ideal village if we able to establish one). He reiterated that too only on proper utilisation of village resources, an ideal village may be developed and that through the united strength of the villagers. He did not like the people to depend upon outside charity, though help is necessary but with' self-respect. He said : "মানুষ কোনোদিন কোনো যথার্থ হিতকে ভিক্ষারূপে গ্রহন করিবে না, ঋনরূপেও না, কেবলমাত্র প্রাপ্য বলিয়াই গ্রহন করিতে পারিবে।"[19] (Man will never accept real benefit as an object of charity, neither as loan. He will accept it only as something that is his due). He thought that health, education and economical programmes should receive top priority.

HEALTH : Rabindranath felt the real condition of rural life during the supervision of zamindari estate. He witnessed the ill health and the diseases which untold sufferings to the village people. He gave us a vivid picture about the miserable condition of the villages. He explained : "এত কষ্ট এত অনারাম মানুষের কী করে সয় আমি ভেবে পাই নে - এর উপরে প্রতি ঘরে ঘরে বাতে ধরছে, পা ফুলছে, সর্দি হচ্ছে, জর হচ্ছে, পিলেওয়ালা ছেলেগুলো অবিশ্রাম ঘ্যান্ ঘ্যান্ করে কাঁদছে। কিছুতেই তাদের বাঁচাতে পারছে না - একটা একটা করে মরে যাচ্ছে।"[20] (I can not imagine how such misery and leisureless life can be suffered by man. Apart from this pathetic general scenario, there are people in every house who are suffering from gout swollen legs, cold and fever, liver affected children are weeping naggingly whose lives can never be saved, dying one by one). He decided to solve the health problems first and began to serve within the range of his capability. He believed in homeopathic treatment and carried on that treatment among villagers. He not only provided medical treatment but also made the village workers aware of the ignorant villagers against superstition and directed them: "রোগিদের হোমিওপ্যাথি চিকিৎসার জন্য কুঠিবাড়ীতে নিয়ে আসবে আর কঠিন রোগীদের সরকারী ডাক্তারখানায় পাঠাবার ব্যবস্থা করবে। খবরদার ঝাড়ফুক করাতে দেবে না।"[21] (Arrangements should be made to bring patients to Kuthibari for homeopathic treatment and serious ones to government hospitals. They should never be treated by an exorcist) Rabindranath founded also an indoor hospital for sick people "পদ্মানদীর কোলে কুমিরে ধরা একজন চাষির জীবনরক্ষার জন্য দুইমাসের জন্য হাসপাতালে Indoor চিকিৎসার ব্যবস্থা হয়।"[22] (The farmer who was bitten by a crocodile inside the Padma river should be brought to the indoor ward and treated for two months) Rabindranath established a society in his zamindari estate with the help of villagers and it was a registered society.

Rabindranath laid emphasis on the situation of drinking water problems. Tagore desired that these problems could also be solved by the villagers themselves. Being moved by the distress of the rural people regarding their drinking water scarcity, he told the villagers to dig the well with their labour. He assured that he would provide some financial help to complete the well. But superstitious villagers refused the proposal. Rabindranath told us through a lecture about the incident : "তারা বললে, মহাশয়, আপনি কি মাছের তেল দিয়ে মাছ ভাজতে চান? আমরা খরচ দিয়ে কুয়া খুড়ব আর স্বর্গে যাবেন আপনি।"[23] (They said, "Sir, do you want to derive double benefits from the same source? We shall dig the well incurring expenses and you will reap the benefits (and go to heaven). As Tagore believed in self-help, he refused to help them to dig a well to solve their drinking water problem. Some people also responded to his suggestion and he immediately helped them to complete their well. Zealously and lack of unity among the villagers are the main reasons which stand in the way to solve the problems of the villagers. He remarked with frustration! "নিজেদের পরস্পর চেষ্টা-দ্বারা পরস্পর কল্যানের প্রবৃত্তি কারও মনে জেগে ওঠে না, সকলের যাতে কল্যান হয় সে চেষ্টা আমাদের দেশে হল না, তাতে দুর্গতির এক শেষ হয়েছে।"[24] (Nobody is inspired by rendering benefits to one another by common efforts. The spirit of commonality of welfare does not inspire our countrymen. As a result, people suffer from unbearable misery). The poet and philosopher noticed that there were hundreds of problems but these could not be solved for the lack of unity among the villagers. Villagers did not take interest in the active participation for the solution of the outstanding village oriented problems. Rabindranath rued: "মধ্যাহ্নে অতিথি আসিয়া জল চাহিলে এক গন্ডুষ জল দিতে গৃহির হাত সরে না।"[25] (A householder flinches while offering a drop of drinking water to a thirsty guest!") India is famous for her hospitality, but when a guest came to his house, the owner could not offer a glass of drinking water to that guest. Tagore observed this helplessness of the household owner and at the same time he also observed the helplessness of the owner to solve that type of problem which could easily be solved if there was unity among villages and a unified organisation in the village. Rabindranath also noticed that ignorance superstition and illiteracy are mainly responsible for the backwardness and miseries of the rural people.

EDUCATION: Having bitter experience regarding the solution of drinking water problem at that time, Tagore realised that lack of proper organisation among villagers was one of the reasons for this distress. He felt that proper education could only remove superstition, ignorance, which would be in turn useful to organise the villagers themselves for their welfare. So he emphasised on extension of education among villagers to enrich their inner and exterior power. He thought that education is the main tool for the welfare of mankind. For this reason he wanted to make the people aware of the value of proper education. He reminded us that : "মানুষের সকল সমস্যা-সমাধানের মূলে হচ্ছে তার সুশিক্ষা।"[26] (Good education is the only means to solve all the problems of mankind). As we mentioned elsewhere he took various educational programmes and established school, Night school, Adult school in the villages of his zamindari estate to educate villagers. Rabindranath desired to reconstruct the village in all its aspects. He believed that proper education is one of the main tools through which many problems could be solved. He regarded the utility of education: "রাস্তাঘাট, ড্রেন-পুকুর, ঘরবাড়ি তৈরী, হঠাৎ কোনো সাংঘাতিক আঘাত প্রভৃতির উপস্থিতমত চিকিৎসা ও কৃষিবিদ্যা প্রভৃতি বিষয় সম্বন্ধে মোটামুটি শিক্ষা দেবার ব্যবস্থা থাকা কর্ত্তব্য।"[27] (It should be our duty to make arrangements for imparting at least minimum training and education towards making roads, drains, ponds, building houses, first aid treatment for treating seriously injured patients). He established Nights schools for those people who were busy during day to earn their livelihood. Rabindranath aspired to build the village through rendering proper education. He thought, proper education could enrich the leadership quality among the villagers. They would be able to take up the responsibility to develop their village in future. It was known that benevolent zamindar did not get any obstruction to set up schools, because tenants were interested in educating their deprived children in those schools: "প্রজাদের মধ্যে লেখাপড়া শেখার আগ্রহ অত্যন্ত বেশী। তারা যে-শিক্ষা থেকে বঞ্চিত হয়েছে তাদের ছেলেরা যাতে সেই শিক্ষা পাবার যথেষ্ট সুযোগ পায় তাদের একান্ত আকাঙ্খা।"[28] (Great interest is found among the subjects for deriving benefits from education. But they have been deprived of that. It is their earnest desire that their children get the opportunity for education.) Rabindranath also emphasised women's education. He advised the rural women to study in their leisure time. It was known, after the establishment of Sriniketan, Rabindranath went further to his zamindari estate in July 1937 for the last time. He appealed and advised the villagers regarding the extension of education.

The great philosopher emphasised to make rural economy self-reliant through the use of modern science and technology. Basically agriculture and rural industries were emphasised to make economy self sufficient through the co-operative efforts of the villagers.

AGRICULTURE : Rabindranath wanted to develop Indian agriculture. It is well known that in the year 1906 he sent her own son, Rathindranath, friend's son Sontosh Chandra Mazumdar and son-in-law Nagendranath Gungali to study agriculture and dairy system in USA. His aspiration was that after completing their study, they would devote themselves to develop Indian agricultural products. He reminded them : "তোমরা দুর্ভিক্ষপীড়িত প্রজার অন্নগ্রাসের অংশ নিয়ে বিদেশে কৃষি শিখতে গেছ - ফিরে এসে এই হতভাগ্যদের অন্নগ্রাস কিছু পরিমানেও যদি বাড়িয়ে দিতে পার তা হলে এই ক্ষতি পূরন হয়ে মনে স্বান্ত্বনা পাব।"[29] (You have gone to a foreign country for getting training in agriculture with the help of the part of means of the living of famine-stricken subjects. If you can increase their means of living to some extent then this loss would be compensated and I shall be consoled.) The poet realised that it could not be possible to develop agriculture if cultivation was done by traditional system. He tried to apply modern science and technology in agriculture to improve the production of crops. He told us through *'Bhumilakshmi'* Patrika which was published from Birbhum district : "আজ শুধু একলা চাষীর চাষ করিবার দিন নাই, আজ তাহার সঙ্গে বিদ্যানকে, বৈজ্ঞানিককে যোগ দিতে হইবে।"[30] (This is not the day for the farmer to till the land all alone along with him, the learned, a scientist have to contribute to their efforts). Rabindranath deeply sympathasised with the sufferings of farmers during his supervision of zamindari estate. He witnessed that village farmers had to harvest premature paddy for untimely heavy rain. He tried to remove that helpless condition of the villagers and asked them to cultivate other crops during summer to supplement their income. Many enterprising farmers cultivated paddy crops instead of one in a year and were benefited. Rabindranath not only advised the farmer but he also devoted himself to cultivate on an experimental basis through the application of improved technology and seeds. It was known from his letter which was written to the famous scientist Jagadish Chandra Bose "আমার চাষবাসের কাজও মন্দ চলিতেছে না।"[31] (My farming is not running bad either). He collected improved seeds of American Maize, Madrasi Paddy etc. Only for the development of agriculture. Besides, it was known from the *'Annual Report of 1899'* about Rabindranath's cultivation "Experiment with Nainital Potatoes were made by Mr. Rabindranath in the Tagore Estate at Shelidah"[32] Rabindranath also paid attention to sericulture cultivation in his zamindari estate. Tagore tried to free the farmers from the grip of money lenders: "An agricultural bank had been founded to advance loans particularly seasonal loans on reasonable rates of interest to the cultivators."[33] It was known that after harvesting the farmer repaid the loan with interest. In this way Rabindranath tried to introduce a system which the farmers could have followed for their own interest. He also emphasised on rural industries to make village economy self-reliant. He realised that only agricultural development could not make them self-sufficient in economy. He observed in regard to the significance of rural industry in the village : "এখানকার চাষাদের কোন Industry শেখানো যেতে পারে সেই কথা ভাবছিলুম। এখানে ধান ছাড়া আর কিছুই জন্মায় না।"[34] (I was thinking if some science of Industry could be taught to the farmers of this place. Here nothing else other than paddy is grown). Thus Rabindranath emphasised to develop village economy through rural industry along with agricultural development.

RURAL INDUSTRY : Tagore wrote a letter in the year 1911 to his son regarding the rural industry to his zamindari estate such as pottery, umbrella-making, cup-plate making etc. He emphasised proper utilisation of village resources to make self-reliant economy. He inspired the villagers to make yarn from the leaves of Annas. Rabindranath arranged suitable training and education for the farmers to develop the rural industries in his zamindari estate. A weaving school was set up at Kusthia and great efforts were made to stimulate the cottage industry. He was a firm believer in co-operative principles. He wanted to bring a small furnace and operate it through the co-operative efforts of villagers. He always advised all classes of people to co-operate with another for the development of village society and economy. He said regarding co-operation : "জমিদার, জোতদার আর চাষি এই তিন রকমের স্বার্থভোগীদের হাত মেলাতে হবে।"[35] (Three types of interested parties that the land lords the Jotdars and the farmers have to join hands). He realised that without co-operative attitude among villagers it would not be possible to reconstruct the village for self-reliance. That is why he always put emphasis on the united force of villagers for rural reconstruction.

CO-OPERATIVE SYSTEM : He advised villagers to use advanced technology unitedly for their self-reliant economy. He reminded the people : "য়ুরোপে আমেরিকায় কৃষির নানা প্রকার মিতশ্রমিক যন্ত্র বাহির হইয়াছে — নিতান্ত দরিদ্রবশত সে সমস্ত আমাদের কোনো কাজেই লাগিতেছে না — অল্প জমি ও অল্প শক্তি লইয়া সে সমস্ত যন্ত্রের ব্যবহার স ব নহে।"[36] (Many labour-saving mechanical devices have been marketed in Europe and America for farmers, due to our sheer poverty we can not utilise them. In fact, it is not possible to use these devices with the possession of small land and little power). He realised that without co-operative system it could not be possible to make the villages self-reliant. He said : "যে দিন সমবায় মূলক জীবিকার কথা প্রথম শুনি আমার মনে জটিল সমস্যার একটা গাঁট যেন অনেকটা খুলে গেল।"[37] (The day I heard the idea of co-operative employment, the complex knots of the problems were, to a great extent, resolved). It has already been mentioned earlier that he established a cooperative agricultural bank through the united efforts of the village farmers. As a humanitarian with deep faith on cooperative principles, he desired to associate both Hindus and Muslims in rural reconstruction programmes. He know that there was no good relationship among Hindus and Muslim; in rural reconstruction programmes. He said : "আমাদের দেশে মধ্যে মধ্যে সামান্য উপলক্ষে হিন্দু মুসলমান বিরোধ বাধিয়া ওঠে, সেই বিরোধ মিটাইয়া উভয় পক্ষের মধ্যে প্রীতি শান্তি স্থাপন, উভয় পক্ষের স্ব-স্ব অধিকার নিয়মিত করিয়া দিবার বিশেষ কর্তৃত্ব সমাজের কোনো স্থানে যদি না থাকে, তবে সমাজকে বারে বারে ক্ষত বিক্ষত হইয়া উত্তরোত্তর দুর্বল হইতে হয়।"[38] (Off and on Hindu-Muslim disputes arise on flimsy grounds. The society gets worn and torn and weakened, progressively if there are no authorities to settle these disputes to establish friendliness and peace and to regularise the individual rights among the parties concerned). He felt the necessity of holding fairs and festivals for making good relationship between Hindus and Muslims: "এই সকল মেলায় যদি তাঁরা হিন্দু-মুসলমানের মধ্যে সদ্ভাব স্থাপন করেন – কোনো প্রকার নিস্ ল পলিটিক্সের সংস্রব না রাখিয়া, বিদ্যালয়, পথ ঘাট, জলাশয়, গোচরভূমি প্রভৃতি সম্বন্ধে জেলার যে সমস্ত অভাব আছে তাহার প্রতিকারের পরামর্শ করেন, তবে অতি অল্পকালের মধ্যে স্বদেশকে যথার্থই সচেষ্ট করিয়া তুলিতে পারেন।"[39] (They can really activate the people of the country within a very short time if they can establish amity among Hindus and Muslims. During this fairs without associating with fruitless politics and if they can redress the grievances in regard to problems of schools, roads, bathing ghats, ponds and grazing grounds in the district).

Like Mahatma Gandhi he also endeavoured to make the villagers aware regarding the evils of untouchability and advised them to avoid such hateful practice. Because, all communities have make construction to build up the nation. He significantly remarked through the drama *Kaler Yatra* : ""আমরাই তো জোগাই অন্ন, তাই তোমরা আছ; আমরাই বুনি বস্ত্র, তাতেই তোমাদের লজারক্ষা"[40] (It is we who are supplying food for your survival and it is we who are weaving cloths for covering your bodies) He advised that all villagers should take collective part actively in rural reconstruction programmes and avoid casticism superstitions etc. To quote again from the same drama which sound like Marxian theory : "শুদ্রদের টানে রথ চলিল, মহাকালের জাত গেল ও তাহার গতি হইল।"[41] (The chariot was driven by the power of the Sudras and it then only secured power. Due to this power the eternity achieve the higher status). So it is clear that Rabindranath wanted to reconstruct the village for self-reliance through cooperative efforts of all classes of people irrespective of caste and community.

ROLE OF YOUTH : Rabindranath believed that youths were the main force that could reconstruct villages in all its aspects. So he called the youth force to take the leadership in rural reconstruction. He thought that only youth could make the society progressive fighting all decaying forces. He inspired the youth in a play called *'Falguni'* "যুবকেরা বললে – আনব সেই জড়াবুড়োকে বেঁধে, সেই মৃত্যুকে বন্দী করে।"[42] (The youth said that they would get death imprisoned by finding up the worn-out and the old and we shall bring them infront.) What he wanted to say through some other dialogues that old decaying force could not resist the youth force. The youth force must take the leadership to build up the nation. He told the traditional minded old people : "দেশের নব যৌবনকে তাঁহারা আর নির্বাসিত করিয়া রাখিতে পারিবেন না। তাঁহারা চন্ডীমন্ডপে বসিয়া থাকুন, আর বাকী সবাই পথে ঘাটে বাহির হইয়া পড়ুক সেখানে তারুণ্যের জয় হউক।"[13] (They will not be able any more to confine the rising youth of the country in exile. They could sit on Chandimandap and let the rest come out and spread themselves all over may the youth triumph. He was happy to see the role of youth in the nation-building activities. He blessed them through his speech in Pradeshik Sammelan : "বর্তমানকালে আমাদের দেশের যে সকল দৃঢ়নিষ্ঠ যুবক সমস্ত সংকট উপেক্ষা করিয়াও স্বদেশ হিতের জন্য স্বেচ্ছাব্রত ধারন করিতেছেন, অদ্য এই সভাস্থলে তাঁহারা সমস্ত বঙ্গ দেশের আর্শিবাদ গ্রহন করুন।"[44] (All those determined young people of the country who ignoring all the crisis are attending this meeting and taking up the vow of voluntarily serving the country, may accept the blessing of all our country men) Through some poems (ref: Sabujer Abhijan) in *'Bolaka'* he inspired the youth to take active part in building up the village friendly nation. The youth force should also ready to participate in the nation building activities. It is known from a lecture of Rabindranath "আজ এই সভায় যাঁরা উপস্থিত তাঁরা অনেকেই যুবক ছাত্র, দেশের কাজ করবার জন্যে তাদের আগ্রহ পরিপূর্ন হয়ে উঠেছে।"[45] (Many of those who are present in the meeting today are either young people or student, they are throbbing with the patriotic feelings to serve the country). But Rabindranath cautioned them to control their emotional traits and advised them to go to a village with determination for a good relationship with the villagers and devote themselves in rural reconstruction programmes.

Rabindranath gave priority to health and chose physicians and teachers carefully for rural reconstruction programmes because they had the good opportunity to have close relationship with the rural folk. He wanted to provide training to rural youth and villagers through suitable village workers. For this reason, he established farm, for agricultural development. He advised them to set up a club or VDS where all villagers would assemble to study various aspects of village activities.

VILLAGE ORGANISATION : Rabindranath always put emphasis on the united efforts of villagers to reconstruct the village. But without having any proper organisation that purpose could not be materialised. In a village organisation villagers would assemble, discuss and participate in various rural reconstruction programmes. He tried to solve the drinking water problem of the village through the organised force of the villagers. He told all about the importance of proper organisation : ""বর্তমান কালের প্রকৃতির সহিত আমাদের দেশের অবস্থার সামঞ্জস্য করিতে না পারিলে আমাদিগকে বিলুপ্ত হইতে হইবে। বর্তমানের সেই প্রকৃতিটি জোটবাঁধা, ব্যূহবদ্ধতা, অর্গানিশ্যেন।"[46] (We are doomed to lose everything unless we know how to adjust tne situations in the country with the current trends. Among these are group-forming, invincible camp forming and organisations.) He also devoted himself to organise the village in his estate in order to solve the various problems. He wrote in a letter : "গ্রাম-পল্লীকে Organise করে তোলবার যে প্রস্তাব আমার বর্ক্তৃতায় করেছি সেটা আমি কাজে খাটবার জন্যে পূর্ব হতেই চেষ্টায় প্রবৃত্ত হয়েছি।"[47] (I have been engaged before hand to implement the resolutions that 1 mooted out in my speech in regard to the organisation of the villages around). Tagore directed the village worker to organise the village. Kalimohan Ghosh was an ideal village worker who devoted himself to develop rural society according to Tagore' s idea. Since then Ghosh dedicated himself to that mission until death. One of his friends established a social organisation named 'Bangiya Hitasadhan Mandali'. Rabindranath set up some aims and objects for that organisation and implemented them in his zamindari estate through village organisation. The aims and objectives were[48]

(১) নিরক্ষরদিগকে অন্ততঃ যৎসামান্য লেখাপড়া ও অংক শেখানো।

(To teach three R's to the illiterate)

(২) ছোট ছোট 'ক্লাস' ও পুস্তিকা প্রচার দ্বারা স্বাস্থ্য রক্ষা, সেবা শুশ্রূষাদি সম্বন্ধে শিক্ষা দান।

(To teach something about health and sanitation through small classes and Booklets and also through nursing.)

(৩) ম্যালেরিয়া, যক্ষা, নানাবিধ অজীর্ন ও উদরাময় রোগ প্রভৃতির প্রতিষেধের জন্য সমবেত চেষ্টা।

(To make joint efforts to take precaution against attacks of Malaria, Tuberculosis and many elements concerning the stomach)

(৪) শিশুমৃত্যু নিবারনের উপায় নির্ধারন ও অবলম্বন।

(To prevent child mortality by finding our and adopting the solutions accordingly)

(৫) গ্রামে উৎকৃষ্ট পানীয় জলের ব্যবস্থা।

(To arrange the purest drinking water in the village).

(৬) গ্রামে গ্রামে যৌথ ঋনদান সমিতি ইত্যাদী প্রতিষ্ঠা ও দরিদ্র লোকদিগকে ইহার উপকারিতা প্রদর্শন।

(To establish cooperative societies for providing loan etc. for the security and progress of the poor people and to show them the benefit there off.)

(৭) দুর্ভিক্ষ বন্যা, মড়ক প্রভৃতির সময়ে দুঃস্থ দিগকে বিবিধ প্রকারে সাহায্য।

(To render help to the distressed people during famine, floods and epidemic etc.)

The poet divided villagers into some mandalis and wanted to solve the various village disputes through this mandali. He said : "প্রত্যেক গ্রামে বাসিন্দারা তাদের নিজেদের মধ্যে থেকে একজনকে প্রধান মনোনীত করত। ... অল্প স্বল্প ঝগড়াঝাটি গ্রাম-প্রধানরাই মিটিয়ে দিত।"[49] (The villagers used to nominate their chief among themselves ..... these chiefs used to settle the petty disputes. He said in regard to village based administration : "কতকগুলি পল্লী লইয়া এক-একটি মন্ডলী স্থাপিত হইবে। সেই মন্ডলীর প্রধানগন যদি গ্রামের সমস্ত কর্মের এবং অভাব মোচনের ব্যবস্থা করিয়া মন্ডলীকে নিজের মধ্যে পর্যাপ্ত করিয়া তুলিতে পারে তবেই স্বায়ত্বশাসনের চর্চা দেশের সর্বত্র সত্য হইয়া উঠিবে। নিজের পাঠশালা শিল্প, শিক্ষালয়, ধর্মগোলা সমবেত পণ্যভান্ডার ও ব্যাংক স্থাপনের জন্য ইহা দিগকে শিক্ষা সাহায্য ও উৎসাহদান করিতে হইবে। প্রত্যেক মন্ডলীর একটি করিয়া সাধারণ মন্ডপ থাকিবে, যেখানে কর্মে ও আমোদে সকলে একত্র হইবার স্থান পাইবে।"[50] (A group will be formed comprising some villages if those group chiefs can arrange to remove all the wants of the villages and help in the activities there of and this way can make those group enough helpful amongst them. Only then the cultivation of self rule (autonomy) can become reality every where. We have to educate these people and help and inspire them in regard to artefacts and to organise primary schools, educational institutions, grain stores and cooperative harvest stores. Every group will have a general canopy which will be a place for meeting together for various activities and recreations). He thought that only organised force of villagers could look after their own welfare and it would not be possible to bring about in all round improvement, unless they were organised. He warned them about the consequences of the absence of proper, organisation : "পৃথিবীতে চারিদিকে সকলেই জোট বাঁধিয়া প্রবল হইয়া উঠিতেছে। এমন অবস্থায় যাহারাই বিচ্ছিন্ন একক-ভাবে থাকিবে তাহাদিগকে চিরদিনই অন্যের গোলামী ও মজুরী করিয়া মরিতে হইবে।"[51] (Everywhere in the world we find organisation is gaining momentum. Under the circumstances those who will live in isolation will have to become slaves to others for ever and have to die by labouring hard). The poet devoted himself to form an organisation in Kaligram paragana of his zamindari estate, named 'Kaligram Hitaisee Sobha' through the cooperative efforts of villager. He endeavoured to make a self-reliant ideal village before the country through that organisaton. He was often worried about the activities of the people of 'Kaligram paraganas'. He wrote in a letter to Atul Prasad Sen regarding his anxiety : "কালিগ্রামে কাজ সম্বন্ধে আমার মন অত্যন্ত উদ্বিগ্ন ছিল — এমন কি রাত্রে ঘুম থেকে জেগে আমি ঐ কথা, আলোচনা করে ঘুমুতে পারি নি।"[52] (I was very anxious about the reconstruction work at Kaligram. Even I used to wake up at night and could not sleep after remembering the problems of the village). It is known that the following rural reconstruction programmes were implemented by Hitaisee Sabha at Kaligram paragana[53] : Extension of education, weaving, agricultural growth, fish business, Road making, solution of village disputes through mutual efforts, solutions of the problem of the scarcity of water, establishment of Dharmagola* against famine etc. The rural reconstruction

* Dharmagola (Co-operative grain store).

programmes were carried in three phases in his Zamindari estate. (1) হাতে কলমে কৃষি-শিক্ষা, (To learn agriculture through practical experience), (2) আদর্শ গ্রাম তৈরী, (To set up ideal villages (3) ব্রতী বালক দল গঠন (To form Brati organisations) As a model he took up 'Lahini' a village in his zamindari. His aim was to eradicate the ills that the villagers were suffering from. As a result, the other villages would also be gradually improved towards self-reliance and gradually in turn the entire country would be developed. He called the youth to take up the leadership and to build up at least one village through the organisation of villages. He observed in Pabna Pradeshik Sammelan : "তোমারা যে পারো এবং যেখানে পারো এক-একটি গ্রামের ভার গ্রহন করিয়া সেখানে গিয়া আশ্রয় লও। গ্রামগুলিকে ব্যবস্থাবদ্ধ করো। শিক্ষা দাও, কৃষি শিল্প ও গ্রামের ব্যবহার সামগ্রী সম্বন্ধে নূতন চেষ্টা প্রবর্তিত করো; গ্রামবাসীদের বাসস্থান যাহাতে পরিচ্ছন্ন স্বাস্থ্যকর ও সুন্দর হয় তাহাদের মধ্যে সেই উৎসাহ সঞ্চার করো; এবং যাহাতে তাহারা নিজেরা সমবেত হইয়া গ্রামের সমস্ত কর্তব্য সম্পন্ন করে সেই রূপ বিধি উদ্ভাবিত করো।"[55] (Who ever amongst you and where even possible to take up the charge of one Village each and stay there. 'Make the villages well organised, educate them and introduce the new devices in regard to farming and rurally usable goods. Create enthusiasm amongst villagers about keeping their dwellings clean, hygienic and beautiful. Further, find out the ways, which will help them in discharging all their duties in a limited manner). It is known that after establishment of Sriniketan, various activities were going on in the villages of his zamindari estate. Tagore also established in his estate another PSV to carry on rural reconstruction programmes. It is known,[56] some young instructors went there to provide training on weaving, Satranj making, knitting and Bratı organisation.

From the early period when he took the responsibility to look after the zamindari estate, Tagore established Sriniketan as a separate development centre adjacent to Santiniketan to continue the development activities which he had started in his zamindari estates. He knew[57] that Kaligram paragana might slip down from his grip. He realised the significance of establishing Sriniketan, which would be the model centre of rural reconstruction for the whole of India. He established Sriniketan in the year 1922 on 6th February and implemented a lot of rural reconstruction programmes in the surrounding villages of Sriniketan. Some well known leading persons like L.K. Elmhirst and the renowned social worker Kalimohan Ghosh assisted him. Although villages around Sriniketan were not within his zamindari estate, yet he became successful to organise VDS and to implement rural reconstruction programmes to make a self-reliant village through the united force of villagers.

The Sriniketan activities are discussed in detail in the following chapter. This discussion will try to give a clear picture about Sriniketan activities.

REFERENCES

1. Sachindranath Adhikary : *Silaidah O Rabindranath,* Jijnasa, Calcutta, January 1974, p. 10.
2. Rathindranath Tagore : "Father as I knew him" *A Centenary volume, Rabindranath Tagore* (1861-1961); Aspects of Indian Culture; edited by Mahendra Kulasrestha, Sahitya Akademi, New Delhi, November 1961, p. 22.
3. Rathindranath Tagore : *Pitrismriti,* Jijnasa, Calcutta, Agrahayan 1378 B.S., p. 42.
4. Rabindranath Tagore : Patraboli; 15th November 1934; *Palliprakriti,* Visva-Bharati Granthan Vibhaga, Calcutta, Magh 1368 B.S., p. 196.
5. Rabindranath Tagore : Swadeshi Samaj, Bhadra 1311 B.S., *Swadeshi Samaj* (Essay), Visva Bharati, Calcutta, Pous, 1369 B.S. p.6
6. Rabindranath Tagore : Barjito Rachangsha, *Swadeshi Samaj,* Visva-Bharati, Calcutta, Pous 1369 B.S., p.99.
7. Rabindranath Tagore : Marma Katha, Agrahayan 1336 B.S. *Swadeshi Samaj,* Visva-Bharati, Calcutta, Pous, 1369 B.S., p.3.
8. Rabindranath Tagore : `Ebar Firao Morae' (Poem), 23rd Falgun 1300 B.S.; *Sanchayita* (collection of poems), Visva-Bharati Granthan Vibhaga, Calcutta, 1338 B.S., 10th edition 1389 B.S., p. 219.
9. Rabindranath Tagore: A letter; Silaidah 10th May 1893; *Palliprakriti,* (also *Chhinnapatra* 1891-94, p.81), Visva-Bharati Granthan Vibhaga, Calcutta, Magh 1368 B.S., p. 204.

10. Rabindranath Tagore : A letter; Sajadpur 20th Magh (1891); *Palliprakriti,* Visva-Bharati Granthan Vibhaga, Calcutta, Magh 1368 B.S., p.203.
11. Rabindranath Tagore: A letter to Abala Basu, April 1908. *Palliprakriti,* Visva-Bharati Granthan Vibhaga, Calcutta, Magh 1368 B.S., p. 229.
12. Rabindranath Tagore : *Palli Samaj* (Pabna Bangyia Pradeshik Sammellanir Adhibesane) February 1908, *Palliprakriti,* Visva-Bharati Granthan Vibhaga, Calcutta, Magh 1368 B.S., p. 222.
13. Rabindranath Tagore : Objectives of Palli Samaj, February 1908, *Palliprakriti,* Visva-Bharati Granthan Vibhaga, Calcutta, Magh 1368 B.S., pp. 222-224.
14. Amlan Datta: "Aspects of Gandhian Economic Thought", *The Visva-Bharati Quarterly,* Gandhi number, Edited by. Sisir Kumer Ghosh, Vol. 35 (Nos.1, 2, 3 & 4) Santiniketan, West Bengal, 1971, p. 174.
15. *Ibid.,* p. 174.
16. *Ibid.,* p. 174.
17. *Ibid.* p. 177.
18. Srimati Bina Mukhopadhyay : *Chithipatre Rabindranath,* Navana, Calcutta, Agrahayan 1372 B.S., p. 73.
19. Rabindranath Tagore : Lokahita, Bhadra 1321 B.S. *Kalantar,* Visva-Bharati Granthan Vibhaga, Calcutta, Vaisakh, 1344 B.S., Revised edition 1367 B.S., p. 37.
20. Rabindranath Tagore : A letter (Digha patia Jalapathe), 20th September 1894; *Palliprakriti,* Visva-Bharati Granthan Vibhaga, Calcutta, Magh 1368 B.S., pp. 209-10.
21. Sachindranath Adhikari : *Silaidah O Rabindranath,* Jijnasa, Calcutta, January 1974, p. 72.
22. Sahindranath Adhikari : *Silaidah O Rabindranath,* Jijnasa, Calcutta, January, 1974 p. 429.
23. Rabindranath Tagore : Malaria (Anti-malaria Societyte Kathito), 23rd February 1924; *Palliprakriti,* Visva-Bharati Granthan Vibhaga, Calcutta, Magh 1368 B.S., p. 132.
24. *Ibid.* p. 133.
25. Rabindranath Tagore : Jalakasta (Srimati Kanistha), Jyaistha 1312 B.S., *Swadeshi Samaj,* Visva Bharati, Calcutta, Pous 1369 B.S., p. 68.

26. Rabindranath Tagore : Third letter 25th September 1930, *Russiar Chithi,* Visva-Bharati Granthan Vibhaga, Calcutta, Vaisakh 1338 B.S., p.22.
27. Rabindranath Tagore : Pallir Unnati (Hitasadhan Mandalir Sabhai Kathito) Vaisakh 1322, B.S., *Palliprakriti,* Visva-Bharati Granthan Vibhaga, Calcutta, Magh 1368 B.S., p. 35.
28. Rathindranath Tagore : *Pitrismriti,* Jijnasa, Calcutta, Agrahayan 1378 B.S. p. 249.
29. Rabindranath Tagore : A letter to Nagendranath Gangopadhyay, 12th Kartik 1314, B.S., *Palliprakriti,* Visva-Bharati Granthan Vibhaga, Calcutta, Magh 1368 B.S., p. 230.
30. Rabindranath Tagore : Bhumi Lakshmi, Aswin 1325 B.S. *Palliprakrili,* Visva-Bharati Granthan Vibhaga, Calcutta, Magh, 1368 B.S., pp. 39-40.
31. Rabindranath Tagore : A letter to Jagadishchandra Bose, 10th Ashara 1306 B.S., *Palliprakrili,* Visva-Bharati Granthan Vibhaga, Calcutta, Magh 1368 B.S., p. 211.
32. Sachindranath Adhikari : *Silaidah O Rabindranath,* (land records of Agriculture 1899), Jijnasa, Calcutta, January 1974, p. 424.
33. Sudhir Sen : *Rabindranath Tagore on Rural Reconstruction and Community development in India,* Visva-Bharati, Calcutta, 1943, Revised and enlarged edition, 1991., p. 142.
34. Rabindranath Tagore : A letter to Rathindranath Tagore (1911-1912), *Palliprakriti,* Visva-Bharati Granthan Vibhaga, Calcutta, Magh 1368 B.S., p.246.
35. Sachindranath Adhikary : *Silaidah O Rabindranath,* Jijnasa, Calcutta, January, 1974, p. 365.
36. Rabindranath Tagore : Sabhapatir Abhibhasan (Pabna pradeshik Sammelani) Falgun 1314 B.S., *Palliprakriti,* Visva-Bharati Granthan Vibhaga, Calcutta, Magh 1368 B.S., p.2.
37. Rabindranath Tagore : Charka, Bhadra 1352 B.S., *Kalantar,* Visva-Bharati Granthan Vibhaga, Calcutta, Vaisakh 1344 B.S., Revised edition, 1367 B.S., p.261.
38. Rabindranath Tagore : Swadeshi Samaj, 1311 B.S. *Swadeshi Samaj* (Essay), Visva-Bharati, Calcutta, Pous 1369 B.S.,p.25.
39. *Ibid.,* p. 13.
40. Rabindranath Tagore : *Kaler yatra* (Drama), Visva-Bharati Granthan Vibhaga, Calcutta, Bhadra 1339 B.S., p. 34.

41. Charu Chandra Bandapadhyay : *Rabirashmi* (Vol.2), College Street Publication Private Limited, First College Street edition, 1396 B.S., Second College Street edition, 1401 B.S., p. 317.

42. Charu Chandra Bandapadhyay : *Rabirashmi,* (Vol.2), College Street Publication Private Limited, First College Street edition, 1396 B.S., Second College Street edition, 1401 B.S., p. 134.

43. Rabindranath Tagore : Bibechana O Abibechana, Vaisakh 1321 B.S., *Kalantar,* Visva-Bharati Granthan Vibhaga, Calcutta, Vaisakh, 1344 B.S., Revised edition, 1367, B.S. p. 35.

44. Rabindranath Tagore : Sabhapatir Abhibhasan (Pabna pradeshik Sammelani) Falgun 1314 B.S. *Palliprakriti,* Visva-Bharati Granthan Vibhaga, Calcutta, Magh 1368 B.S., p. 10.

45. Rabindranath Tagore : Pallir Unnati (Hitasadhan mandalir Sabhai Kathito) Vaisakh 1322 B.S., *Palliprakriti,* Visva-Bharati Granthan Vibhaga, Calcutta, Magh 1368 B.S., p. 25.

46. Rabindranath Tagore : Sabhapatir Abhibhasan (Pabna Pradeshik Sammelani) Falgun 1314 B.S., *Palliprakriti,* Visva-Bharati Granthan Vibhaga, Calcutta, Magh 1368 B.S., p. 12.

47. Rabindranath Tagore : A letter to Nagendranath Gangopadhyay, Falgun 1314 B.S., *Palliprakriti,* Visva-Bharati Granthan Vibhaga, Calcutta, Magh 1368 B.S., pp. 230-231.

48. Sajanikanta Das : *Rabindranath Jibon O Sahitya,* Satabdi Grantha Bhavan, Calcutta, Rathayatra, 1367 B.S., p. 75.

49. Rathindranath Tagore : *Pitrismriti,* Jijnasa, Calcutta, Agrahayan 1378 B.S., p.42.

50. Rabindranath Tagore : Sabhapatir Abhibhasan (Pabna Pradeshik Sammelani) Falgun 1314 B.S., *Palliprakriti,* Visva-Bharati Granthan Vibhaga, Calcutta, Magh 1368 B.S., p.l.

51. *Ibid.,* p. 2.

52. Rabindranath Tagore : A letter to Sri Atul Sen, Agrahayan 1322 B.S. *Palliprakriti,* Visva-Bharati Granthan Vibhaga, Calcutta, Magh 1368 B.S., p. 255.

53. Rathindranath Tagore : *Pitrismriti,* Jijnasa, Calcutta, Agrahayan 1378 B.S., p. 250.

54. Sachindranath Adhikary : *Silaidah O Rabindranath,* Jijnasa, Calcutta, January, 1974 p. 71.

55. Rabindranath Tagore : Sabhapatir Abhibhasan (Pabna Pradeshik Sammelani) Falgun, 1314 B.S., *Palliprakriti,* Visva-Bharati Granthan Vibhaga, Calcutta, Magh 1368B.S., p. 11.
56. Sachindranath Adhikary : *Silaidah O Rabindranath,* Jijnasa, Calcutta, January, 1974, p. 362.
57. Sachindranath Adhikary : *Silaidah O Rabindranath,* Jijnasa, Calcutta, January, 1974, p. 17.

4

Establishment of Sriniketan and Role of Village Organisation Towards the Rural Reconstruction Programmes: A Detailed Discussion

Maharshi Devendranath Tagore was one of the founder members of Bramha Samaj. Once he was invited by Lord Sinha Family of Raipur. On his way to Raipur he saw a vast land where there was only one tree named 'chhatim'. He took rest under that tree during a severe summer season. At that moment he felt a unique indescribable joy, happiness and peace in his mind "তিনি আমার প্রাণের আরাম মনের আনন্দ, আত্মার শান্তি" (he is my life's comfort, mind's joy and soul's peace). At once he felt a desire to set up an Ashrama in such a peaceful environment. He bought those twenty bighas of land and acquired hereditary right over that land from the owner Pratap Narayan Sinha of Raipur. He built a house near the chhatim tree. It was named Santiniketan and later on the entire Ashrama area was called by the same name. He ritually preached Brahma religion on 22nd December, 1843. In order to commemorate that day, till now the famous Pousmela an annual fair is organised every year at Santiniketan. Besides Pousmela, various functions and festivals are organised throughout the year at Santiniketan.

To Rabindranath, this day was an important one not only to Brahma Samaj but for the Ashramiks too. He said: "শান্তিনিকেতনের সাম্বৎসরিক উৎসবের সফলতার মর্মস্থান যদি উদ্‌ঘাটন করে দেখি, তবে দেখতে পাব, এর মধ্যে সেই বীজ অমর হয়ে আছে, যে বীজ থেকে আশ্রম-বনস্পতি জন্মলাভ করেছে, সে হচ্ছে সেই দীক্ষা গ্রহনের বীজ।"[1] (If we look into the source of the success of annual functions and fair of Santiniketan, we shall see that out of that immortal seed has grown up the Ashrama giant tree and the genesis of that success is nothing but the capacity to be initiated to godhood).

The Ashrama was established in the year 1888. Villages around Santiniketan spontaneously participated on that occasion. As the institution grew in the rural area the founders of the institution tried to build a rapport with people of the surrounding villages of Santiniketan. The Bramha Upasana Mandir had been founded on 7th December in the year 1890 and in the next year, 1891, on 21st December the construction of the Mandir was completed and opened for religious service. The younger son of Maharshi, Rabindranath started a Brahma Vidyalaya like hermitage in the year 1901. This school was started with only six boys. He wished to administer the school, which was completely different from other schools. He realised from the experience of his childhood that there was no possibility to make a complete man through the monotonous school teachings. He drove home to the people the significance of Ashrama centric school : "ছেলেদের মানুষ করে তোলবার জন্যে যে একটা যন্ত্র তৈরী হয়েছে, যার নাম School, সেটার ভিতর দিয়ে মানব শিশুর শিক্ষার সমপূর্ণতা হতেই পারে না। এই শিক্ষার জন্য আশ্রমের দরকার, যেখানে আছে সমগ্র জীবনের সজীব ভূমিকা।"[2] (The machine that has been created to bring up the boys is known as school. But completion of the education can never be achieved through that machine. Ashrama is required for that purpose which has the live role of total living). He wished to render education for the service to mankind and motivated the students for a progressive society. He reiterated the objectives of Ashrama school thus : "আমি যে বিদ্যানিকেতনের কল্পনা করেছি, পড়া মুখস্থর কড়া পাহারা ঠেলেঠুলে তার মধ্যে পরস্পরের সেবা ও পরিবেশ রচনার কাজকে প্রধান স্থান দিয়েছি।"[3] (The institution that I have projected in my mind is a place where overcoming all the strict vigilance of the system for cramming lessions, the students will have top priority of mutual service and the creation of proper environment). The poet created a new society, which was not the tradition-bound, in which the people would be free from all kinds of servitude. He wanted the formation of such a type of an Ashrama at Santiniketan. He said: "শিলাইদহে পদ্মাতীরে সাহিত্য চর্চা নিয়ে নিভৃতে বাস করতুম, একটা সৃষ্টির সংকল্প নিয়ে সেখান থেকে এলেম শান্তিনিকেতনের প্রান্তরে"[4] (I used to live a secluded life on the banks of Padma river at Silaidah for cultivating literature. From these I came over to the meadows of Santiniketan with vow to create some thing). When political movement for independence was at its peak. Rabindranath desired to make an ideal self-governing administration in a small area of Santiniketan: "লোকহিত ও স্বায়ত্ব শাসনের যে দায়িত্ব বোধ আমরা সমস্ত দেশের কাছ থেকে দাবি করে থাকি। শান্তিনিকেতনের ছোট সীমার মধ্যে তারই একটি সমপুর্ন রূপ দিতে চাই। এখানকার ব্যবস্থা ছাত্র ও শিক্ষকদের সমবেত স্বায়ত্ব শাসনের ব্যবস্থা দরকার।[5]" (The commitment that we expect about service to people and self rule from the whole country was projected in my mind for giving a complete safe to that within the narrow limits of Santiniketan. There should be cooperative sense of self-rule amongst the students and teachers of this institution). He aspired to solve all the major problems of India in a small area of Santiniketan. He told "অল্প পরিমানে একজায়গাতেই আমরা ভারতের সমস্যার সমাধান করব।"[6] (We shall solve the problems of India in the same place in a small scale). Tagore emphasised that education of Ashrama should be based on truth. He endeavoured to remove miseries of Indians through this special type of education. Tagore believed: "The object of education is to give man the unity of truth"[7] we came to know from the above remark that Rabindranath desired to make education man oriented and inspired the student in the nation-building activities.

We know that Rabindranath wanted to reconstruct the Indian Village, to help the countrymen in their struggle for independence in a way, which was distinguished from that of other freedom fighters. He at first started such type of programme in his zamindari estate and thought that would be a model for the whole of India. With the same objectives he instructed the voluntary workers to implement various rural reconstruction programmes in the surrounding villages of Santiniketan from the beginning of the establishment of Ashrama. It was known that 'Ashrama Sammelani' would help the poor students from outside and destitute persons. Various rural reconstruction programmes were implemented at that time in the nearest village 'Bhubandanga' Rabindranath admired this kind of social service and wrote a letter in the year 1907: "তোমাদের গ্রামের কাজ ভালো চলছে শুনে আমি ভারী খুশী হয়েছি।"[8] (I am very glad to know that the rural activities of yours are going on well). He concentrated his activities at Santiniketan for the development of whole India. Even it is known that 'Swadeshi' songs of Rabindranath were sung in the Villages around Santiniketan under the leadership of Kalimohan Ghosh some young students established Night Schools at near by Santiniketan villages and devoted themselves to teach the illiterate villagers.

Gradually he felt that the villagers had many problems but those problems could not be solved by the students of Santiniketan Ashrama Vidyalaya. In the year 1912 he bought 'Surul Kuthibari' with twenty bighas of land from Narendra Prasanna Sinha of Raipur. In due course when he got the opportunity he associated 'Surul Kuthibari' with Santiniketan and formed Visva-Bharati; later on the 'Surul Kuthibari' and the entire area was named 'Sriniketan' (a graceful abode). Although Visva-Bharati was formed in a small area, its objectives were all embracing. Visva-Bharati was meant to be an international centre of culture and all round education where the world meets in a single nest. The motto of Visva-Bharati in Sanskrit language "যত্র বিশ্বম উন্নতি এক নীড়ম" Rabindranath instructed the students and teachers to go to the villages and to take the responsibility of redressing the sufferings of the villagers and make them self-reliant. He explained the significance of Visva-Bharati: "ভারতবর্ষে যদি সত্য বিদ্যালয় স্থাপিত হ.য় তবে গোড়া হইতেই সেই বিদ্যালয় তাহার অর্থশাস্ত্র, তাহার কৃষিতত্ত্ব, তাহার স্বাস্থ্যবিদ্যা, তাহার সমস্ত ব্যবহারীক বিজ্ঞানকে আপন প্রতিষ্ঠা-স্থানের চর্তুদিকবর্ত্তী পল্লীর মধ্যে প্রয়োগ করিয়া দেশের জীবনযাত্রার কেন্দ্রস্থান অধিকার করিবে। এই বিদ্যালয় উৎকৃষ্ট আদর্শে চাষ করিবে, গোপালন করিবে, কাপড় বুনিবে এবং নিজের আর্থিক সম্বল-লাভের জন্য সমবায় প্রণালী অবলম্বন করিয়া ছাত্র শিক্ষক ও চারিদিকের অধিবাসীদের সঙ্গে জীবিকার যোগে ঘনিষ্টভাবে যুক্ত হইবে। এইরূপ আদর্শ বিদ্যালয়কে আমি 'বিশ্বভারতী' নাম দিবার প্রস্তাব করিয়াছি।"[9] (If schools in a true sense are established in India, then its sciences of Economics, Agriculture, Hygiene and impact, all its operative sciences, should be spread out to the surrounding rural areas, centering round the original institution. This institution will then occupy the central place of Indian life style. This institution will arrange tilling in the best way, look after the cattle and weaving in ideal manner and by adopting cooperative method will achieve financial self-sufficiency. They will have to associate with neighbouring residents intimately, I have proposed to name this kind of institution as Visva-Bharati). Joy and freedom are two basic instructions of Rabindranath that is what the great poet has put into practice in Visva-Bharati where the students will be living its own life not only in contact with books but also with soil and nature. In fact Tagore's educational principle was, as he beautifully said that enrichments of emotions and intellect in the living presence of Nature. When the poet bought the house 'Surul Kuthibari' he had not any clear-cut idea about the utility of this house. Some of his followers thought that it was a haunted house and requested him to sale it but Rabindranath had a mission to set up an ideal rural reconstruction centre. He immediately took a decision to make full use of this house. We know that Rabindranath got by his side the dedicated services of the young foreigner named L. K. Elmhirst, who wished to devote himself in rural reconstruction programmes in India. Elmhirst records in his book: "It was in Newyork in November 1920 that I first met Tagore........... My dearest ambition was to get back to India and to work there in some Indian Village."[10] At first Rabindranath Tagore discussed with L.K. Elmhirst in regard to the harsh realities of Indian rural areas. He invited him to tackle the village problems through his expertise. Tagore told Elmhirst that "I have established an educational enterprise in India which is almost wholly academic. It is situated well out in the countryside of west Bengal at Santiniketan. We are surrounded by villages, Hindu, Muslim, Santali. Except that we employ a number of these village folk for various menial tasks in my schools, we have no intimate contact with them at all inside their own communities. For some reason these villages appear to be in a state of steady decline. In fact they are all in decay. Some years ago I bought from the Sinha family a farm just out side the village Surul, a little over a mile from my school. I hear that you might be interested in going to live and work in such a farm in order to find out more clearly the causes of this decay".[11] L. K. Elmhirst, motivated by Tagore's missionary zeal come to Santiniketan in the year 1921 in November. At first he emphasized to learn Bengali, Ehmhirst recounted "Early in January 1922. Tagore called me into his room and said; the ten of our college students, who say they want to become farmers, are impatient to start work. They and the members of your staff are all Bengalis and all know English. I can't wait any longer. How soon can you all take up your residence on the farm at Surul? Stop your Bengali lessons. If you learn too much Bengali yourself you'll want to go on your own to the village to ask them your questions. You will then make the great mistake of trying to become indispensable to this enterprise like any missionary. I want you never to go alone to any village but always to take with you either a student or a member of your staff to act as interpreter. Only in this way they will learn what kind of questions you ask just how the farmers and villagers frame their answers. These answers they will then have to interpret back to you. In this way they will never forget the experience"[12] L. K. Elmhirst led the rural reconstruction programmes at Sriniketan. He may be called a pioneer in this field. The noble dream of Tagore could not have materialised with out the acute involvement and financial support of L. K. Elmhirst. Kalimohan Ghosh was another person who assisted Tagore on rural reconstruction programmes. In the year 1922 on 6th February Sriniketan was formally opened L.K. Elmhirst recounts : "On February 17th 1922 we all set out for Surul together on our Ford lorry with our Pots, pans and tools".[13] He instructed to social workers to establish developmental organizations through cooperative efforts of villagers which may solve all village problems in such a manner that villagers could help them selves, Rabindranath always emphasised on 'organized force' to reconstruct the Indian village in all its aspects. For this reason a separate organisation was built up at Sriniketan named 'Palli Samgathana Vibhaga' (PSV). The discipline was a key-factor in this venture. Some of eminent social workers and followers participated in the organisation to implement the Tagore's rural reconstruction programme. Tagore wanted to utilise modern resources to develop the village life in all its aspect through the proper village organisation. He thought it would not be possible to develop the village without organised force of the villagers. According to Tagore's desire., social workers of Sriniketan would go to the village to make aware the villagers to follow cooperative principle and establish village organisation. They tried to develop the leadership qualities among the rural youth for the development of their own village. Various village organisations were established in the village, after the Sriniketan model. This type of village organisations would contribute towards reconstruction of the villages in all its aspccts specially health, education and village economy.

Rabindranath had acquired sufficient knowledge about village life and the problems during his supervision of his zamindari estate. He noted his experience thus: "ক্রমে এই পল্লীর দুঃখ দৈন্য আমার কাছে সুস্পষ্ট হয়ে উঠল, তার জন্য কিছু করব এই আকাঙ্খায় আমার মন ছটপট করে উঠেছিল।"[14] (Gradually, weak points of this village became clear to me. I was suffering from a tense desire to do something for this place). We all know that he disliked the outside charity and desired to utilise village resources. Tagore was worried about the upliftment of village life: "কী করলে এদের মনের উদ্‌বোধন হয়, আপনাদের দায়িত্ব এরা আপনি নিতে পারে। আমরা যদি বাইরে থেকে সাহায্য করি তাতে এদের অনিষ্টই হবে। কী করলে এদের মধ্যে জীবন সঞ্চার হবে, এই প্রশ্নই তখন আমাকে ভাবিয়ে তুলেছিল।"[15] How to awaken their minds and how they can discharge their duties on their own. They will be harmed if we help them from outside. I was then, in fact, worried about how to improve and reform their lifestyle. He farther observed: "পল্লীর মধ্যে সমগ্রভাবে প্রাণ সঞ্চার হলে তবেই সেই প্রাণের সমপূর্ণতা নিজেকে প্রতিনিয়ত রক্ষা করবার শক্তি নিজের ভিতর থেকেই উদভাবন করতে পারবে কেমন করে সেটা হবে সেই তত্ত্বটাই কাজে ও কথায় কিছু কাল থেকে ভাবছি।"[16] (If enthusiasm is created amongst villagers then only a sense of fulfilment of life will constantly try to save them by deriving power from within themselves. I was thinking for sometimes as to how that theory could be given a practical shape). Tagore and Gandhiji both wanted to make village dependent on its own resources. But Gandhiji wanted this to serve the political purposes. "The initial differences of approach of these two men, Tagore and Gandhiji to the idea of a free and self governing India, remained".[17] Of course Gandhiji tried to get theoritical help from Tagore in his political movement for 'Swaraj' Gandhiji told Rabindranath : "Gurudev, you were yourself a leader and promoter of the Swadeshi (National) movement some twenty years ago. You always wanted Indians to stand on their own feet as Indians and not to be poor copies of westerners. My 'Swaraj' movement today is the natural off spring of your own Swadeshi."[18] Gandhiji understood Tagore's aspiration, but at that time no national political leaders responded to Tagore's call. "যখন এ কথা কাউকে বলে - কয়ে বোঝাতে পারলুম না যে, আমাদের স্বায়ত্বশাসনের ক্ষেত্র হচ্ছে কৃষিপল্লীতে, তার চর্চা আজ থেকেই শুরু করা চাই, তখন কিছুক্ষনের জন্যে কলম কানে গুঁজে এ কথা আমাকে বলতে হল – আচ্ছা, আমিই এ কাজে লাগব।"[19] (When I failed to convince the people that the idea of self rule should start from the villages of farmers and that cultivation of the same should start right from today. I for sometime kept tight-lipped. Then I vowed that I should myself take up the job). He empathetically declared that only one village in any part of the country could be reconstructed by undertaking various programmes and by developing that single unit through the cooperative efforts of villages which should be a model village. "আমার প্রস্তাব এই যে, বাংলাদেশের যেখানে হোক একটি গ্রাম আমরা হাতে নিয়ে তাকে আত্মশাসনের শক্তিতে সমপূর্ণ উদ্বোধিত করে তুলি। সে গ্রামের রাস্তাঘাট, তার ঘরবাড়ির পারিপাট্য, তার পাঠশালা, তার সাহিত্যচর্চা ও আমোদপ্রমোদ, তার রোগীর পরিচর্যা ও চিকিৎসা, তার বিবাদ নিষ্পত্তি প্রভৃতি সমস্ত কার্যভার সুবিহিত নিয়মে গ্রামবাসীদের দ্বারা সাধন করাবার উদ্যোগ আমরা করি।"[20] (This is my proposal that let us take up a particular village of Bengal and it inspire it by injecting mental power towards autonomous rule. We shall see to it that the villagers become self-sufficient enough to make roads, arrange health centers for the nursing and treatment of the rural people, entertainment programmes and set up peoples court to settle disputes etc. all efficiently). He devoted himself to make villagers stand on their own feet through the establishment of Sriniketan. In his various speeches the poet expressed his vision by saying that if he could build only two or three model villages through their own resources that would be a concrete ideal for the country "আমি যদি কেবল দুটি-তিনটি গ্রামকেও মুক্তি দিতে পারি অজ্ঞতা অক্ষমতার বন্ধন থেকে, তবে সেখানেই সমগ্র ভারতের একটি আদর্শ তৈরী হবে।"[21] (If I can set free only two or three villages from ignorance and incapacity then it will produce an ideal symbolic center for whole of India). We can realise from these speeches the significance of Sriniketan as a model rural reconstruction centre in India.

For the development of agriculture and there by to develop village economy, he established at Surul the 'Department of agriculture and village Economies' in 1922. In the year 1930 Rabindranath visited Russia witnessing the experimental activities of Russian people. He was deeply impressed and his own projects, still a mere vision were reinforced. The Russian people had already been implementing those programmes to make themselves self-reliant. He recorded in *Russiar Chithi*: "আমি যা বহুকাল ধ্যান করেছি, রাশিয়ায় দেখলুম এরা তা কাজে খাটিয়েছে"[22] (That what I pondered upon for long has been practically implemented by Russia. Which I have myself witnessed). He at once decided that it would be better if he could send some of his workers of Sriniketan to undertake training in Russia from where they could take lessons in rural reconstruction. He noted: "আমরা শ্রীনিকেতনে যা করতে চেয়েছি এরা সমস্ত দেশজুড়ে প্রকৃষ্টভাবে তাই করেছে। আমাদের কর্মীরা যদি কিছুদিন এখানে এসে শিক্ষা করে যেতে পারত তা হলে ভারি উপকার হত।"[23] (That what we wanted to do at Sriniketan has been very efficiently practiced by the Russians throughout their country. It would have benefited our workers if they could learn something from the Russian experiments by visiting the country). He had a desire that the Indian rural people would also be inspired like the Russian to develop their own country and he wanted that Sriniketan should take up such a responsibility. He realised that:

"এটা খুব করে বুঝেছি, আমাদের সবচেয়ে বড়ো কাজ শ্রীনিকেতনে। সমস্ত দেশকে কী করে বাঁচাতে হবে ঐখানে ছোট আকারে তারই নিষ্পত্তি করা আমাদের ব্রত।"[24] (I have thoroughly realised that our greatest ideal could only be experimented at Sriniketan. Our task would therefore be to bring into reality at that very place even if in a small scale, our aim of saving the country). He endeavoured to make villages self-dependent around Sriniketan and implemented there various rural reconstruction programmes through utilizing the rich collective power of the villagers. For successful implementation of the programmes he gave some guidelines. These are as follows:[25]

(1) To win the friendship and affection of the villagers and cultivators by taking a real interest in all that concerns their life and welfare, and by making a lively effort to assist them in solving their most pressing problem.

(2) To take the problems of the village and the field to the classroom for study and discussion and to the experimental farm for solution.

(3) To carry the knowledge and experience gained in the classroom and experimental farm to the villagers in the endeavour to improve their sanitation and health, to develop their resources and credit, to help them to sell their produce and by their requirements to the best advantage ; to teach them better methods of growing crops and vegetables and of keeping live stock; to encourage them to learn and practice arts and crafts, and to bring home to them the benefits of associated life, mutual aid and common endeavours.

(4) To work out practically and all round system of elementary education in the village based on the boy Scout ideal and training, with the object of developing ideas of citizenship and public duty such as may appeal to the villagers and be within their means and capacity

(5) To encourage in the staff and students of the department it-self a spirit of sincere service and willing sacrifice in the interest of and on terms of comradeship with their poorer, less educated and greatly harassed neighbours in the village.

(6) To train the students to a due sense of their own intrinsic worth, physical and moral and in particular to teach them to do their own hands everything

which a village house holder as a cultivator does or should do for a living if possible, more efficiently.

(7) To put the students in the way of acquiring, practical experience in cultivation, dairing, animal husbandry, poultry keeping, carpentry, smithing, weaving, tanning, practical sanitation work and in the art and spirit of cooperation.

(8) To give the students elementary instruction in sciences connected with their practical work, to train them to think and observe accurately, and to express and record the knowledge acquired by them for their own benefit and for that of their fellow men.

Besides the above guidelines, Rabindranath instructed his village workers to adopt three principles to implement various plans and programmes to make self-reliant village. These are as follows:

(1) The people must be helped by helping themselves.

(2) When services are given to the villagers it must be given with respect.

(3) We can not help merely by our willingness to help. There is nothing so dangerous as inexpert service. If we want to serve we must learn.

So we come to know that Rabindranath wanted to reconstruct the village through acquiring sufficient knowledge about the problems and concluded that it should be solved by the united efforts of the villagers. He desired to help the villagers by asking them to help themselves. Tagore wanted to reconstruct the village in such a manner that they could comprehend their problems and solve them unitedly through the effective utilisation of the village sources. He implemented various programmes to improve health education and economy through the cooperative efforts of villagers. For this purpose he directed his followers to establish village organisations, to tackle all types of village problems.

HEALTH: Unluckily when Tagore began the programmes of Sriniketan, he witnessed the epidemic form of Malaria, the villages around Sriniketan, like as other places in the country "Even an ordinary preventable decease like malaria caused more then 18 million deaths between 1901-1921"[26]. So he significantly remarked: "এই কাজ হাতে নিয়ে দেখা গেল — রোগের ছবি"[27] (when the job was taken up, the dismal picture of sickness emerged). He realised that villagers were in a dying state and immediately instructed his social workers to undertake such health and educational programmes which would free the villagers from the grip of malaria. He emphasized on ones own power and united efforts to control the disease and tried to improve the village health. The poet told the villager "শত্রু যত বড়োই হোক, তাকে মানব না, মশাকে রাখব না, যেমন করে পারি উচ্ছেদ করব — এ সাহস যদি হয় তবে কেবল মশা নয়, তার চেয়ে বড়ো শত্রু নিজেদের দীনতার উপর জয় লাভ করব।"[28] (However great the enemy may be we shall ignore it. We shall destroy the mosquitoes at any cost. If we can dare this menace, then, not only the mosquitoes but our greatest enemy our inferiority would be won over). At that time Sriniketan used to help the villagers only through outside expertise and with the participation in the various programmes, which were organised by the villagers: "It did not take long to realise that any scheme involving charity will defeat its own object. The problem was to devise a scheme of health work which could be maintained by the people themselves."[29] The procedure of work is known to us from the following lines[30]: "It would seem to us that the first steps in approaching the village health problem would be: (1) to find out that the health problem really is, (2) To prevail upon the villagers to purchase cooperatively as much of the means of solving the problem as they are capable of doing." Sriniketan would help the villagers only to organise cooperative health society to solve the health problem in the village: "The health societies run by the villagers themselves are an excellent example of self-help and cooperation both from financial as well as organisational points of view. Sriniketan acts in relation to the functioning of these societies, merely as helper."[31] This way the work was started to improve the village health through cooperative efforts of villagers around Sriniketan. An American lady named Mrs. Grichen Green came to Sriniketan to serve the villager in the year 1923. She was much inspired with Tagore's ideal of rural reconstruction programme. She nursed the villager with out any hesitation. A clinic and a health centre were established by her efforts. Besides this, another foreigner named Dr. Harri Timbers came for survey on behalf of American Friends Society in the year 1929. Rabindranath gave due respect to those foreigners who devoted themselves to Sriniketan programmes "বিদেশী লোকের কাছে সাহায্য পেয়েছি, সে কথা কৃতজ্ঞতার সহিত স্বীকার করছি"[32] (Let me gratefully acknowledge that I have received help from foreign friends). In the year 1927, Sisir Kumar Basu commemorated his late two daughters "Aruna and Amita" and donated ten thousand rupees to provide Medicines and sick diet to the local patients. Aruna Amita endowment fund was formed with this money. We knew that Rabindranath put emphasis on the village organisation to solve the village problem, so he sent Kalimohan Ghosh to a foreign country to study rural health organisation in the year 1930. The health societies were well organised under his suitable leadership in the surrounding villages of Sriniketan. At that time with the help of the judge of Birbhum district some government grants were received and the number of health societies were increased in the district. Various village sanitation work were done through the cooperative efforts of the villagers as jungle cleaning, filling up pits, distribution of quinine and kerosinisation to check the breeding of mosquitoes in stagnant waters etc. The 'Brati' organisation was formed among young boys and girls and they were trained on different village welfare work for making suitable village worker in future.

EDUCATION : Tagore thought education was the main means for the development of the Indian villages. He wanted to free villagers from ignorance and incapability through proper educational extension programme. He said: "নূতন একটা কর্মের দিকে আমার চিত্ত ধাবিত হল, মনে হল শিক্ষার ভিতর দিয়ে সমস্ত দেশের সেবা করব"[33] (My heart was driven towards a new task. I thought that I could serve the whole country through education). Because according to Tagore, education should not be dragged out of its national elements the life current of the people. He adds economic life covers the whole wide of the fundamental basis of the Society, because its necessities are the simplest and most universal. Educational institutions in order to obtain their fullness of truth must have a close association with the economic life. Our centre of culture should not only be the centre of intellectual life of India, but the centric economic life also. It must cooperate with the villages around it, cultivate land, breed cattle spine cloths, press oil from oilseeds, It must produce all necessities devising the best means, using the best material and calling science to it's aid.

The cardinal principles of his educational philosophy are: (1) Freedom of mind, (2) Creative self-expression, (3) Active communion with nature and man, (4) Self-realisation and (5) The study of ancient heritage for the education of the whole. Tagore criticised the present education system. Regarding the basic philosophy of education he said that education in all its different forms and channels has its ultimate purpose in the evolving of a luminous sphere of human mind from the nebula that has been rushing round ages to find in it self and eternal centre of unity. Tagore said that our education should be in full touch with our complete life, economical, intellectual, aesthetic, social and spiritual; and our educational institutions should be in the very heart of our society connected with it by the living bonds of varied co-operations. Tagore wanted to relate education to the needs and aspirations of human life. According to him, education should help to create a new social order and the good for each individual to live and work. It should help for betterment of social, cultural, political and economic life of every individual and the nation. With this aim he established Visva-Bharati and particularly Siksha Satra at Santiniketan later on shifted to Sriniketan. It was unfortunate that the villagers were not aware of Tagore's ideals of education due to ignorance. Rabindranath tried to remove their ignorance and superstitions through imparting scientific knowledge. He inspired them to cooperate with one another in their development activities. He emphasized on education because he believed that only education could remove their selfishness and help them to cooperate among themselves. He said: "তাহাদের পরস্পরের মধ্যে

একটা রাস্তা থাকা চাই, সেটা যদি রাজপথ না হয় তো অন্তত গলিরাস্তা হওয়া চাই। লেখাপড়া শেখাই সেই রাস্তা।"[34] (There should be way out in regard to their mutual selves. That should at least be a small lane if not a high road and that is imbibing knowledge through education). He realised that villagers were deprived of education and removal of illiteracy was essential. In his scheme education was to be extended for all people. He said: "আজ আমাদের সকলের চেয়ে বড়ো দরকার শিক্ষার সাম্য।"[35] (Our main requirement today is the principle of social equality in this sphere of education). Rabindranath aimed at to develop the village-centric India through education. In view of the efforts that are being made to day to reorient educational system to meet the needs of people of free India. Tagore about 75 years ago gave a concrete shape in Siksha Satra. According to him, we must show endeavour that a power from within the villages themselves may be working along side of us albeit indiscernible by us.

Rabindranath wanted to enrich the quality of human beings and their own power through extension of real education. He wished to free only two or three villages bonds on ignorance and weakness, there will be built on a tiny scale, and ideal for the whole of India. Education for all should be winds of joy blowing across the villages. He selected Santiniketan as an ideal place to implement his idea. He observed : ল্লআজ প্রায় চল্লিশবছর হল শিক্ষা ও পল্লী সংস্কারের সংকল্প নিয়ে পদ্মাতীর থেকে শান্তিনিকেতন আশ্রমে আসন বদল করেছি।"[36] (Forty years have rolled by since I changed my sit from the bank of Padma to Santiniketan with a vow to take up the job of imparting education and rural reconstruction). We know that Ashrama vidyalaya was established in 1901 and students took their lesson under trees. Tagore wanted that education should close to life and nature so that the students in future would be suitable workers of the country. After independence we have introduced work education programme but Tagore introduced this programmes in his Ashrama Vidyalaya and also in Siksha Satra long ago. He was of the opinion that education should not be confined within the four walls of school. He had a bitter experience in his early school days. We come to know from his *'Jibansmriti'* "আমার দিনগুলি নর্মাল স্কুলের হাঁ-করা মুখ-বিবরের মধ্যে তাহার প্রাত্যহিক বরা গ্রাসপিন্ডের মতো প্রবেশ করিতে

লাগিল।"[37] (My days at normal school were being devoured like mouthful 'mosels there daily dues). For this reason he established another type of school like after the ideal of hermitage situated in a forest. He believed on plain living and high thinking. He gave a clarion call to the students to lead a simple life and to concentrate on their India's past glory. He told the students: "ভোগের পথে নহে, ভিক্ষার পথে নহে, কর্মের পথে। দেশের কাব্যে গানে ছড়ায়, প্রাচীন মন্দিরের ভগ্নাবশেষে কীটদ্রষ্ট পুঁথির জীর্ন পত্রে, গ্রাম্য পার্বনে, ব্রত কথায়, পল্লীর কৃষি কুটিরে, প্রত্যক্ষ বস্তুকে স্বাধিন চিন্তা ও গবেষনার দ্বারা জানিবার জন্য - তোমাদিগকে আহ্বান করিতেছি।"[38] (Neither through following the ways of materialistic enjoyments, nor through begging, but through work. I invite you all to enrich you through the means of country's poetry, songs limericks, ruins of temples, ancient work out pages of scripts rural festivities, narrations and farmers cottages. All this should be done with the help of research and free thinking). He desired that education should be useful to the students so that in near future they would be suitable village workers and village leaders would grow among themselves. He expected the future leadership of the village to come from these educated boys and girls. For this reason another school was established named Siksha Satra for village youth. The objective of the school was to teach the students in such a manner that they could take a part in their lessons through practical experience, which would help those students to take leadership in their village reconstruction programme. Rabindranath while underlining the importance of Siksha Satra said : "I had to start a parallel school where the villagers who do not have ambitions for finding government employment or employment in merchant offices."[39] The students of Siksha Satra were taught various aspects of modern science. Rabindranath desired that the students of Siksha Satra would take up the leadership of their village and participate in all aspects of social life to release the villagers from the darkness of ignorance and superstition. The students of Siksha Satra would be helpful to built up the scientific attitude among villagers: "শিক্ষাসত্রের ছাত্ররা যে সর্ব্বাঙ্গীন শিক্ষা পাইবে তাহার দ্বারা তারা যে কেবল আপনাদের জীবিকা অর্জন করিবে তাহা নহে, তাহারা গ্রামে গিয়া গ্রামের উন্নতি করিতে পারিবে তাহার হইবে Village Leaders"[40] (The all-round education that the Siksha Satra students will receive may help them not only do earn their living but they will also take up the village reconstruction work. Thus they will become village leaders). So, in the year 1927 Siksha Satra was transferred from Santiniketan to the appropriate place like Sriniketan where a rural reconstruction centre was established.

A teachers training centre was also established at Sriniketan in the year 1937 by the help of government grants. The name of this centre was Siksha Charcha. Various aspects of village life were taught through this centre. Another project was started for the training of village teachers. Every Sunday, local teachers would come at Sriniketan. They were taught on various aspects of teaching methods, health and sanitation, basic agriculture, Brati organisation, language, literature, geography and science.

We know that Rabindranath emphasized on women education to make them self-reliant and a girl's school was established in the year 1923. The girls are given instruction in needle work, embroidery, cooking and gardening".[41] One could note here also that Tagore wanted to enrich woman power, so that they would take active part in rural reconstruction programmes. He felt that some books on nutrition and child care should be written in simple bengali to help mothers. Different problems of women were also discussed in the school and Mahila Samity. Rabindranath was very keen to raise the social status of women and by the year 1935, he kindly agreed inaugural to a Mahila Sammmelan organised right at Sriniketan.

Another programme was launched at Santiniketan in the year 1937. It was named 'Loksiksha samsad'. This programme was later on transferred to Sriniketan in the year 1943. It was in fact mass education programme, the system of Loksiksha samsad was like to days 'distance education', the people, irrespective of age, sex, and status would receive education at their door step. This programme would be organised through a separate board of Visva-Bharati. After Tagore's death it had been continuing for long years, but unfortunately it discontinued due to lack of proper leadership. Night Schools were opened in the surrounding villages of Santiniketan and Sriniketan for the illiterate villagers who were busy during day time. It was known that boys of Ashrama took up responsibility to teach the villagers: "আশ্রমের এক-একটি ছেলে এক-একটি ছাত্রের ভার লইত।"[42] (Each students of the Ashrama used to take care of one student). In the year 1927, `Prasad Smriti Welfare Fund' was established for organising Night School. Within three years after the establishment of rural reconstruction Centre in the year 1925, library service was extended to the villages. A mobile library was also started. Various books on rural economics, cooperative movement, dairy and allied subjects were collected in Sriniketan library. Besides educational activities, Rabindranath emphasised on research and survey in the surrounding villages of Sriniketan, because it was clear to him that without having any knowledge about the village problems no reconstruction could be taken up.

AGRICULTURE : India lives in villages and during that period most of the villager's main occupation was agriculture. So Rabindranath emphasised on the importance of agriculture to make village economy self-reliant. He realised it could not be possible to develop economy without improved agriculture. So he took up various programme on agriculture through proper utilisation of science and technology in the surrounding village of Sriniketan. According to Tagore the cooperative efforts of villagers and proper utilisation of village resources could build a self-reliant village. In the year 1922 he established a separate department to develop agriculture and to make self-reliant economy. He himself ploughed in 'Halakarshana Utsav' to inspire the villagers for cultivation. According to him, agriculture is not an undignified profession. He said "আজ সুরুলে হল চালনা উৎসব হবে। লাঙল ধরতে হবে আমাকে। বৈদিক মন্ত্র-যোগে কাজটা করতে হবে বলে এর অসম্মানের অনেকটা হ্রাস হবে।"[43] (The ploughing festival will be held today at Surul. I have to pick up the plough. As the work will be introduced with vedic hymns the disrespectability attached to it will be reduced to great extent). He planned different programmes and collected information for the agricultural development in the surrounding villages of Sriniketan. As we said earlier he desired to make

Sriniketan a model for the whole of India. He wrote in a letter "যেখানে জলের অত্যন্ত অভাব সেখানকার জন্যে অস্ট্রেলিয়ার কি একটা গাছ লাগিয়ে ভারতবর্ষের কোথাও কোথাও বিশেষ ফল পাওয়া গেছে – সেই গাছ গোরুর খাদ্য। গাছটা কি জানলে বোলপুরের জন্য চেষ্টা করা যেতে পারে।"[44] (Some tree belonging to Australia, were planted at the place where there is due need of water, it has produced good result in India. That tree is in fact fodder for the cow. The name of the tree if known, may be brought to Bolpur). Realising the psychology of the villagers, he felt that the villagers would not follow the method of cultivation if that was not demonstrated to them and so he established a demonstrating agricultural farm at Sriniketan. Rabindranath took various plans and programmes and directed his workers to implement those programmes in the surrounding villages of Sriniketan. He liked to provide expert knowledge to the village farmer through Sriniketan and he wanted attention to be given to specified problems and solution found for them. For the reason he wanted agricultural demonstration to be given on the peasants plots in addition to those carried out on institute's own farm. Besides these activities, Rabindranath composed some songs to inspire village farmer, L. K. Elmhirst informed us 'Amra chash kori Anande'. We plough with joy and this song was adopted by our chasas as the appropriate song of Surul".[45] Animal husbandry and fishery was also developed to improve the village economy. He wrote a letter: "সন্তোষ পাঁচটি গোরু নিয়ে বোলপুর বিদ্যালয়েই একটি ছোটোখাটো Dairy খুলেছে। বোলপুরে গোরু রাখার বিস্তর অসুবিধা, ঘাস নেই — তবু দেখা যাচ্ছে লোকসান হবার আশঙ্কা বেশী নয়।"[46] (Sontosh has opened a small dairy farm right at Bolpur school with five cows. Bolpur has many problems to keep cows, scarcity of fodder yet we find that there is little fear of loss). We came to know that Rabindranath tried to plant Australian tree at Bolpur as a fodder. At that time milk and milk products were sold from Sriniketan dairy. In the year 1924 a poultry and goatery were established. In the year 1927 two big ponds were dug for the purpose of irrigation and Fishery. Rabindranath used to collect information about weather through news papers like an eminent agriculture scientist. He was worried about the sufferings of village farmers. He wrote in a letter. " এরকম মেঘছায়া শ্যামল বর্ষন মুখর দিন মোটের উপর আমার ভালোই লাগে। কিন্তু এই

সময়টা, মাঠে যখন আউস ধান কাটবার দিন আসন্ন হয়ে এল, তখন মনের থেকে উদ্বেগ কিছুতেই যেতে চায় না ... তাই প্রতিদিন খবরের কাগজটা খুলে সব প্রথমে আমি Weather report টা দেখে নিই।"[47] (On the whole I rather like this kind of sky overcast with dark raur-soaked clouds. But at this time when the season for reaping the ous-paddy comes near worries constantly trouble us. That is why I first have a look over the weather chart in the daily newspaper). A small meteorological centre was established at Sriniketan in 1929. Indian meteorological department provided some assistance to the centre.

RURAL INDUSTRY : Rabindranath wanted to develop rural Industry along with agriculture for self-sufficient economy of the village. He inspired villagers to earn money through rural Industry in their leisure time. Mahatma Gandhi emphasized on spinning for making khadi in leisure time of villagers, but Rabindranath opposed to Gandhi's emphasis on spinning only and put emphasis on different kinds of rural industry in the village so that villagers would enjoy their creativity and as well earn money. In the year 1922, Tagore established a centre named 'Bichitra studio' for the development of rural Industry in the village. Under the supervision of his daughter in law that centre started its functioning. In the year 1928 this centre was transferred to Sriniketan with a new name 'Silpa Bhavana'. Rabindranath tried to develop rural industry in the village providing suitable training to the local artisans and village youth. He invited some eminent artisans from different countries to Sriniketan for more attractive productions at 'Silpa-Bhavana'. At that time the production of Silpa Bhavana was famous 'The goods produced at Silpa-Bhavana, by the villagers'of the surrounding area flooded the markets of all major towns and villages of India".[48] Different cottage industries were started at Silpa Bhavana like weaving, leather work, wood work, pottery, Batik, book-binding, fruit preservation and canning, embroidery etc. In the year 1938 Silpa Bhavana was converted to a separate department. It may be mentioned here, later on the department is called 'Silpa Sadana'.

COOPERATIVE : We can imagine that a believer in internationalism had little faith in individualism for improving the quality of human beings, without cooperation among the individuals that could not be achieved. So Tagore put much emphasis on cooperation. He wanted to use science and technology in rural reconstruction through cooperative principle. As he thought that outside charity could not be developed the Indian village. He put emphasis on own power and united efforts of villagers for the utilization of village resources in rural reconstruction programme. He wrote in a letter: "চাষীকে আত্মশক্তিতে দৃঢ় করে তুলতে হবে, এই ছিল আমার অভিপ্রায়। এ সম্বন্ধে দুটো কথা সর্বদাই আমার মনে আন্দোলিত হয়েছে — জমির স্বত্ব ন্যায়ত জমিদারের নয়, সে চাষীর; দ্বিতীয়তঃ সমবায়নীতি অনুসারে চাষের ক্ষেত্র একত্র করে চাষ না করতে পারলে কৃষির উন্নতি হতেই পারে না।"[49] (We have to empower, the farmer with the idea of self-reliance and make them determined and this is my intention. I toy always with two ideas: The ownership of the land does not justifiably belong to the 'zamindar' himself but to the farmer; secondly no improvement in farming is possible if we do not till the land by collecting together, the lands for farming according to cooperative principles). He inspired the villagers to unite their cultivated land pieces and adopt scientific method of cultivation through cooperative efforts. He told the village farmer: "তোমরা সমস্ত জমি এক সঙ্গে চাষ করো, সকলের যা সম্বল আছে, সামর্থ আছে তা একত্র করো, তাহলে অনায়াসে ট্রাক্টর দিয়ে তোমাদের জমি চাষ করা চলবে। সকলে একত্র কাজ করলে জমির সামান্য তারতম্যে কিছু যায় আসে না"[50] (You till the land all together, collect together whatever provisions and capacity you have. Then you can till the land easily with the help of tractors. It does not matter if some qualitative differences in land measurement occur in this united effort) To him cooperation was the best method through which the villagers would come close to each other and be able to improve not only their economic conditions but also social status and moral values. He said : "যারা দুর্বল, পরস্পরের প্রতি বিশ্বাস তাদের দূর্বল। নিজের পরে অশ্রদ্ধাই অপরের প্রতি অশ্রদ্ধার ভিত্তি"[51] (Faith in one another gets weak in the case of those who are themselves weak. The cause of disrespects for others is due to one's lack of respect for one self). He realised that it could not be possible to develop the Indian villages without cooperation. He warned the social workers and villagers and advised them not to depend on charity. According to him, charity creates helplessness among man and it destroys cooperative attitude among the people: "মনের যে দৈন্যে মানুষ আপনাকে অন্যের সঙ্গে বিচ্ছিন্ন করে সেই দৈন্যেই সে সকল দিকেই মরতে বসে, তখন বাইরের দিক থেকে কেউ তাকে বাঁচাতে পারে না।"[52] (Deficiency of mind that separates a man from other man makes one's existence at stake on all accounts and then no body can save him from outside). As Indian farmers are poor and plots of land are small, he advised them to pool up their individual resources including land to cultivate it in a cooperative method. He said: "ইহা দিগকে বুঝাইয়া দিতে হইবে, যাহা একজনে না পারে তাহা পঞ্চাশজনে জোট বাঁধিলেই হইতে পারে।"[53] (We have to make them realised what that one can not do can be done through united effort of fifty persons). Indeed he gave much emphasis on cooperative principle: "এই কো-অপারেটিভ প্রণালীই আমাদের দেশকে দারিদ্র হইতে বাঁচাইবার একমাত্র উপায়"[54] (This cooperative method is only way to save the country from poverty). Not only in the field of agriculture but also in all socio-economic schemes, he wanted to adopt cooperative method. He observed: "ভারতবর্ষে জীবিকা যদি সমবায়নীতির উপর প্রতিষ্ঠিত হয় তবে ভারত সভ্যতার ধাত্রী-ভূমি গ্রামগুলি আবার বেঁচে উঠবে ও সমস্ত দেশকে বাঁচাবে"[55] (If earning in India is based on cooperative method then the nursing source up Indian culture, the villages, will be revived again). So he always desired to follow cooperative principle and further said: ""আমাদের দেশে আমাদের পল্লীতে পল্লীতে ধন-উৎপাদন ও পরিচালনার কাজে সমবায়নীতির জয় হোক, এই কামনা করি"[56] (I wish the success of cooperative principle in the sphere of capital production and management in the village). So in all activities of Visva-Bharati, he tried to introduce cooperative system. He often consulted his social workers and took joint decision In his opinion: "আর সকল দেশ এগিয়ে চলেছে, আমরা অজ্ঞানে অশিক্ষায় স্থাবর হয়ে পড়ে আছি। এ-সমস্তই দুর হয়ে যাবে যদি নিজের শক্তি সম্বলকে সমবেত করতে পারি। আমাদের এই শ্রীনিকেতনে জনসাধারণের সেই শক্তি সমবায়ের সাধনা।"[57] (All the other countries are progressing fast, but we are lying as fossils in the darkness of ignorance and lack of education. All this will be removed, if we can collect together all the power we possess. Our efforts are aimed at bringing together at Sriniketan this power of the people). L.K. Elmhirst reported us: "We decided to offer major or minor projects for each student to work on and to try and established cooperation among the local farmers in buying, selling and for credit"[58]. The Visva-Bharati central Bank was established to free the villagers from the grip of moneylenders.

Some cooperative societies were established through their united efforts. Cooperative health society was established for the improvement of village health and sanitation. These societies were established by under the suitable leadership of Kalimohan Ghosh. Besides this, under the leadership of Sriniketan workers various cooperative societies were organised such as irrigation societies, Dharmagola Samity to offer loan of grains at that time of scarcity of food. Agricultural credit society was there to offer loan for cultivation.

ROLE OF YOUTH: Rural youths were the force, which could motivate the villagers and could take the responsibility for the village development activities through united efforts. From the beginning of Ashrama, Rabindranath inspired the students to participate in the various constructive programmes in the surrounding villages of Santiniketan. Students of Ashrama were instructed to help in times of danger. Many times the Ashrama students went to help the villagers when fire broke out. Tagore established a significant organisation among youth named 'Sahayak Sangha' or 'Brati organisation' who would devote themselves in rural upliftment programmes. He tried to build up a second line leadership in the village development activities. Various suitable training programmes were arranged to provide training to these rural young boys and girls: "In order that the youth could play a vital role in helping to push forward the general programme of rural reconstruction".[59] According to Tagore's aspiration the rural young boys and girls would actively participate in the reconstruction programme with other villagers. The poet and philosopher believed in the strength of organised youth force and "he built a volunteer force recruited from the village youth. He advised them to take the vow of service to the villages. To remind them constantly of the spirit with which they were expected to serve the country, he named them the 'Brati Dal'".[60] Brati organisation was trained about various aspects of rural reconstruction that they could lead the villagers: 'To teach the village boys the idea of Social service, ... A training camp is held each year for the training of village boys as leaders of Brati Balakas in their own villages.[61] Brati organisation was the most important programme of Rabindranath. He thought that Brati education is not less important than any other educational programmes. At first Brati organisation was started in the nearest village of Sriniketan named 'Mahidapur' and in the thirty decades of the nineties Brati organisation were formed in the surrounding villages of Sriniketan. Cadres of brati dal actively participated in various rural reconstruction programmes in their own village like road-making, jungle-cleaning, distribution of quinine for malaria treatment to patients, Brati organisation volunteers participated in the kerosinisation in the stagnant water, cleaning the drain and filling up the pits etc. They participated in games and drills for their physical and mental development. They collected data on malaria and took preventive measures against cholera. They collected and distributed cloths and diet to the patients.

There were two divisions of Brati organisation, one was 'Brati Balaka organisation' and another was 'youth organisation'. After sixteen years of their age, the membership of the youths could be shifted to 'youth organization'. This youth organization took active part in rural reconstruction programme and led the villagers towards health, education economy etc. The youth organization would communicate between their village and Sriniketan to reconstruct the village looking after all its needs. They involved to solve various village problems through the help of Sriniketan. This way we can realise the important role of youth force in rural reconstruction programme at Sriniketan.

VILLAGE DEVELOPMENT ORGANISATIONS : A self-reliant village through cooperative efforts of villagers and utilisation of village resources were the main objectives of Tagore's rural upliftment programme. He instructed his followers to establish village organization where villagers would be assembled and solve their village problems through cooperative efforts. According to his idea various village development organization were established in the surrounding villages of Sriniketan. The poet wanted village development organization to be grown out of the need of the villagers so that they could help themselves through this organization. He explained: "আমি বলেছি সমাজের ভিতর থেকে সমাজের শক্তিকে জাগাতে হবে, পরস্পর সকলের সমবেত চেষ্টা-দ্বারা শক্তিলাভ করবে। এ সম্বন্ধে চেষ্টাও করেছি, পল্লী সমিতি বল্মলে সমিতি গড়ে তুলেছি।"[62] (I have said that strength of the society should be aroused from within the society itself. I have also tried to instill the idea that with mutual cooperation this strength can be gained. I have also founded village society). Tagore's idea on rural reconstruction programme was such type of programmes that he was very much proud of as they would enable the villagers to make their own fortune through their united efforts. It was like today's sustained socio-economic programmes. He believed that: "গ্রামবাসীদের সঙ্গে যোগ দিয়ে জনশক্তিসমবায়ের দ্বারা এই যে জলাশয়ের উদ্ধার ঘটেছে তার গৌরব আরও বেশী। এই রকম সমবেত চেষ্টাই আমরা সমস্ত দেশের হয়ে কামনা করি"[63] (On behalf of the country we wish to introduce such cooperative efforts by which, with the help of the villagers in a united and cooperative way, to bring in reformation, one of which we have already implemented that is to revive the local pond). It is known that rural reconstruction programme in all it's aspect was done through village development societies in the village. "All these activities were reflected through the village development societies, organised by the rural people at the grass root level".[64] At that time of Rabindranath, rural reconstruction programme of Sriniketan progressed rapidly through different constructive programmes. It was meant to make villages self dependent with the help of the villagers. Day Schools as well as Night Schools were established for helpless and ignorant people, Library service, health society, rural industry, cooperative store, mutual settlement of village disputes, road-making and various folk culture projects were rolled on through the united force of villagers. He wanted that villagers would depend on their own source. So he implemented various constructive programmes in the surrounding villages of Sriniketan for the development of not only West Bengal villages but also the development of the whole country.

A BRIEF REPORT ON BALLAVPUR VILLAGE (1925-1930)

It is clear from the above discussion that Tagore's idea of rural reconstruction programme was not of a piece meal nature. He targeted the whole village and tried to solve those problems simultaneously. We can get a clear picture regarding the development of village Ballavpur by surveying its development within a sort period (1925-1930) Ballavpur is one kilometer away from Sriniketan. Sriniketan started its work in this village. In the year 1925, we can get an idea from the following activities that were undertaken by the villagers themselves through their newly created village organization under the leadership of Sriniketan'workers.

Health: At first health and Sanitation programmes were implemented, villagers were involved to distribution of quinine to prevent malaria, kerosinisation in the stagnant water, vaccination to prevent pox, jungle cleaning, filling up the pits, drain-washing and road-making at Ballavpur.

Education: Adult education and Night Schools were established to extend education among the villagers. Meetings and discussions were held to discuss different problems in the village. Magic lantern show, Ramayana and Mahabharata readings, kathakatha etc. were organised in the villages to make the villagers aware of the various problems and the cultural heritage of India. A village survey was done and the report was submitted in 1926 for further development planning by Kalimohan Ghosh. Four women of Ballavpur were trained for devoting themselves in social service in the surrounding village of Sriniketan. A Mahila Samity. was organised and trained rural women on embroidery work, maternity work, nursing, child care etc. Various village cultural activities were taken up along with economic activities such as Harisava, Radhastami, Janmastami, Nandotsava, etc.

Agriculture: As agriculture was the main occupation of the villagers agricultural demonstration was organised at Sriniketan, various types of crops were cultivated and poultry farm was set up in the village.

Rural Industry : A weaving school was established at Ballavpur and the villagers were trained on weaving and yarn colouring.

Role of Youth : But all these projects were implemented through a newly created village development organisation. Brati organisation was established, young boys and girls were belonging to Brati organisation. They participated in drill and games, Bratidal participated in various welfare activities. Panchayat Samity was established where different village disputes were solved.

We have tried to draw a sketch in chapter V about the various activities of Sriniketan from the beginning. Three phases have been discussed: (1) During Tagore's life time (2) After the death of Tagore and (3) After independence when the centre took up Visva-Bharati as it is Protege.

REFERENCES

1. Satish Chandra Chakraborty (edited by): *Maharshi Devendranath Thakurer Atmajibani,* Visva-Bharati Granthalaya, Calcutta 1927, 4th Edition 1962, pp.369-370.
2. Rabindranath Tagore : *Ashramer Rup O Bikash,* Visva-Bharati Granthan Vibhaga, Calcutta, Ashara 1348 B.S., p.8.
3. *Ibid.,* p. 14.
4. *Ibid.,* p. 24.
5. Sudhir Chandra Kar: *Santiniketaner Siksha O Sadhana,* Orient Book Company, Calcutta, 1360 B.S., 3rd edition, 1370 B.S., p. 18.
6. Rabindranath Tagore: *Visva-Bharati,* (Essay), Visva-Bharati Granthan Vibhaga, Calcutta, Pous 1358 B.S., p. 130.
7. Tanayendranath Ghose: "Rabindranath's Contribution to Education in India", *The Visva-Bharati quaterly,* Education number, Signet Press, Elgin road Calcutta, May-Oct. 1947, p. 18.
8. Rabindranath Tagore: A letter to Ajit Kumar Chakraborty, 29th Pous 1314 B.S., *Palliprakriti,* Visva-Bharati Granthan Vibhaga, Calcutta, Magh 1368 B.S. p. 225.
9. Rabindranath Tagore: Visva-Bharati (Essay), Vaisakh, 1326 B.S., *Rabindra Rachanavoli* (collected works) Vol. 14, Visva-

Bharati Granthan Vibhaga, Calcutta, Aswin 1398 B.S., p. 244.

10. L.K. Elmhirst: *Poet and Ploughman,* Visva-Bharati, Calcutta, 1975, p. 15.
11. *Ibid.,* p. 16.
12. *Ibid.,* p. 18.
13. *Ibid.,* p. 18.
14. Rabindranath Tagore: Sriniketaner Itihas O Adarsha (Sriniketaner Karmider Sabhai Kathito), 1346 B.S. *Palliprakriti,* Visva-Bharati Granthan Vibhaga, Calcutta, Magh 1368 B.S. p. 98.
15. *Ibid.,* p. 98.
16. Rabindranath Tagore: Rioter Katha (Sriman Pramatha Nath Chowdhury, Kalyanesu), Ashara, 1333 B.S. *Kalantar,* Visva-Bharati Granthan Vibhaga, Calcutta, Vaishak 1344 B.S., Revised Edition 1367 B.S., p. 299.
17. L.K. Elmhirst, *Poet and ploughman,* Visva-Bharati, Calcutta, 1975, p. 30.
18. *Ibid.,* p. 20.
19. Rabindranath Tagore: *Russiar Chithi* (4th letter), 28lh September 1930, Visva-Bharati Granthan Vibhaga, Calcutta, Vaishak 1338 B.S., p. 25.
20. Rabindranath Tagore: Pallir Unnati, (Hitasadhan Mandalir Sabhai Kathito), Vaishak 1322 B.S., *Palliprakriti,* Visva-Bharati Granthan Vibhaga, Calcutta, Magh 1368 B.S., p.34.
21. Rabindranath Tagore: Sriniketaner Itihas O Adarsha (Sriniketaner Karmider Sabhai Kathito), 1346 B.S., *Palliprakriti,* Visva-Bharati Granthan Vibhaga, Calcutta, Magh 1368 B.S., p. 104.
22. Rabindranath Tagore: A letter to Pratima devi, Chithipatra-3, 1930, *Russiar Chithi,* Visva-Bharati Granthan Vibhaga, Calcutta, Vaisakh 1338 B.S., p. 155.
23. Rabindranath Tagore: 1st letter 20th September, 1930, *Russiar Chithi,* Visva-Bharati Granthan Vibhaga, Calcutta, Vaisakh 1338 B.S., p. 11.
24. Rabindranath Tagore: A letter to Rathindranath Tagore, Chithipatra-2, 31st October 1930, *Russiar Chithi,* Visva-Bharati Granthan Vibhaga, Calcutta, Vaisakh 1338 B.S., p. 156.

25. *Visva-Bharati Bulletin* No.6, 'The Institute of Rural Reconstruction- Sriniketan (Prospects of apprenticeship and training camp)', November 1925, pp. 1-3.
26. G. Kausal: *Economic History of India* (1757-1966), Kalyani Publishers, New Delhi 1996, p. 65.
27. Rabindranath Tagore : Samabaye Malaria Nivaran (Antimalaria Societyte Kathito), 29th August 1923; *Palliprakriti,* Visva-Bharati Granthan Vibhaga, Calcutta, Magh 1368 B.S., p. 123.
28. *Ibid,* p. 127.
29. *Visva-Bharati Bulletin* No.25, 'Health Cooperatives, Institute of Rural Reconstruction' edited by Rathindranath Tagore, July 1938, p.3.
30. Hard G. Timbers: "A Village Health Programmes'" *Visva-Bharati News* (Vol. 1, No. 1), July 1932, p. 5.
31. Sugata Dasgupta: *Poet and a Plan,* Thacker spink & Co. (1933) Private Limited, 3, Esplanade East, Calcutta-1, p. 64.
32. Rabindranath Tagore: Samâbaye Malaria Nivaran (Antimalaria Societyte Kathito), 29th August 1923, *Palliprakriti,* Visva-Bharati Granthan Vibhaga, Calcutta, Magh 1368 B.S., p. 123
33. Rabindranath Tagore : Sambhasan (Santiniketane Sammilito Rabibasarer Sadasyader Prati) 30th Falgun 1343 B.S., *Palliprakriti,* Visva-Bharati Granthan Vibhaga, Calcutta, Magh 1368 B.S., p. 167.
34. Rabindranath Tagore : Lokahita, Bhadra 1321 B.S.; *Kalantar,* Visva-Bharati Granthan Vibhaga, Calcutta, Vaisakh 1344 B.S., Revised edition, 1367 B.S., pp. 45-46
35. Rabindranath Tagore: Palli Seva (Sriniketan Barsik Utsave Kathito), 6th February 1940 *Palliprakriti,* Visva-Bharati Granthan Vibhaga, Calcutta, Magh 1368 B.S., p. 113.
36. Rabindranath Tagore: Abhibhasan (Sriniketan Silpa Bhandar Udbodhon) 22nd Agrahayan 1345 B.S., *Palliprakriti,* Visva-Bharati Granthan Vibhaga, Calcutta, Magh 1368 B.S., p. 89.
37. Rabindranath Tagore: Bahire Yatra, *Jivansmriti,* Visva-Bharati Granthan Vibhaga, Calcutta, 1319 B.S, pp. 34-35.
38. Rabindranath Tagore: Chhatrader Prati Sambhasan, Vaisakh 1312 B.S., *Sankalan,* Visva-Bharati Granthan Vibhaga, Calcutta, 1332 B.S., p. 19.

39. *Visva-Bharati Bulletin* No. 15; 'Rabindranath Tagore in Russia', edited by P.C. Mohalanobis, November 1930, p. 34.

40. Prabhat Kumar Mukhopadhyay : *Rabindra Jiboni O Rabindra Sahitya Prabeshak* (Vol.4), Visva-Bharati Granthan Vibhaga, Calcutta, 1363 B.S. Third edition, Ashara 1401 B.S., p. 129

41. Prem Chand Lal : *Reconstruction and Educaton in Rural India,* London George Alien & Unwin Ltd., Museum street, 1932, p. 81.

42. Sri Jatindramahon Mukhopadhyay: Rabindra Smriti; *Desh* 23rd Sravan 1349 B.S., *Palliprakriti* Visva-Bharati Granthan Vibhaga, Calcutta, Magh 1368 B.S., p. 226.

43. Rabindranath Tagore: A letter to Srimati Nirmal Kumari Mohalanobish, 25th Sravan 1336 B.S., *Palliprakriti,* Visva-Bharati Granthan Vibhaga, Calcutta, Magh 1368 B.S., p. 278.

44. Rabindranath Tagore : A letter to Rathindranath Tagore, 1910. Chithipatra-2; *Palliprakriti,* Visva-Bharati Granthan Vibhaga, Calcutta, Magh 1368 B.S., p. 290.

45. L.K. Elmhirst: *Poet and Ploughman,* Visva-Bharati, Calcutta, 1975, p. 122.

46. Rabindranath Tagore: A letter to Nagendranath Gangopadhyay, 30th Falgun 1313 B.S., *Palliprakriti,* Visva-Bharati Granthan Vibhaga, Calcutta, Magh 1368 B.S., p. 233.

47. Rabindranath Tagore : Patraboli, 29h October 1929; *Palliprakriti,* Visva-Bharati Granthan Vibhaga, Calcutta, Magh 1368 B.S., pp. 182-183.

48. Sugato Dasgupta : *Poet and a Plan,* Thacker spink & Co. (1933), Private Limited, 3 Esplanade East, Calcutta-1, p. 51.

49. Rabindranath Tagore : *Russiar Chithi,* 28th September 1930, Visva-Bharati Granthan Vibhaga, Calcutta, Vaisakh 1338 B.S., p. 25.

50. Rabindranath Tagore : Sriniketaner Itihas O Adarsha, (Sriniketaner Karmider Sabhai Kathito), 1346 B.S., *Palliprakriti,* Visva-Bharati Granthan Vibhaga, Calcutta, Magh 1368 B.S., p. 102.

51. Rabindranath Tagore : *Russiar chithi,* Upasanghar, Visva-Bharati Granthan Vibhaga, Calcutta, Vaisakh 1338 B.S., p. 124.

52. Rabindranath Tagore : Bharat Barshe Samabayer Bisishtata, Sravan 1334 B.S. *Samabay Neeti,* Visva-Bharati Granthan Vibhaga, Calcutta, 1360 B.S., p. 26.

53. Rabindranath Tagore : Samabay-1, Sravan 1325 B.S., *Samabay Neeti,* Visva-Bharati Granthan Vibhaga, Calcutta, 1360 B.S., p. 15.

54. *Ibid,* p. 14.

55. Rabindranath Tagore : Samabay Neeti, 1325 B.S., *Samabay Neeti* (essay), Visva-Bharati Granthan Vibhaga, Calcutta, 1360 B.S., p. 51.

56. Rabindranath Tagore : Patrabali, 1337 B.S., *Palliprakriti,* Visva-Bharati Granthan Vibhaga, Calcutta, Magh 1368 B.S., p. 193.

57. Rabindranath Tagore : Gram Basider Prati (Sriniketan Batsarik Utsave Kathito), Chaitra 1337 B.S., *Palliprakriti,* Visva-Bharati Granthan Vibhaga, Calcutta, Magh 1368 B.S., p. 73.

58. L.K. Elmhirst : *Poet and Ploughman,* Visva-Bharati, Calcutta, 1975, p. 62.

59. Sugato Dasgupta: *Poet and a Plan,* Thacker spink & Co. (1933), Private Limited, 3, Esplanade East, Calcutta, p. 78.

60. Hiranmay Banerjee: *Experiments in Rural Reconstruction,* Visva-Bharati, Calcutta, 1966, p. 78

61. *Visva-Bharati Bulletin* No. 11, 'Sriniketan; The Institute of Rural Reconstruction', December 1928, p. 6.

62. Rabindranath Tagore: Malaria (Antimalaria Societyte Kathito), 23rd February 1924. *Palliprakriti,* Visva-Bharati Granthan Vibhaga, Calcutta, Magh 1368 B.S., p. 137.

63. Rabindranath Tagore: Jolotasarga (Bhubandangai Jalasai Pratistha Upalakshe Kathito), 7th Bhadra 1343 B.S.; *Palliprakriti,* Visva-Bharati Granthan Vibhaga, Calcutta, Magh 1368 B.S., p. 164.

64. Arun Mukherjee: "Tagore's Concept of Population Education and Rural Reconstruction". *Centenary volume : L.K. Elmhirst* (1893-1993), Edited by Manjula Bose, Tagore Research Institute, Calcutta, 1994, p. 22.

5

Activities of PSV (Based on Visva-Bharati Annual Reports and Audited Accounts) Since 1922 to 1995-96

Rabindranath with his limited resources desired to set up a model village and to develop the Indian socio-economic scenario through the establishment of Sriniketan. He in fact, wanted to reconstruct the villages through the co-operative efforts of the villagers. He wanted that the villagers should utilise their village resources and follow their own culture so as to improve their quality of life. Tagore implemented various kinds of programmes in the surrounding villages of Sriniketan since the inception of the institution, PSV, in the year 1922.

Tagore adopted various strategies to solve the rural problems of the villages around Sriniketan, such as health, sanitation, education, culture and economy. He had a deep faith in applying co-operative methods for social and economic growth. He inspired the villagers to establish village development organisation through which the village problems would be solved by their own power. He told the villagers to take active part in their village reconstruction work. Rabindranath instructed his social workers to form various co-operative societies among the villagers so that they could be helped to help themselves. To enrich the leadership capabilities among rural young boys and girls, the Brati organisation was formed in the village. This organisation was made for the future leadership of rural reconstruction programmes. Various development programmes were implemented in the villages through these village organisations and the social workers of Sriniketan would only actively help them.

Tagore's experiments on rural reconstruction programme has been continuing through various extension activities even after his death and recognition of Visva -Bharati as a central university. An attempt has been made here to discuss and analyse chronologically these extension programmes with the help of data collected from the Annual Report of Visva-Bharati. This discussion is made keeping in view three phases,

1. In the first phase, during the period, 1922 to 1941, the various reconstruction programmes introduced in Tagore's lifetime have been discussed.
2. In the second phase (1942 to 1950), that is the post-Tagorean period, the village extension programmes which were running under PSV have been discussed.
3. In the third phase, from 1951 to 1995-96, when Visva-Bharati came under the ambit of the Central government, the extension activities under taken by PSV have been discussed.

Table No. 5.1 shows the various village extension programmes which had been implemented in the surrounding villages of Sriniketan during Tagore's lifetime (1922-1941).

Sriniketan was established in the year 1922 on 6th February. At that time the malaria broke out in the villages in an epidemic form. Rabindranath took various programmes to protect the villagers from the grip of the disease through co-operative efforts of the people around Sriniketan. Tagore wanted that in each rural reconstruction programme the villagers would take initiative by themselves so that in near future they could solve their own problems. His emphasis was on the improvement of health, sanitation and illiteracy and economic condition. Tagore emphasised to form village development organisation through the co-operative efforts of the villagers themselves. Tagore directed to form Brati organisation to develop the leadership qualities among rural young boys and girls for the future leadership of their village.

At first, in the year 1922, the rural reconstruction programmes were started at only two nearest villages, one of these was Surul, a Hindu dominated village and another was Mahidapur, a muslim dominated village. The workers of PSV not only established general rapport with the villagers but made individual friendships with the villagers. The number of villages was gradually increased around Sriniketan. In the year 1922 Sriniketan activities worked in only two villages, but those extension activities were so effective that in the year 1932, within eleven years (1922-1932), Sriniketan workers with the joint efforts of the villagers covered twenty-one villages. These villages were devided into different village centres to implement the programmes in more effective manner. In the year 1933, Sriniketan functioned in fifty-eight villages in extensive form. In the year 1934, number of villages decreased but large number of programmes was better implemented in the village.

At first, Tagore instructed his workers to undertake the health programmes. This was because at that time villagers were suffering from malaria. Workers of Sriniketan tried to protect the villagers from malaria through these co-operative efforts.

Health: From the beginning of Sriniketan different kinds of health programmes were undertaken. Already we know at that time malaria was spreading its clutches very rapidly. Rabindranath instructed his workers to motivate the villagers so that they could undertake various measures to protect their health from various types of ailments. Various types of preventive measures were undertaken and implemented in the surrounding villages of Sriniketan, like jungle cleaning, tank cleaning, kerosinisation of the stagnant water, application of quinine and other suitable preventive programmes for the treatment of malaria patients. These programmes were formulated through co-operative efforts of villagers under the suitable guidance of Sriniketan staff. A charitable dispensary was established at Sriniketan. It was known that about fifteen hundred patients were medically treated in the beginning at Sriniketan. In the year 1925 medicine and sick diet were provided to the villagers to remove malnutrition through Aruna Amita relief work. Tagore realised the necessity of such programmes to improve mother's health and check the child mortality rate. He advised his workers to start child welfare and maternity work in the villages around Sriniketan. Today we noticed the 'Integrated Child Development Services Scheme'. (ICDS) programmes for this purpose, but Tagore at that time realised the significance of such type of programme. Lantern lecture (a visual programme) was arranged to make villagers aware on health and sanitation programme side by side, in the year 1929, villagers were given vaccination against cholera and small pox for the preventive measures. During the year medical treatment was arranged for snakebite during monsoon in the villages around Sriniketan. At that time, villagers followed'some superstition against snakebite, but Tagore desired to create scientific attitude among villagers. Sriniketan dispensary as central health unit functioned and guided the villagers from outside. In the year 1930 Aruna Amita nursing work was more extensive. Sriniketan covered twenty-five villages and provided sick diet and medicine to six hundred thirteen patients. Maternity work was continued in eight villages for the benefit of mother and child of the village. Tagore gave more emphasis on this programme and directed his followers to arrange training programmes for Dai (village midwife) who were devoted to serve the new born baby and the mother. Four Dais were trained during the year 1930. For the better health of the villagers, one homeopathic dispensary was also established at Bandhgara.

In the year 1931, more extensive work continued in the twelve villages. These villages were devided into three village centre as Ballavpur, Binuria and Bandhgara. Different kinds of health programmes were implemented through the village development organisations specially health co-operative society. In the year 1932, for the better implementation of health programmes, One health survey was carried out in the surrounding villages of Sriniketan. During the year 1933, health programmes were continued more extensively in fifty-eight villages. In the year 1934 different kinds of health programmes were implemented in seventeen villages and these villages were devided into four village centres. It is interesting to note that Tagore believed in methodical and systematic, work and at the same time he tried to help the villagers in such a manner that they could help themselves. He did not want to control all the developmental activities held at Sriniketan. So he tried to establish a common platform for villagers like village development centre at different suitable places. Another health survey was done in the year 1935 in the surrounding villages of Sriniketan for implementing future plan. At that time Sriniketan was more active, during this year about two thousand nine hundred sixty patients were benefited through 'out door' treatment of Sriniketan. Besides this, one co-operative society inauguarated at Bandhgora by public health minister. Public health extension programmes continued through Bandhgora and Binuria health projects. The social workers of Sriniketan were devoted to improve the village health through the united force of the villagers. In the same year, Aruna Amita nursing work covered twenty-three villages to cater sick diet and medicines. It is seen that Sriniketan not only helped the villagers from outside but also tried to solve the village health problems through their own effort. In the year 1940 it was unfortunate that eminent social worker named Kalimohan Ghosh died on 12th May. He was the main guiding force of Sriniketan. Next year a health visitor of Sriniketan supervised to improve all types of health programme in the village.

Tagore believed in co-operative method to uplift a village. So he directed his social workers to improve village health by establishing co-operative organisation in the village, like co-operative health society, co-operative dispensary. In the year 1923 first co-operative health society was established experimentally at Ballavpur village and within three years the villagers around Sriniketan realised the importance of such type of society and by the year 1926 twelve health co-operative societies were established around Sriniketan. During Tagore's lifetime, government also recognised the activities of these societies and sponsored to organise the health societies. During the year 1939 twelve health co-operative societies were functioning in the whole district of Birbhum under the guidance of PSV and in the year 1940 i.e. within one year, the number of health co-operative societies increased to fifteen for the improvement of the health in the villages.

Besides health co-operative society, one co-operative dispensary was also established at Sriniketan to improve the health condition of the village. As a result of proved effective role, co-operative dispensaries were increased gradually. In the year 1935 six co-operative dispensaries were functioning in the villages. It is noticed that during Tagore's lifetime, village health problem was successfully tackled through cooperative methods in the village.

Besides health co-operative societies, rural reconstruction societies or VDS were established and involved to solve the village health problems. This type of village development organisation proved more active. In the year 1931, VDS was functioning to improve the village health and various types of programmes were undertaken by the society. The members of VDS took active part in the village welfare programmes specially antimalarial drive and participated to establish health union to improve the village health condition. During the last phase of Tagore's life VDS was established in every village around Sriniketan. Social workers of Sriniketan guided the villagers according to Tagore's ideals. The village health problems were solved to a great extent through the effective policies applied by village society and the rural society become self-reliant on health.

Education: Tagore wanted to reconstruct the Indian village by rendering real education to the rural people. He noticed that villagers were ignorant and illiterate. So Rabindranath desired to relieve the sorrows and sufferings of the villagers by educating the villagers. He said "নূতন

একটা কর্মের দিকে আমার চিত্ত ধাবিত হল, মনে হল শিক্ষার ভিতর দিয়ে সমস্ত দেশের সেবা করব।"[1] (My heart was driven towards a new task. I thought that I could serve the whole country through education). From the inception of Sriniketan, he dreamt of different kinds of educational programmes to enrich the quality of villagers and gradually he turns them into reality.

In the year 1922, Night Schools were founded in the villages around Sriniketan for those villagers, who were busy during day time for their livelihood. They were meant specially for the depressed class villagers. By the way, today, we notice that various kinds of developmental programmes have been undertaken by the state and central governments for the upliftment of depressed class. But Tagore realised the significance of all-round development of such depressed classes when nobody could think of providing education to those people. British government also recognised the importance of village Night Schools and provided five rupees per month to each Night School. Day Schools were also run along with Night Schools in the villages. Gradually, the numbers of Night Schools were increased in the villages around Sriniketan. In the year 1925, seven Night Schools were set up in different villages. Library service was also provided to extend education among villagers. In the year 1926, twelve circulating libraries were functioning in the village. Villagers would study various books on religion, health, agriculture and juvenile literature. At the time of Rabindranath, emphasis was given for extending education among women also. Today our society realises the significance of the role of women in nation building activities. Tagore helped in taking up various projects to make women self-reliant, he was the pioneer in this field. Rabindranath gave emphasis on and took initiative to develop women folk through suitable education and training. In the year 1929 one girls' school was established at Sriniketan to fulfil this noble objectives. Two girls' schools were established at Goalpara and Paruldanga village in the year 1934 and 1939 respectively. In the year 1930 girl's Night School was also started at Bhubandanga. Sriniketan took the responsibility to educate villagers on various aspects of rural development like public health, co-operative movement, 'child welfare and maternity' and the activities of Sriniketan through mass media like lantern lecture, meetings, etc. Tagore emphasised to educate weaker section of the community like Santals. So one primary school was established at the Santal village to educate santals who belonged to the lowest stratum of the society. In the year 1934, two primary schools were established at Santal village named Bonerpukur and Chumkapara through the Sramdan of the Santal people. Village Night Schools were gradually increased to extend education among Santal community. During the year 1930, seven Night Schools were established at seven Santal hamlets. Besides this, other five Night Schools were set up in five villages. We learn from the extension and popularity of Night Schools that these Night Schools were more effective to extend education among villagers. Gradually, Night Schools were increased to cater to the needs of education among the weaker section around Sriniketan. In the year 1933, thirty two Night Schools were established for the 'Horizon' Boys and girls belonging to all classes. In this way, during the time of Rabindranath, emphasis was given on upliftment of the lifestyle of the weaker section community. Tagore not only desired to extend education but he also wanted to develop the teaching quality in the primary schools. A conference was organised for three days at Sriniketan in the year 1936.

Tagore put emphasis on 'distance education' throughout the country. He realised that countrymen would be busy for their livelihood and deprived from higher education. So he established a 'distance education' unit named 'Loksiksha Samsad' in the year 1937 and after four years in 1941, Loksiksha Samsad was organised through a separate Board.

Training: Tagore directed his followers to provide training to the villagers on rural reconstruction. Tagore desired that village youth should take the responsibility of their own village and involve the other villagers in rural reconstruction programme. Various kinds of training programmes were conducted every year to make the village self-reliant. In the year 1926, a training camp was organised for the village workers. The training was given to the boys and girls of Brati organisation on agriculture and rural industry. During the year 1930, training programme was also arranged on different aspects such as (a) Brati organisation, (b) Village sanitation and First aid (c) Rural Reconstruction and Real Education (d) Cottage crafts, (e) Elementary knowledge on Agriculture. After two years, another training camp was organised on rural reconstruction to improve the quality of teachings in the village schools.

Village survey: Social workers of Sriniketan had done some village survey for better implementation of rural reconstruction programme. Tagore believed in scientific study prior to any type of practical work in the villages. Different kinds of survey were conducted. Among these surveys socio-economic survey got much importance. It is already mentioned that in the year 1926, Ballavpur survey was done by Kalimohan Ghosh and the survey was completed in the year 1929. In 1930, another survey was done at Bhubandanga, Islampur and Benuria around Sriniketan and a survey report of Raipur was published from Sriniketan during this year. According to the suggestion given in the survey reports, rural reconstruction programmes were implemented in the surrounding villages of Sriniketan.

Cultural activities: Tagore not only desired to extend education through establishing schools but also followed traditional culture of our village. He tried to provide recreation through the cultural activities. He wanted to develop the rural economy through the introduction of different festivals among village farmers. In the year 1930, 'Halkarshan utsav' was organised at Santal village and various religion based festivals and folk culture were celebrated at Ballavpur. During the year 1933, an exibition was arranged along with village festivals. After four year in (1937), 'Halkarshan' and 'Vriksha ropana' were celebrated at Santal centre to encourage the people to develop agriculture along with environment. In the year 1940, 'Basanta utsav' (Dol-Yatra) was celebrated at Sriniketan, Bandhgora and Goalpara. This year, an exhibition was also organised at Suppur village on the occasion of Rash mela.

Agriculture, Animal husbandry and fishery: Rabindranath Tagore wanted to develop the village economy through agriculture. We all know that agriculture is the main base of rural economy of our country, so it is not possible to develop the village economy without agriculture. He established experimentally the 'Surul department of agriculture and village economy' in the year 1922. The objectives were to make village economy self-reliant. Many new crops were introduced and cultivated in the surrounding villages of Sriniketan and villagers derived knowledge about scientific cultivation through this. In the year 1930, villagers were involved to cultivate vegetables, sugarcane, potato, onion and cotton etc. New crops were introduced at Bandhgora after two year (1932) for the betterment of the cultivation, seed and seedlings were distributed among villagers from 'Surul agricultural farm'. In the year 1934, seeds of vegetables were distributed among fifty eight villagers to develop the cultivation and different kinds of methods were followed to make the villagers aware regarding agriculture. In the year 1932, training on the scientific methods of cultivation followed and after this year agriculturists and officers supervised the scheme for the development of agriculture. During the year 1936, agricultural demonstration farm was organised in five villages. Government recognised Tagore's ideal of Sriniketan and sponsored grants to set up demonstration farm. Folk schools were organised to provide knowledge to the village farmer on production and marketing so that they could develop their own economy. A training camp was arranged on agriculture and dairy to develop the village economy. Sriniketan took initiative when there was economical problem through suitable economical programmes. In the year 1940, the agricultural work was hampered due to unprecedented drought, Sriniketan provided adequate knowledge to village farmers to overcome the problem, leaflets were distributed among villagers. Lectures and discussions were held at villages alongwith demonstration on agriculture. In the year 1937, a pond was excavated for irrigation.

Animal husbandry: Tagore wanted to make economy self-sufficiency not only of agriculture but also through other activities like poultry, dairy and fishery. In the year 1924, the activities of poultry farm, animal husbandry got more importance. In the year 1938, another poultry farm was established in the village named Ballavpur.

Fishery programme was undertaken to make economy self-reliant in the village. In 1928, four ponds were cleaned for fishery. After this year, in 1929, fishery continued to develop the village economy around Sriniketan.

Rural Industry: Tagore emphasised on rural industry to develop the rural economy along side agriculture. From the beginning of Sriniketan different kinds of programmes were undertaken to develop village industry. Tagore emphasised on all types of rural Industry. At first, in the year 1922, training was given to village tanner and in the year 1934, three-month training was given on Sandel making to seven village cobblers of Bahadurpur village. It is known that Tagore wanted to develop leather work in the village. In the year 1923, training on weaving was arranged at Santal para to develop village economy of the Santals and, in the year 1927, the students of Visva-Bharati and local teachers were involved in weaving in their own village to develop the village economy. Those activities covered in thirty six villages around Sriniketan. During Tagore' s life time, emphasis was given on weaving to make the rural economy self-reliant.

Tagore always emphasised on local resources of the village and co-operative efforts of the villagers to develop the rural area. We noticed from the activities of Sriniketan during Tagore' s life time that various kinds of economical programmes were undertaken to make economy self-reliant for making a model village before the country. So from the beginning of Sriniketan, programmes were undertaken to develop village economy like agriculture and rural industry. Tagore directed his followers to take such economical programmes in which villagers could be able to participate.

Co-operative Organisation: Tagore emphasised on cooperation as an important aspect of rural reconstruction. He realised that it would not be possible to make self-reliant economy without co-operative efforts of the villagers.

He believed that the villagers could be reorganised in all its aspects through the proper utilisation of village resources and co-operative efforts of the villagers. His observations regarding the significance of co-operative principles are worth quoting "যেদিন সমবায়মূলক জীবিকার কথা প্রথম শুনি আমার মনে জটিল সমস্যার গাঁট যেন অনেকটা খুলে গেল।"[2] (The day I heard the idea of co-operative employment, the complex knots of the problems were, to a great extent resolved). He adopted this principle, when he worked at his zamindari estate. After this work he desired to reconstruct the village successfully by establishing Sriniketan. He directed his followers to establish different type of co-operative organisations to solve all types of problems of the villages. According to his direction different cooperative organisations were established in the village. These were health co-operative society, Dharmagola society to prevent famine and other types of co-operative organisations. It is already discussed about health co-operative society and here we shall discuss about the other aspects of co-operative organisation.

In the year 1922, a co-operative store was established for the development of village. A Co-operative Bank was established at Bolpur to cater to the credit needs of the farmers at a low rate of interest. During this year, one co-operative credit society was established at Mahidapur near Sriniketan. Villagers were not able to cultivate their land for financial problems and they could not be self-reliant. So villagers were benifited by the loans provided by the society. Rabindranath realised that irrigation was the main input of cultivation. So at that time irrigation co-operative society was established at Raipur to solve the problem. After this year the number of irrigation and credit societies were increased in other villages. It is clear from these activities that such types of co-operative organisations were more active and useful to help the villagers to revive their economy and society. In the year 1930, a conference on cooperative society was held at Sriniketan. Within four years (1927-1931) gradually a number of credit societies were increased in the surrounding villages of Sriniketan. Nine such societies were established and started their work.

Dharmagola society was established through the co-operative efforts of villagers in the villages around Sriniketan. This society was established to save the village farmers from scarcity of food. In the year 1932 six Dharmagola societies were functioning, fishery co-operative society was established by the villagers to develop the village economy. In the year 1928, one such society was established at Ballavpur. During Rabindranath's time rural reconstruction programmes were undertaken through the co-operative efforts of the villagers, but the different castes and subcastes were not united due to superstition. So rural reconstruction programmes were not implemented according to the ideology of Rabindranath. To eradicate such type of problems, in the year 1932, the programmes were undertaken against untouchability. Motivated workers assembled and involved all castes in rural reconstruction programme.

It may be noted from the analysis that Rabindranath believed that a self-reliant village economy would be more useful for sustained development and to enrich the quality of life of the villagers. The villagers took the guidance from PSV workers and establish different co-operative organisations to solve all types of problem of the village. These co-operative organisations were very much useful to the villagers. As a result, the number of co-operative organisations was increased in the surrounding villages of Sriniketan. At the present situation, we can realise the significance of cooperative principles in the developmental programmes. We know that co-operative method have been able to develop the economical conditions in the state Gujrat and Maharastra.

Role of Youth: Rabindranath used to inspire the youth to take responsibility on rural reconstruction programme. He thought that only youth force could reconstruct the village in all its aspects providing proper leadership. He directed his followers to take suitable programmes so that the youth could take the leadership and be able to mobilise villagers in rural reconstruction programmes. Different training programmes were arranged for this youth force to turn them into village leaders. Brati organisation was formed by the leadership of Dhirananda Roy. Rural young boys and girls are the member of this organisation. These organisations were formed from the beginning of Sriniketan. At first the name of this organisations was 'Sahayak Sangha' (helping group). In the year 1922, Brati organisation was started in the near by two villages. In 1923, this organisation was founded in five villages around Sriniketan. Brati organisations participated in different developmental programmes. The rural young boys and girls were trained in village health programmes and they also participated in these programmes. At that time they participated to improve the health conditions of the village. During the year 1929, they also participated in antimalarial work. These young boys and girls involved themselves in such programmes along with their school education. The rural young boys and girls also participated to develop the village economy. In the year 1926, training was arranged for them to make self-reliant economy of the village. In the year 1938, seed and seedlings were distributed for vegetable gardening We understand from Visva-Bharati Annual Report that to encourage the Brati organisation in agricultural activities arrangement was made to distribute prize to Brati organisation for vegetable gardening. Tagore desired to reconstruct the Indian villages through adopting co-operative principles. So he directed his followers to organise a co-operative store by the voluntary work of Brati organisations, the rural young boys and girls of this organisation arranged a demonstration on rural handicraft.

Brati organisations participated in all types of developmental programmes in the village. To extend education in the village, they organised and supervised Night Schools and other activities. This organisation went out on excursion to different villages to know about the actual village problems and how to solve it, within ten years these organisations were increased in the surrounding villages of Sriniketan. In the year 1932, Brati organisations were functioning in twenty two villages. This organisation was the pillar of rural reconstruction programmes. Tagore wanted those young boys and girls of Brati organisation should take the whole responsibility of the village. Suitable social workers of Brati organisations would participate to solve village problems. They served the village patients and distributed rice to the poor.

The trained dedicated workers organised musical club and swimming clubs for entertainment and physical exercise.

It is realised from the above analysis that during Tagore's lifetime rural youth forces took the responsibility to reconstruct their own villages. According to the ideology of Rabindranath, the members of Brati organisation participated in all types of rural reconstruction programmes in the villages. Social workers of Sriniketan gave suitable training to make them future leaders of the village. It is clear that it would not, be possible to implement rural reconstruction programmes in the village without active participation of rural youth.

Mahila Samity or Mahila Organisation: Rabindranath wanted that women should join in rural reconstruction programmes. Side by side, he desired to develop the overall condition of women and make them self-reliant. Rabindranath suggested ways and means to form women organisations which could be able to develop the woman power. During Tagore's life time Mahila Samity was organised under the leadership of Smt. Nanibala Roy and after her, under Pratima Tagore (Daughter in law of Rabindranath). Women were trained on maternity and child care to check the child mortality and participate in the rural handicraft schemes for a self reliant economy.

In the year 1929, two Mahila Samities were organised at Surul and Mahidapur. It is obvious that Tagore gave importance to Mahila Samity and discussion was held to form more Mahila Samities in the villages. Within a short period of time a number of Mahila Samities were increased in the year 1935. In total, five Mahila Samities were organised in the villages. At the time of Rabindranath even the muslim women actively participated in the Mahila Samities and discarded their traditional purdah. In the year 1937, two Mahila Samities were established among muslim women. They participated in rural reconstruction programmes. We know that muslim community is more conservative and the women are not free to open society. But it is noticed that Muslim women responded to the call of Rabindranath.

Village Development Societies (VDS): Rabindranath established a centre of rural reconstruction named Sriniketan. A number of followers of Rabindranath assembled here. They devoted themselves in rural reconstruction programmes according to the direction of Rabindranath. Side by side, Rabindranath directed the social workers to form centres in each of the adopted villages. Those village organisations were the common platforms for the villagers from where rural reconstruction programmes were implemented in the village under the able guidance of Sriniketan authority. Villagers took the responsibility to develop their own village society and economy through the proper utilisation of village human and material resources. Obviously, VDS took up a vital role to reconstruct the village in all its aspects.

In the year 1925 one VDS was established at Ballavpur. Next year Dom Community of twelve villages established societies. This society was more active to develop the social and moral development of the Dom community. In the year 1928, another VDS named 'Santal Sahayak Samity, was established among santals. Socio-economic development of the Santal community was implemented through this society. Kalimohan Ghosh established a Santal Welfare Association. School, credit society, rural industry etc. were formed through this association to improve the Santal community. Panchayat Board was also organised to develop the village economy. In the year 1934, Panchayat Board and Palli Seva Samity was organised at Santal centre. Next year, in 1935, Santal Sahayak Samity and Panchayat were established to develop the Santal community in eight villages around Sriniketan.

It is clear from the above discussion that at the time of Rabindranath, all developmental activities were performed in the village through VDS and emphasis was laid for developing the weaker sections of the community through their own organisations (VDS) and different kinds of programmes were implemented in the village to develop health, education and economy. These programmes were implemented in the villages. It may be noted that village development organisation was established through the united efforts of the villagers of backward community.

As a matter of fact, these programmes constituted a model for the whole of India. Rabindranath directed his followers to implement different programmes in the village through VDS. He endeavoured to relieve the sufferings of villagers by establishing such ideal centre. At first, rural reconstruction programmes were started through VDS in two villages near Sriniketan. But within a short period of time, the programmes were covered in twenty five villages. Rural reconstruction programmes were implemented in these villages through the united efforts of the villagers under a common umbrella named VDS. All that time social workers of Sriniketan emphasised on co-operatve efforts of villagers and proper utilisation of village resources. VDS were also established to solve all types of village problem. In Rabindranath's time the programmes of Sriniketan were implemented successfully in the village through VDS and collective efforts of the villagers. Some eminent social workers, motivated by Tagore's ideology, dedicated themselves to the cause of rural reconstruction programmes at Sriniketan.

Table No. 5.2 shows the activities of Sriniketan extension programmes after the death of Rabindranath Tagore, prior to the period, when Visva-Bharati was declared as a central university by the Govt. of India i.e. from 1942 to 1950.

During these nine years (1942-1950) what kind of rural reconstruction programmes were being implemented in the surrounding villages of Sriniketan are discussed here. The table shows that the tempo of the rural reconstruction programmes were not continued and implemented in the villages according to Tagore's ideology which had been done through the united efforts of the villagers at the life time of Tagore. Two major reasons could be traced behind such poor performance: (1) financial problem and (2) lack of proper leadership.

Health: In the year 1943, financial problem was so acute that medicine and treatment could not be provided to the villagers. No preventive measures were taken against the epidemic form of malaria. As a result, a large number of patients died due to lack of proper treatment. Co-operative scheme i.e. co-operative health society could not continue due to financial crisis. Only one health society was functioning at Sitalpur village and another health society was reorganised at Binuria village. In spite of the acute financial problem, health and sanitation work was tried again to continue in the villages by the co-operative efforts of the villagers. Next year in 1944 sixty five villages were covered under health and sanitation programme. These villages were divided into fourteen village centres. Health societies were revived in each village centre. Although a large number of villages were adopted by Sriniketan PSV, actual rural reconstruction programmes were not followed according to the ideology of Rabindranath. In this year, relief measures were provided to the economically distressed people of south Birbhum. These relief measures were collected from the source of official and non-official sources. But we all know that Rabindranath generally disliked the outside charity. He wanted to reconstruct the villages through the proper utilisation of local resources. In the year 1945, health condition of the villages deteriorated due to malaria disease and mal-nutrition. Health society was not established and most of the existing health societies were not functioning properly as desired by the villagers. 'American friend service committee' provided medicine to the villagers through Sriniketan. Villagers were also gradually dependent on outside help due to lack of proper guidance. This weakness was realised in the year 1946 and Sriniketan emphasised on self-help and cooperation for rural reconstruction. In the year 1950, a serious effort was made to implement different health programmes such as antimalarial work, maternity and child welfare, health and sanitation etc. by PSV with the active co-operation of the villagers.

It may be clear from the above analysis that the health programmes were not undertaken to develop the village health through the united efforts of the villagers. But during Tagore's life time, the health programmes were implemented in the villages by the villagers themselves. Self-development was the key-note in all Tagorean constructive endeavours.

Education: After the death of Tagore, 'Loksiksha Samsad' programmes were continued and in the year 1943, the execution responsibility of these programmes was transferred to Sriniketan. Mobile libraries functioned in the surrounding villages of Sriniketan. The educational programmes were continued in sixty five villages through fourteen village centres. Schools functioned in each centre. 'Loksiksha Samsad' took vital role on national education schemes and a number of centres of 'Loksiksha Samsad' were established. Emphasis was put on study and research on different subject.

We can understand that new educational programmes among the people could not be taken up except by 'Loksiksha Samsad' which had been undertaken during Tagore's lifetime.

During Tagorean days the followers of Sriniketan took different methods to make the villagers aware of different aspects of their problems. Educational programmes were undertaken for the upliftment of weaker sections. Side by side, emphasis was put to extend education among women. But, unfortunately, those education and training programmes were not undertaken seriously after the Poet's death. During this period, no cultural programmes were held to provide entertainment to the villagers.

Agriculture, Animal husbandry and fishery: In the year 1943, the programmes were undertaken on agricultural development. But during this time, emphasis was laid only on the campaigning for 'grow more food'. Fishery programme was followed in the surrounding villages of Sriniketan. Scientific study and research was encouraged for the development of village economy. However, during this critical period, developing agriculture and animal husbandry was emphasised.

But it is noticed at the same time that co-operative efforts of the villagers and proper utilisation of village resources could not be carried on to develop agriculture for self-reliant economy of the villagers. After the death of Tagore, lack of proper leadership was the main cause for going all Tagorean schemes astray.

Rural Industry: After the death of Tagore emphasis

was not laid on rural industry. But costly goods were produced by Silpa Sadana. Villages were helped from outside. Local fishermen and weavers were provided with temporary employment only. In the year 1950, during this time some youths were trained on handicraft and rural industry was set up for their self-employment.

Surprisingly no report about all this training programmes was recorded for the development of rural industry at the village level. We know that Rabindranath put much importance on agriculture and rural industry to revive the village economy and it is he established 'Silpa Bhavana' in the same year 1922, when Sriniketan was established. He arranged to provide training to the villagers on weaving, leather technology etc for the development of villagers. But, unfortunately, those activities of Sriniketan were not followed according to Tagore's ideology.

Role of Youth: We find that Brati organisation continued their work in the villages upto the year 1944. But there was no report on activities of this organisation during the later period.

On the other hand, it is noticed that there were no village development organisations in the village except the health co-operative society and Brati organisation. The later organisation was indispensible for village development work and to train up future village leaders.

In the year 1951, on 14th May Visva-Bharati became an autonomous body guided by central government. The administrative structure and work procedure was recognised, Silpa Bhavana and rural reconstruction centre of Sriniketan were also revitalised with different programmes like village extension activities which are being administered by PSV even today.

The discussion attempted above shows that programmes of rural reconstruction had been deteriorating during this time. The progress of work was slow. There were many reasons for this deterioration due mostly to financial crisis and lack of suitable leadership. Rabindranath collected money from different sources, but after the death of Tagore, followers could not be able to collect money for continuing the Sriniketan programme.

It is admitted that the central government realised the importance of Tagore's ideology and felt the utility of Visva-Bharati being recognised by our government and then the financial crisis was solved.

I have tried to discuss village extension activities of Sriniketan and the role of VDS since the period 1951 when Visva-Bharati has declared central (federal) university. This discussion has been extended (from the year 1951 to 1995-96) to the next analysis.

Table No. 5.3 shows the village extension activities of Sriniketan PSV, after Visva-Bharati was taken over by central government. We learn from reports that rural reconstruction programmes were not being properly implemented in the village after the death of Tagore. There were different reasons behind it. Lack of able leadership is one and the other is lack of economic infrastructure to counter the rural problems. The financial problem was solved to some extent after Visva-Bharati was undertaken by Central Government and Sriniketan functioned under the suitable leadership of Dhirananda Roy, Tarak Chandra Dhar, Jnanendra Nath Ghosh and many other village level workers. So it would be relevant to discuss the kind of activities that were undertaken by PSV to reconstruct the village according to Tagore's ideology. How much these activities were effective when the India government tried to implement different kinds of programmes. In the year 1952-54, Sriniketan, (PSV) covered eighty three villages and these villages were devided into sixteen village centres. VDS were either revived or formed in every village. Social workers of Sriniketan along with the members of VDS tried to engage themselves in different development programmes in their adopted villages.

Health: In the year 1957-58, different kinds of health programmes were implemented in the village. Maternity and child welfare training centre and milk canteens were set up to distribute milk to the destitute children in the villages. These schemes were formulated and implemented by the social workers of Sriniketan. In this period, a small number of Health co-operative societies were functioning in the village. Youth club and Brati organisation participated in these welfare activities. Antimalarial work was also continuing in the village. During this year a leprosy centre was established with the financial help, provided by Gandhi leprosy foundation. The motto of this centre was to control leprosy in the villages. A sewing machine was also donated by UNICEF for poor mothers, for making garments for themselves as well for as their babies. Baby show was organised in the village for inspiring village-mothers to develop child health. In spite of outside financial help it is noticed that the number of Health Co-operative Societies decreased after Visva-Bharati was taken over by the Central government. In the year 1956-57 out of fifteen, only ten Health Co-operative societies functioned and within a few years Health Co-operative Societies gradually decreased in number. During the year 1981-82, only one Health Co-operative society was in existence in a village and only four health service units functioned. In the year 1979-80 two of them were working in the tribal area. Aruna Amita endowment fund provided medicines and sick diet to the needy villagers. Village people got doctors' advice up to the year 1987-88. Since the introduction of pulse polio vaccination scheme, PSV takes active part in this programme.

Thus, only a few health programmes were undertaken to improve the village health around Sriniketan. But such type of health programmes are not sufficient to make the village self-reliant. During this period PSV did not try to discourage the villagers to received outside help rather in some cases it emphasised to get out side help, which Tagore disliked. But PSV do not take initiative to chalk out such plan which could be implemented by the co-operative efforts of the villagers themselves. For this reason, Co-operative Health Societies could not continue in the village and gradually became defunct. On the other hand, villagers did not participate in the health programmes unitedly to improve their health condition due to lack of proper guidance. Only three health service units had been functioning for a few years but these units too were also abolished in course of time.

Only true, some Co-operative Health Societies continued in the villages around Sriniketan after Visva-Bharati was declared a central university by the Govt of India. But within a short period of time, this type of self-help health programmes were not followed. On the other hand, Sriniketan PSV projected different kinds of health programmes in the villages through the help of VDS machinery. But-VDS unfortunately do not take any plan to develop the village health. Rabindranath desired to make the village self-reliant at all levels. He instructed his followers to establish health co-operative societies in the village to tackle the village health problems by the villager's united efforts. During Tagore's lifetime village health problem was solved to some extent by this society and gradually the number of this type of Health Society increased. But after Visva-Bharati became central government undertaking, PSV did not or could not follow Rabindranath's ideology. Actually PSV is not able to provide proper guidance and leadership to the villagers to make the village self-reliant as Tagore aspired.

Education: Loksiksha Samsad Continued their work for some years during this period. It is unfortunate that it was stopped in the year 1982, when different universities are trying to introduce the distance education system. 'Indira Gandhi National Open University' has also been established for this purpose. Due to lack of such programmes -our country men are deprived of education. We know that Rabindranath emphasised education to reconstruct Indian villages. At first, this programme was more effective in the whole area. In this period and at present, except distance education system, there are different kinds of educational programmes like adult education centre, library service, literacy programme etc. These educational programmes were implemented through affiliated VDS and PSV's direction which helped VDS to participate in this programme. Side by side, Panchayat is also involved in literacy programmes. Mass Literacy Programme and literacy programmes are being introduced in the district by the Government through

Zilla Sakhshrata Samity and District Resource Unit.

At present, affiliated VDS units are not interested in listening to the direction of PSV unless financial help is provided. In fact VDS are not motivated to undertake the rural reconstruction programmes to make the village self-reliant. So at present VDS want only financial help to increase the society funds. Frankly the members of VDS do not come forward to undertake any plan to extend education among villagers. So educational extension programmes are not totally followed according to Tagore's ideology. Rabindranath desired to extend education by establishing suitable village schools or educational centres through the co-operative efforts of the villagers. In this field he wanted that rural youth should take up the responsibility. But at present villagers are dependent on outside agencies for their education. Educated villagers do not take any plan or programme to extend educational programmes in their own villages. The present PSV workers have failed to motivate the villagers to become self-reliant in this aspect.

Training: During this period, different kinds of training programmes were arranged in the villages through PSV. The object of PSV was to make the villages self-reliant. During the year 1954-55, a training camp was organised in the village for thirty days. Rural youth participated in this camp according to the direction of PSV. They were involved in constructive work, like road making, pond cleaning etc. Next year on wards training was given by PSV to the leaders of Brati Organisation, adult education teachers and co-operative workers for rural reconstruction. In the year 1961-62, social service training camp was organised and training was given to the village farmers for the improvement of agriculture. Besides training, during this period, seminar workshop, etc were organised. Village workers and the members of VDS participated in this seminar and workshop. Training was given to the librarian of the rural library which was run by affiliated VDS. During the year 1990-91 training was given to the villagers for their socio-economic development. Rural women were trained for self-dependence. In the year 1978-79 crafts training was given to rural women for their economic development. In the year 1984-85, one hundred women were trained on cutting, tailoring, weaving, etc. in order to meet some of their financial needs.

PSV made attempts to develop the village in all its aspects through training. But it is noticed that the objectives of PSV were not fulfilled, villagers did not apply their acquired skill. They were habituated to depend on outside agency and wanted immediate solution to their pressing problems. Women were not independent in their own affairs. Rabindranath desired that villagers could solve their own problems unitedly and Sriniketan should only guide them from outside. He wanted village resources should properly be utilised for the economic self-reliance. But we can realise that Tagore's aspiration was not being materialised. On the other hand, villagers depend on material help provided by PSV, specially in the matter of finance. For this reason villagers only responded to the direction of PSV. Village people participated in some special training programmes of PSV but did not take any scientific practical knowledge which is very essential for their development.

Culture: PSV arranged varieties of cultural and recreational programmes like cinema, yatra, kavigan, kirtan, kathakatha, dramatic performance and observed special days. The objectives of PSV were to provide enjoyment and knowledge through these programmes. In the year 1993-94, PSV arranged to teach songs to the village boys and girls. PSV also tried to revive the dying folk culture. For this reason Radio programme was arranged.. Villagers participated in this Radio programme.

Though different cultural programmes were being arranged in villages, including the so-called western culture. Our traditional culture were being gradually extinguished. During Tagore's life time different kinds of folk culture were followed to extend rural education among villagers. PSV was also trying to bring the lost folk entertainment and were providing financial help in this regard. Yet it is noticed that instead of folk culture various kinds of other harmful elements were entering in the village and destroyed the positive aspects of rural tradition. No initiative was being taken by the members of VDS to make the villagers aware of the significance of traditional folk culture.

Agriculture: During this period, different kinds of agricultural extension work were formulated in the village. Sriniketan agricultural department and PSV took initiative to develop agriculture and select the surrounding villages of Sriniketan for experiment. Besides this, for the agricultural development, 'Grow more food' campaign was held and some training was arranged for village farmers. Farmers were made aware of this and they introduced kitchen gardening. Villagers were getting financial and other help from government of West Bengal for the development of agriculture. But PSV did not take any step to develop agriculture and animal husbandry to make the village self-dependent

During Tagore's life time Sriniketan exphasised on the formation of different kinds of co-operative organisations through the utilisation of human resource in the village. These organisations played a vital role to tackle the agricultural problems. Cooperative irrigation society was established to solve the irrigation problem. But it is unfortunate that no irrigation societies were formed after the death of Tagore. On the other hand, some irrigation societies got defunct which was established in Tagore's life time. In the past, agriculture credit society was formed to provide financial help and Dharmagola society to provide rice during lean period. During this period, no action was taken to bring life to defunct agricultural credit and Dharmagola societies. Villagers around Sriniketan were not being much benefited in the field of agriculture from PSV or agricultural department of Visva-Bharati.

Rural Industry: During this period, Silpa Sadana department of PSV arranged to provide training to youth for self employment. But no action was taken to develop the existing rural industries in the villages. Only PSV endeavoured to rehabilitate villagers through self-employment. But villagers were not benefited according to their need. There are arrangements to sell the produced goods of Silpa Sadana. But no programmes were taken up to develop the village economy by establishing rural industry or to market their products.

It is realised that though some programmes were undertaken by PSV at Silpa Sadana, no effort was given to enhance the economical status of the villagers. On the other hand, there were some rural industries in the village, but due to lack of proper guidance these industries were maintained half-heartedly. If Silpa Sadana tried to mobilise the rural industries, villagers would have been economically benefited. Now villagers are dependent on outside help but they were not involved to utilise their existing resources. At present, it is observed that PSV did not take any action to make the villagers aware to develop the rural economy according to Tagore's ideologies.

Co-operative Organisation: During this period, in the initial stage a small number of co-operative societies functioned in the village around Sriniketan, but after that, a large number of co-operative societies were defunct. PSV also realised about the deterioration and during the year 1979-80, PSV has tried to revive the co-operative organisation and Dharmagola society. In the year 1979-82, three health services units were running but within some years these programmes were totally abolished. But PSV tried to give emphasis on co-operative principles for the development of the village around Sriniketan.

Tagore desired to develop the village at all levels only by implementing cooperative principles among villagers. So he directed his followers to establish different kinds of co-operative organisations to tackle all types of village problems through the united efforts of the villagers. Rabindranath wanted that villagers would be self-reliant through their co-operative efforts. But it is known from the discussion with the villagers that after the death of Tagore PSV did not try to continue these co-operative organisations which had been established in Tagore's life time. It is noticed from the table that gradually these co-operative organisations were abolished. One old man of the village around Sriniketan said that at present villagers are not united. They were only interested in their self centred prosperity, but not the entire village. But Tagore believed that without co-operative efforts of villagers rural reconstruction programme could not be implemented and sustained.

Role of Youth: During this period, Brati Organisation continued in the villages around Sriniketan. PSV continued the programme through VDS in the village. VDS followed the direction of PSV properly regarding the implementation of Brati organisation. This organisation had been formed during Tagore's lifetime. The members of this organisation involved in different kinds of welfare programmes. The young boys and girls were afso trained in village welfare. But *it* is unfortunate, at present these organisations do not participate in village work as in Tagore's time. Rabindranath desired to build up the leadership qualities among younger generation of the village and make them suitable village workers. Different kinds of training had been arranged for them. But during this period, there were no training programme of this kind. Only in the year 1995-96 leadership training was given to the Brati Organisation in a new action plan to revive the actual role of Brati Organisation. During the period Brati Organisation was involved in various developmental work at the initial stage of this period, but it is observed that after the initial stage, the Brati Organisation did not participate in the welfare programmes of the village except the year 1995-96. No programmes were undertaken to make suitable village worker among rural young boys and girls. So the rural younger generation are not interested to work for the village as a result, leadership capability is not developed among them. But it is true, that at present situation Tagore's ideology regarding the Youth, is more necessary to built up the village oriented nation.

Mahila Samity: During this period, Mahila Samity was not organised in the village. Only during the year 1991-93 emphasis was given to organise Mahila Samity and training was given to the members of Mahila Samity on rural handicraft. During Tagore's life time, Mahila Samities were organised and training was imparted to them for self-reliance and reconstruct the village.

During this period, we find that there were no organised effort to improve the functioning of the village development activities. During Tagore's life time different kinds of co-operative organisations were established for the development of village-economy through united strength of the villagers. But during this period, only VDS were engaged in some of the village development programme which were being offered by PSV. The Rural Extension Centre of Sriniketan does not take action for the villagers awareness regarding the significance of co-operative society which should be the key unit to tackle the village problem. At present PSV formulated different programmes from out side, the PSV workers hardly consult with villagers, which is not the Tagore's ideology.

Youth Club or Village Development Society: Youth Club or VDS was organised in every village by the village youth around Sriniketan. PSV affiliated to these societies, and directed to implement some of the developmental programmes in the village. PSV is not interested to chalk out village development plan according to the felt need of the villagers. It has taken the model programmes from the government, though PSV helped the VDS to continue the organisational function in proper way from out side. VDS also followed the PSV's direction, like health programmes, relief work, Sramdan Project, Cultural programmes, Literacy programme and developing Brati Organisation. Besides these VDS are only interested to participate in such programmes which help to enrich the status of the VDS. But village society does not take any plan to reconstruct the village in all its aspects. VDS supported the agricultural development programmes which are implemented experimentally by agricultural department of Sriniketan. In the year 1984-85, action was taken to develop the village through VDS. During this period, PSV provided financial help to these VDS but did not try to make them self-dependent. It is noticed that VDS are only participating in the developmental programmes as the agent of PSV. But the VDS are not taking any plan to reconstruct the village through the utilisation of village resources and joint venture. VDS emphasised on financial help of PSV but not on expert knowledge.

During Tagore's life time, a large number of village developmental organisations had been established in the village by the leadership of Sriniketan. These organisations planned to tackle all types of problems through unity of villagers But this kind of village development organisations were gradually destroyed for the lack of proper guidance and awareness. Tagore visualised at that time, VDS is the most vital unit through which all types of village problem could be solved in the village through organised effort. PSV at best might help and guide the VDS at the initial stage. In the long run for sustained development the concerned VDS should take initiative on their own.

We observed with regret that the programmes which had been implemented during Tagore's life time, were not followed after his death. Lack of proper leadership and financial problem are responsible for this. But financial problem of Visva-Bharati was solved after the university was undertaken by the Central government. During this period (1951 to 1995-96) rural reconstruction programmes had not been properly implemented according to Tagore's ideology. There are hundreds of problems in the village around Sriniketan. Even some constructive programmes were gradually discarded which are the most valuable at the present changed situations, like the cooperative organisations for village self-reliance and loksiksha samsad for the educational extension. We know about these deterioration not only from my observation but also from some old persons of the villages around Sriniketan. They compared the past (Tagore's lifetime) and present activities of Sriniketan and lamented about the present functioning of Sriniketan.

We know that community development programmes (CDP) have been implemented to develop the rural life since 1952. But these programmes are formulated from outside to the village. One of the objectives of CDP was to involve the beneficiaries with this developmental programmes. But villagers are not involved unitedly to implement these programmes for their development. Today, Panchayat system is the vital organisation to develop the rural community. This organisation is formed by the electoral process in the village. Many political parties participating in the election and their candidates are contesting. Villagers are divided into many political parties. So village people are not being involved unitedly in the developmental activities of the panchayat. All we know that panchayat system is controlled by the political parties and government Bureaucrat but not by the villagers.

Village people are not guided by any organisation that they can utilise local resources to make themselves self-reliant. So villagers are almost dependent on outside charity. Rural folk around Sriniketan are not also free from this system. On the other hand, government failed to meet all the needs of the villagers. So today we must realise the importance of Tagore's views on rural reconstruction to make the village self-reliant.

But unfortunately we notice that PSV is only interested to follow the governmental model programme and take initiative to implement it through the affiliated VDS around Sriniketan. PSV does not take any programmes according to the felt need of the villagers for self-sufficiency through the villagers innerstrength according to the Tagore's aspiration.

We know that, many developmental programmes are being implemented-in the rural community for long, but till now it is not possible to make the village self-reliant. The poet desired that PSV would help and guide the villagers, so that the villagers could help themselves in near future. For this noble purpose he established the unique village development institutions - Sriniketan. During Tagore's life time, workers of Sriniketan worked with a mission so that the villagers could stand on their own feet. But now only a few staff of Sriniketan try to follow Tagore's idea but they are not able to implement Tagore's ideology. Temptation is offered in the shape of subsidy by the government with out having any effective supervision and follow up programmes. We noticed that some of the NGOs are realising the truth and effectiveness of Tagore's ideology and try to follow the Tagore's idea in the course of rural development but gradually Sriniketan is being deprived of its own spirit. An attempt has been made in the next chapter to show.

1. In what way the VDS are implementing the developmental programmes.
2. What are the hindrances to implement these development programmes as desired.
3. How Tagore's ideology on village development programmes could most effectively be implemented by the VDS.

REFERENCES

1. Rabindranath Tagore : *Sambhasan* (Santiniketane Sammilito Rabibasarer Sadasyader Prati), 30th Falgun 1343 B.S. *Palliprakriti,* Visva-Bharati Granthan Vibhaga, Calcutta, Magh 1368B.S., p.167.
2. Rabindranath Tagore : Charka, Bhadra 1332 B.S., *Kalantar,* Visva-Bharati Granthan Vibhaga, Calcutta, Vaisakh 1344 B.S., Revised 1367 B.S. p. 261.

TABLE 5.1
RURAL RECONSTRUCTION PROGRAMMES IN THE VILLAGES DURING TAGORE'S LIFE TIME (1922 TO 1941)

Sl. No.	Year	No. of village	Health and Sanitation	Education and Training	Cultural and Recreational Programme	Agriculture and Animal husbandry	Rural Industry	Village development organisation						Any other activities
								Youth Organisation			Cooperative Organisation			
								Brati org. or Village Scout	Youth club or VDS	Mahila Samity or Mahila organisation	Health Society	Dharma gola	Any other Society	
1	2	3	4	5	6	7	8	9	10	11	12	13	14	15
1	1922	Two	Charitable dispensary and village sanitation	Night school	-	Establish the Surul department of Agriculture and village economics	Tannery for village shoe makers	Scout movement	-	-	-	-	Cooperative store	-
2	1923	Seven	Charitable dispensary and village sanitation	Night school at Santal village and Bhubandanga	-	-	Weaving class at Santal village	Seven Scout movement involve in village sanitation and other activities	-	-	-	-	Cooperative store	-
3	1925	Homeopathic dispensary at Bandgorah	Seven night school and mobile library	-	-	-	-	-	VDS at Ballavpur village	-	Health Society at Ballvpur Village	-	Cooperative Society	-
4	1926	Twelve	Dispensary and village Sanitation	Circulating library village workers training camp	-	Model farm	Cottage industry	Brati Org. was trained up	Dom Samity covered in forty two villages	-	Twelve health societies involve in village sanitation		Credit society cooperative Bank and other two societies	Rural survey

Contd. ...

Sl. No.	Year	No. of village	Health and Sanitation	Education and Training	Cultural and Recreational Programme	Agriculture and Animal husbandry	Rural Industry	Village development organisation							Any other activities
								Youth Organisation			Cooperative Organisation				
								Brati org. or Village Scout	Youth club or VDS	Mahila Samity or Mahila organisa-tion	Health Society	Dharma gola	Any other Society		
1	2	3	4	5	6	7	8	9	10	11	12	13	14		15
5	1927	-	Medical relief and antimalarial work, and other activities	Adult education and Training camp	-	-	-	Brati organisation involves in social service work	-	-	-	-	Coopera-tive Bank Credit society and irrigation society		Rural survey
6	1928	Twelve	Aruna Amita nursing work and antimalarial work and other activities			-	Weaving school in Ballavpur village	Brati Org. involve in different volun-tary service	Santal Sahayak Sangha at Santal para	-	Twelve health society in twelve village	-	Coopera-tive society for fishery credit society at Ballavpur		Rural Survey and different rural reconstruction pro-grammes
7	1929	-	Vaccination antimalarial work and other health programmes	Adult education programme and training camp and others activities	-	Agriculture, Poultry and other activities	Weaving school and other programmes of rural industry	Brati Org. was trained up in welfare work	-	two Mahila Samities	-	-	-		Village survey
8	1930	-	Aruna Amita nursing work and other activities by Sriniketan dispensary	Night school, circulating library and training camp	Halakarshana festival in Santal para	Vegetable gardening	Weaving training centre and other activities	Brati Org. involve in health service	-	two Mahila Samities	Health Society	-	Coopera-tive store and other coopera-tive Organisa-tion		Village survey and confe-rence
9	1931	Twelve village in three groups	Aruna Amita nursing work and Preventive measure	Night school, circulating library and training camp and other programmes	-	Agriculture for economic development	spinning and weaving	Brati Org partici-pate in different progra-mmes	Rural reconstruction society and Santal Welfare Associa-tion	Three Mahila Samities	Health Society	-	Credit Society		-

Contd. ...

Sl. No.	Year	No. of village	Health and Sanitation	Education and Training	Cultural and Recreational Programme	Agriculture and Animal husbandry	Rural Industry	Village development organisation						Any other activities
								Youth Organisation			Cooperative Organisation			
								Brati org. or Village Scout	Youth club or VDS	Mahila Samity or Mahila organisation	Health Society	Dharma gola	Any other Society	
1	2	3	4	5	6	7	8	9	10	11	12	13	14	15
10	1932	Twenty one village	Health Survey	Adult education circulating library, training camp and other educational programmes	-	Agriculture and Animal husbandry and other extension work	-	Brati Org. in twenty two village	-	Women organisation	Health society and Cooperative village dispensary	Dharmagola in six village	-	Programme on untouchability
11	1933	-	Child welfare and Maternity work, Lantern lecture on Public health	Thirty two Night School for Horizon Palli, and lantern lecture on education	Sarva Janin Puja festival	Agriculture and Poultry farm in the village	-	Nineteen Brati Org. involve in different activities	-	Four Mahila Samities	Twelve health societies	Four Dharma-gola	Four Credit Society and depressed class organisation	Exhibition at Bandgoraha
12	1934	Seventeen villages	Charitable dispensary, Maternity work, Village Sanitation and other activities	Girls school and Adult education	-	Agriculture extension in the villages	Weaving school and Sandel making	Brati Org. help rural reconstruction Society	Rural reconstruction society	-	Cooperative dispensary and Health Society	Ten Dharma-gola	Panchayat Board and Palli Seva Samity at Santal Village	-
13	1935	-	Public Health work, Health Project and village sanitary	Adult education and circulating library	-	-	-	Brati Org. involve in Social Service work	Santal Sahak Samity	New Mahila Samity at Goalpara	-	-	Cooperative grocery, Irrigation society.	Relief work at Santal village
14	1936	-	Dispensary and out door programme	Training camp at Ruppur	-	Agriculture demonstration in the village	Weaving School at Santal village	Nineteen Brati Organisation helped the health Society and other activities	-	Mahila Samity in five villages	Cooperative health Society	-	-	Conference on village primary school

Contd. ...

Sl. No.	Year	No. of village	Health and Sanitation	Education and Training	Cultural and Recreational Programme	Agriculture and Animal husbandry	Rural Industry	Village development organisation							Any other activities
								Youth Organisation			Cooperative Organisation			
								Brati org. or Village Scout	Youth club or VDS	Mahila Samity or Mahila organisation	Health Society	Dharma gola	Any other Society	
1	2	3	4	5	6	7	8	9	10	11	12	13	14	15
15	1937	-	Aruna Amita nursing work and preventive measures in the village	Loksiksha Samsad, Adult education and School service in the village	Halakarshana and Vriksha rapana festival in Santal Kendra	Folk School for village farmer	Weaving in the village	Fifteen Brati Organisation	-	Two Mahila Samities for Purdah ladies	Five new health society and dispensaries	Seven Dharmagola	-	-
16	1938	-	Health and Sanitation Programmes	Adult and girls education and other activities	-	Agriculture extension in the village	Village industry	Brati Balaka Organisation involve in Agriculture	-	Women welfare work	Eight health societies	-	-	-
17	1939	-	Antemalarial work . Health and Sanitation Programme	Adult education village primary school and other educational programmes	Amusement and cultural programme	Agriculture extension work in the village	village industry	Fifteen Brati Organisation involve in Health Programme	-	-	twelve health society in the district	-	-	Exhibition on Agriculture and rural handicraft
18	1940	-	Health and sanitation programme	Adult and rural education	Seasonal festivals in Bandgoraha and Goalpara	Agriculture extension work in the village	Village industry	Brati organisation involve in cottage industry and other programmes	Musical and swimming club by youth	-	Fifteen Cooperative health Society	-	-	Exhibitions at Suppur
19	1941	-	Maternity and Child Welfare Programme	Lok Siksha Samsad	-	-	-	-	-	-	-	-	-	-

TABLE 5.2
RURAL RECONSTRUCTION PROGRAMMES IN THE VILLAGES AFTER THE DEATH OF TAGORE (1942-1950)

Sl. No.	Year	Health and Sanitation	Education and training	Cultural and Recreational Programme	Agriculture and Animal husbandry	Rural Industry	Village development organisation						Any other activities
							Youth organisation			Cooperative organisation			
							Brati Org. or Village Scout	Youth club or VDS	Mahila Samity	Health Society	Dharma-gola	Any other society	
1	2	3	4	5	6	7	8	9	10	11	12	13	14
1.	1942	-	Loksiksha Samsad	-	-	-	-	-	-	-	-	-	-
2.	1943	Health and Sanitation work	Loksiksha Samsad and Mobile Library	-	Grow more food and fishery in the village	-	-	-	-	New health Society at Sitalpur village	-	-	-
3.	1944	-	Loksiksha Samsad and establish school & training programme	-	'Grow more food' campaign	-	Brati Organisation involve in Social service work	-	-	Health Society Organised	-	-	Relief measures

Contd. ...

Sl. No.	Year	Health and Sanitation	Education and training	Cultural and Recreational Programme	Agriculture and Animal husbandry	Rural Industry	Village development organisation						Any other activities
							Youth organisation			Cooperative organisation			
							Brati Org. or Village Scout	Youth club or VDS	Mahila Samity	Health Society	Dharma -gola	Any other society	-
1	2	3	4	5	6	7	8	9	10	11	12	13	14
4.	1945	Antimalarial work	Loksiksha Samsad	-	-	-	-	-	-	Health Society	-	-	American Friends service committee help to Health Programme
5.	1946	Health and Sanitation	Loksiksha Samsad and other educational programmes at Sriniketan	-	-	Rehabilitation programme by Silpa Bhavan	-	-	-	Cooperative health service scheme	-	-	-
6.	1950	Maternity and Child Welfare Programmes and other health progammes	Loksiksha Samsad. Study and Research Programme	-	Agriculture and Animal Husbandry	Rural Handicrafts training for refugee Young men	-	-	-	-	-	-	-

TABLE 5.3

RURAL RECONSTRUCTION PROGRAMMES IN THE VILLAGES AFTER UNDERTAKEN BY CENTRAL GOVT.

(1951 to 1995-96)

Sl. No.	Year	Health and Sanitation	Education and training	Cultural and Recreational Programme	Agriculture and Animal husbandry	Rural Industry	Village development organisation: Youth organisation			Cooperative organisation			Any other activities
							Brati Organisation	Youth Club or VDS	Mahila Samity	Health Society	Dharma-gola	Any other society	
1	2	3	4	5	6	7	8	9	10	11	12	13	14
1.	1951	Visva-Bharati became a Central University by the Government of India.											
2.	1952-54	-	Loksiksha Samsad	-	-	-	-	VDS involve in developmental work	-	-	-	-	-
3.	1954-55	Antimalarial and Sanitary Programme	Loksiksha Samsad and Youth Welfare Camp in different villages	-	Agricultural extension work	-	Brati Organisation involve in health programme	Palli Mangal Samity	-	-	-	-	-

Contd. ...

Sl. No.	Year	Health and Sanitation	Education and training	Cultural and Recreational Programme	Agriculture and Animal husbandry	Rural Industry	Village development organisation						Any other activities
							Youth organisation			Cooperative organisation			
							Brati Organisa-tion	Youth Club or VDS	Mahila Samity	Health Society	Dharma-gola	Any other society	
1	2	3	4	5	6	7	8	9	10	11	12	13	14
4.	1955-56	Maternity and Child Welfare, Leprosy Centre and other activities	Thirty one social (Adult) education centre, training camp and other activities	Cultural and recreational Programme in the village	-	Development and extension programme of cottage industry	Brati organisation supervise village school	Youth club	-	Health Society	-	Co-operative Society for rural artisans	-
5.	1956-57	Maternity and Child Welfare Programmes	Loksiksha Samsad and thirty one Social (Adult) education centre	Folk recreational programmes	-	Cottage industry in the village	Twenty nine Brati organisation involve in Social Service	Thirty one Yuba Sangha involve in social education work	-	Health Co-operatives	-	-	Exhibition on health Agriculture and rural industry
6.	1957-58	Maternity and Child Welfare Programmes	Adult education and library service in the village	Folk recreational activities	-	Cottage industry extension and rehabilitation	twenty two Brati organisation involve in community work	-	-	Health Cooperatives	-	-	-

Contd. ...

Sl. No.	Year	Health and Sanitation	Education and training	Cultural and Recreational Programme	Agriculture and Animal husbandry	Rural Industry	Village development organisation						Any other activities
							Youth organisation			Cooperative organisation			
							Brati Organisation	Youth Club or VDS	Mahila Samity	Health Society	Dharma-gola	Any other society	
1	2	3	4	5	6	7	8	9	10	11	12	13	14
7.	1958-59	Maternity and Child Welfare, baby show and other activities	Loksiksha Samsad, Social (Adult) education, library service	Folk recreational Programme	Gardening by Brati Balaka	Cottage industry extension and rehabilitation	Brati Organisation involve in literacy function	Village Youth Club	-	Six health cooperatives covering twenty five villages	-	-	Conference on Krishak samaj
8.	1959-60	Maternity and Child welfare, baby show, milk canteen in the village	Loksiksha Samsad; Social (Adult) education centre, library service, training camp	Folk recreational activities	-	Cottage industry extension and rehabilitation	Thirty two Brati Organisation involve in community work	Forty three Yuba Sangha participated in development work	-	Six Health Cooperatives covering twenty eight villages	-	-	-

Contd. ...

Sl. No.	Year	Health and Sanitation	Education and training	Cultural and Recreational Programme	Agriculture and Animal husbandry	Rural Industry	Village development organisation						Any other activities
							Youth organisation			Cooperative organisation			
							Brati Organisation	Youth Club or VDS	Mahila Samity	Health Society	Dharma-gola	Any other society	
1	2	3	4	5	6	7	8	9	10	11	12	13	14
9.	1960-61	Maternity and Child Welfare	Loksiksha Samsad. Adult education Centre. Library service and two training camp	Cultural functions	-	Cottage industry extension and rehabilitation	Brati Organisation involve in Community work	Youth club	-	Four health Co-operative Society	-	-	-
10.	1961-62	Maternity and Child Welfare	Loksiksha Samsad. Adult education Centre. library service training camp	Folk entertainment and cultural programme	-	Cottage industry extension and rehabilitation Programme	Thirty two Brati organisation involve in Social Service	-	-	Four health co-operative society	-	-	-

Contd. ...

Sl. No.	Year	Health and Sanitation	Education and training	Cultural and Recreational Programme	Agriculture and Animal husbandry	Rural Industry	Village development organisation						Any other activities
							Youth organisation			Cooperative organisation			
							Brati Organisation	Youth Club or VDS	Mahila Samity	Health Society	Dharma-gola	Any other society	
1	2	3	4	5	6	7	8	9	10	11	12	13	14
11.	1963-64	Maternity and Child welfare	Loksiksha Samsad; thirty one Adult education Centre, library service; training camp	Folk entertainment and cultural programme	-	Cottage industry extension and rehabilitations	Brati Organisation involve in community work	Twelve village youth club	-	Four Health Coopera-tive society	-	-	-
12.	1964-65	Maternity and Child welfare	Loksiksha Samsad: Adult education Centre library service training camp	Cultural and Folk entertainment	-	Cottage industry extension and rehabilitation	Seven-teen Brati Organisation involve in community work	Twelve youth club	-	Four Health Coopera-tive society	-	-	-

Contd. ...

Sl. No.	Year	Health and Sanitation	Education and training	Cultural and Recreational Programme	Agriculture and Animal husbandry	Rural Industry	Village development organisation						Any other activities
							Youth organisation			Cooperative organisation			
							Brati Organisation	Youth Club or VDS	Mahila Samity	Health Society	Dharma-gola	Any other society	
1	2	3	4	5	6	7	8	9	10	11	12	13	14
13	1965-66	Maternity and Child welfare	Loksiksha Samsad: Adult education Centre, library service, training camp	Cultural functions	'Grow more food' campaign and kitchen gardening	Cottage industry extension and rehabilitation	Twenty Brati Organisation involve in community work	Fourteen youth club	-	Three Health Co-operative society	-	-	-
14.	1966-67	Maternity and Child welfare, relief work	Loksiksha Samsad: Adult education Centre, library service, training camp	Cultural functions	'Grow more food' campaign	Cottage industry extension and rehabilitation	Fifteen Brati Organisation involve in community work	Four-teen youth club	-	Three Health Coopera-tive society	-	-	-

Contd. ...

Sl. No.	Year	Health and Sanitation	Education and training	Cultural and Recreational Programme	Agriculture and Animal husbandry	Rural Industry	Village development organisation						Any other activities
							Youth organisation			Cooperative organisation			
							Brati Organisation	Youth Club or VDS	Mahila Samity	Health Society	Dharma-gola	Any other society	
1	2	3	4	5	6	7	8	9	10	11	12	13	14
15.	1967-68	Maternity and Child welfare and Relief work.	Loksiksha Samsad: Adult education Centre, library service, training camp	Cultural functions	'Grow more food' campaign and kitchen gardening	Cottage industry extension and rehabilitation	Fifteen Brati Organisation involve in community work	Fourteen youth club	-	Three Health Co-operative society	-	-	-
16.	1968-69	Maternity and Child welfare, and Relief work.	Loksiksha Samsad; Adult education Centre, library service, training camp.	Cultural functions	'Grow more food' effort	Cottage industry extension and rehabilitation	Fifteen Brati Organisation involve in community work	Fourteen youth club	-	Four Health Cooper-a-tive society	-	-	-
17.	1970-71	Maternity and Child Welfare	Loksiksha samsad. Adult education centre. Library service.	Cultural functions	Kitchen gardening, farmer education and Training Centre	Cottage industry extension and rehabilitation	Thirteen Brati Organisation involve in community work	Fourteen youth club	-	Four Health Cooper-a-tive society	-	-	Sramdan Project

Contd. ...

Sl. No.	Year	Health and Sanitation	Education and training	Cultural and Recreational Programme	Agriculture and Animal husbandry	Rural Industry	Village development organisation						Any other activities
							Youth organisation			Cooperative organisation			
							Brati Organisation	Youth Club or VDS	Mahila Samity	Health Society	Dharma-gola	Any other society	
1	2	3	4	5	6	7	8	9	10	11	12	13	14
18.	1971-72	Maternity and child welfare, Aruna Amita Endowment fund	Loksiksha Samsad, Adult education centre, library service.	Cultural programme	Kitchen gardening	Cottage industry extension, and rehabilitation	Fifteen Brati organisation participate in community work	Thirteen youth club	-	Four health co-operative societies	-	-	Sramdan project
19.	1972-73	Maternity and child welfare, Aruna Amita Endowment fund.	Loksiksha Samsad Adult education centre, library service.	Cultural programme	Kitchen gardening	Cottage industry extension and rehabilitation	Fifteen Brati organisation in community work	Youth club	-	Four health co-operative societies	-	-	Sramdan project
20.	1978-79	-	Loksiksha sambad, Adult education, literacy programme	Different occassions.	Agriculture extension.	Crafts training for rural women	Fifteen Brati organisation participated in community drill and physical feat	Twelve Youth club	-	-	-	-	Relief and rehabilitation programme for flood affected area.

Contd. ...

Sl. No.	Year	Health and Sanitation	Education and training	Cultural and Recreational Programme	Agriculture and Animal husbandry	Rural Industry	Village development organisation						Any other activities
							Youth organisation			Cooperative organisation			
							Brati Organisation	Youth Club or VDS	Mahila Samity	Health Society	Dharma-gola	Any other society	
1	2	3	4	5	6	7	8	9	10	11	12	13	14
21.	1979-80	Indigent Patients provided financial assistance	Social education, library service, training camp and seminar	-	Agriculture extension	Rural handicraft training and rehabilitation Programme	twenty Brati Organisation	Twenty five Youth Club	-	Two health society and four health service unit	-	-	Survey and documentation
22.	1980-81	Grants provided for rural poor and preventive operation	Loksiksha sambad; Social education library service training and seminar	-	Agriculture extension work (lab to land)	Rural handicraft training and rehabilitation programme.	twenty Brati organisation	Twenty Youth Club	-	one health society and three health service unit	two Dharagolas were established	-	Programme at Daranda cluster

Contd. ...

Sl. No.	Year	Health and Sanitation	Education and training	Cultural and Recreational Programme	Agriculture and Animal husbandry	Rural Industry	Village development organisation						Any other activities
							Youth organisation			Cooperative organisation			
							Brati Organisation	Youth Club or VDS	Mahila Samity	Health Society	Dharma-gola	Any other society	
1	2	3	4	5	6	7	8	9	10	11	12	13	14
23.	1981-82	Provide grant to purchase medicine, health and sanitation, preventive operation	Loksiksha sambad: Social education centre, library service, training programme	-	Agriculture extension work (lab to land)	Rural handicraft and rehabilitation programme.	Eighteen Brati organisation	Twenty Six Youth Club	-	one health society and health service unit	-	-	-
24.	1982-83	Health extension activities	Literacy Campaigning, library service, training programme	-	Agricultural extension work (lab to land)	Handicraft training for rural women	Brati organisation (40% girls 60% boys)	-	-	-	-	-	-

Contd. ...

Sl. No.	Year	Health and Sanitation	Education and training	Cultural and Recrea-tional Progra-mme	Agricul-ture and Animal husbandry	Rural Industry	Village development organisation						Any other activities
							Youth organisation			Cooperative organisation			
							Brati Organisa-tion	Youth Club or VDS	Mahila Samity	Health Society	Dharma -gola	Any other society	
1	2	3	4	5	6	7	8	9	10	11	12	13	14
25.	1984 -85	Mother and child care, other activities	Adult and nonformal education, Research progra-mmes and other activities	-	Lab to Land progra-mme, for agricultur e extension	Progra-mme for unem-ployed rural youth.	Fourteen Brati troops involved in social service.	VDS func-tioned	-	-	-	-	-
26.	1987 -88	Health extension activities	Adult and nonformal education. Seminar.	Obser-vance of special days.	Income genera-ting progra-mme through Agricul-ture and livestock	Income genera-ting progra-mme through handi-crafts and train-ings.	Brati involve in Socio-economic activi-ties	Fifteen VDS func-tioned	-	-	-	-	-

Contd. ...

Sl. No.	Year	Health and Sanitation	Education and training	Cultural and Recreational Programme	Agriculture and Animal husbandry	Rural Industry	Village development organisation						Any other activities
							Youth organisation			Cooperative organisation			
							Brati Organisation	Youth Club or VDS	Mahila Samity	Health Society	Dharma-gola	Any other society	
1	2	3	4	5	6	7	8	9	10	11	12	13	14
27.	1988-89	-	Adult and nonformal education; mobile library, training programme	Observa-tion days	-	Crafts exten-sion and training	Brati Organi-sation	Village welfare society func-tioned in the village	-	-	-	-	Area develop-ment Appro-ach
28.	1989-90	Help to poor patient; eye operation camp at ; Surul	Adult education centre; rural and mobile library.	Cultural progra-mme and obser-vance day.	-	Crafts exten-sions and trai-ning progra-mme	Brati organi-sation func-tioned in village welfare society	VDS func-tioned in the village	-	-	-	-	-
29.	1990-91	-	Adult education programme library service and other activities	-	Lab to Land progra-mme for agricul-ture extension	exten-sion and train-ing. Produc-tion cum sales unit	Brati Organisa-tion	VDS func-tioned	-	-	-	-	-

Contd. ...

Sl. No.	Year	Health and Sanitation	Education and training	Cultural and Recreational Programme	Agriculture and Animal husbandry	Rural Industry	Village development organisation						Any other activities
							Youth organisation			Cooperative organisation			
							Brati Organisation	Youth Club or VDS	Mahila Samity	Health Society	Dharma-gola	Any other society	
1	2	3	4	5	6	7	8	9	10	11	12	13	14
30.	1991-92	Eye operation camp training for health care	Literacy Programme Jana Siksha Nilay library service, training and seminar	Music and sports competition.	Training for maintenance agricultural equipment	Handicraft training for rural women.	Sixteen Brati dals	VDS functioned in the village	Mahila samity	-	-	-	-
31.	1992-93	Health Programme for poor people	Literacy Programme Jana Siksha Nilay and other activities	Socio-cultural programme	-	Handicrafts training for rural women	Sixteen Brati dals	VDS functioned in the village	Mahila samity	-	-	-	-
32.	1993-94	Child care in the village	Library service and other educational activities	Music teaching and cultural activities in the village	-	Vocational training for unemployed women	Brati Programme	-	-	-	-	-	-

Contd. ...

Sl. No.	Year	Health and Sanitation	Education and training	Cultural and Recrea-tional Progra-mme	Agricul-ture and Animal husbandry	Rural Industry	Village development organisation						Any other activities
							Youth organisation			Cooperative organisation			
							Brati Organisa-tion	Youth Club or VDS	Mahila Samity	Health Society	Dharma -gola	Any other society	
1	2	3	4	5	6	7	8	9	10	11	12	13	14
32.	1995 -96	Pulse polio campaign; Preventive step and other activities in the village	Adult and continuing education, training programme library service and other activities	Cultural activi-ties and various func-tions	Agricul-ture extension progra-mme by Rathin-dra Krishi Vighan Kendra (R.K.V.K.)	Train-ing in differ-ent trade, exten-sion and rehabi-litation progra-mme	Nine-teen Brati Organi-sation partici-pated leadership training	VDS func-tioned in the village around Srini-ketan	-	-	-	-	-

6

Case Study: Analytical Data from Some Selected Villages

It is worth repeating that Rabindranath desired to reconstruct the villages through the co-operative efforts of the villagers themselves and utilise village resources. For this reason he established Sriniketan as a model of rural reconstruction centre in the country. He directed his followers to implement such programmes, which would be implemented through the organised efforts of the villagers. He emphasised on Sriniketan's rural reconstruction activities. As he said: "আমাদের সবচেয়ে বড়ো কাজ শ্রীনিকেতনে"[1] (Our greatest ideal could only be experimented at Sriniketan). He wanted to remove the sufferings of the villagers and as an experiment he limited his activities only to small number of villages. His mission was to do work in villages in such a manner that those villages would set an ideal example before India. Tagore believed in quality not in quantity. Inspired by his vision and earnestness : "আমি যদি কেবল দুটি-তিনটি গ্রামকেও মুক্তি দিতে পারি অজ্ঞতা অক্ষমতার বন্ধন থেকে, তবে সেখানেই সমগ্র ভারতের একটি ছোট আদর্শ তৈরী হবে।"[2] (If I can set free only two or three villages from ignorance and incapacity then it will produce an ideal centre for whole of India). So he choose to work only in two nearest villages of Sriniketan, one was Hindu dominated village named Surul and another was Muslim dominated village named

Mahidapur. After that, gradually, the number of villages were increased. Rabindranath did not like outside charity for the development of the village. He instructed his workers to help the villagers with due respect to their identity. They should not feed that they are being treated in a gratuitous way. He endeavoured to reconstruct the village in their all round aspects through the enrichment of the indigenous resources.

Towards this purpose, PSV, Visva-Bharati affiliated thirty-two VDS. Under forty-six villages upto the year 1995-96. The village extension programmes have been implementing in some of the above villages since Tagore's lifetime and PSV undertook some of the villages for further extension of the experiment after the death of Tagore.

A personal visit to all the villages, adopted by PSV, to have an insight regarding the impact of the PSV's rural reconstruction programme on these villages and the activities undertaken by the villagers themselves through their VDS has been rewarding. Eleven villages where PSV is working at present were selected for this purpose. One representative village Bogdowra was taken up where PSV worked, but does not function now. In total twelve villages have been selected as my study area. To have a total picture of the development activities of the VDS and for a comparative assessment of the activities, these villages have been selected in such a manner as to cover three types of villages:

(1) Villages where the programmes are being implemented since Tagore's lifetime, the number of these selected villages are eight.

(2) Where programmes had not been implemented in Tagore's lifetime, but now PSV is implementing the development programmes there, the number of these selected villages are three.

(3) The rest one village has been selected from the villages where rural reconstruction programmes were undertaken by PSV neither in Tagore's lifetime nor at present.

The following villages and the VDS have been selected:

1. Surul - Surul Anandamayee Samity

2. Mahidapur - Mahidapur Samaj Kalyan Samity

3. Ballavpur - Ballavpur Jyoti Sangha .

4. Binuria - Binuria Jagriti Sangha

5. Ruppur - Ruppur Palli Unayan Samity

6. Laldaha - Laldaha Saraswati Club

7. Santal village (near Sriniketan) - Sriniketan Adibasi Kalyan Samity

8. Jadavpur - Jadavpur Palli Unayan Samity

9. Rajatpur - Rajatpur Kishorimohan Smriti Sangha

10. Nurpur - Nurpur Ambagan Gram Unayan Samity.

11. Khoskadambapur - Khoskhadambapur Palli Seva Samity

12. Bogdowra. - Bogdowra Tarun Samity.

In the first eight villages are under type-1 and PSV started its work during Tagore's lifetime and at present these villages are under the care of PSV's rural reconstruction programmes. The next three villages have been adopted after the death of Tagore and at present PSV has been implementing its development programmes in these villages. The last village Bogdowra was adopted by PSV in the year 1953-54 and continued its work up to the year 1965-66.

Data are collected from the villagers and members of the VDS through structured village schedule and VDS schedules. Group discussions with the villagers and with the members of VDS were organised to collect data and other relevant information, which could not be included in the structured schedules.

Data and other information are collected from the aged persons of the villages regarding the rural reconstruction programmes. Keeping in mind the past performance of the village development organisation and of PSV and also the present activities of these organisations I approached these old persons and received valuable comments. Data are collected from VDS regarding the problems in the way of implementing Tagore's idea in the village. Besides, valuable comments were collected from eminent personalities through interviews. All are related to Sriniketan activities directly or indirectly. So their opinions are very important in this study. From different angles it is judged that their opinions are unbiased and I think, Truth is established by the use of data in regard to these selected villages.

I have made an attempt here to collect and tabulate data and have presented in these data in tables with the following sub-headings:

(6.1) General information of the villages.

(6.2) Occupational status of the households of the villages.

(6.3) Different activities undertaken and are being pursued by the villages at present.

(6.4) Health Programmes in the villages.

(6.5) Educational programmes in the villages.

(6.6) Library service in the villages.

(6.7) Agricultural development programmes in the villages.

(6.8) Cottage industries in the villages.

(6.9) Welfare activities of the VDS. (6.10) Activities undertaken by Brati Organisation. (6.11) Expenditure of the VDS in different activities. (6. 12) Role of PSV.

Interviews were taken with the leaders of the village as well as with the leading members of the VDS. The aged persons who involved in the development activities of the village in the past and at present are also witnessing the activities of PSV and VDS. They have made some significant comments on the nature of functioning of the VDS.

It is known from the ex-social worker of Sriniketan (since retired) about the past activities of Sriniketan. The name of these workers are:

(1) Sri Jnanendranath Ghosh

(2) Sri Sundargopal Debangshi

(3) Sri Sunil Sarkar.

The following, eminent personalities gave their valuable opinions regarding the activities of PSV and village development activities. They are respected, -

(1) Smt Amita Sen (Ashramakanya, mother of Nobel laureate-Amartya Sen)

(2) Smt. Sujata Mitra (Daughter of Kalimohan Ghosh, ex-worker of Sriniketan)

(3) Sri Shantidev Ghosh (Eminent musician, son of Kalimohan Ghosh)

(4) Sri Pannalal Dasgupta (Eminent Social Worker and freedom fighter)

(5) Highly respected noted lady who lived here since her childhood

(6) Prof. Arun Mukherjee -Principal of PSV

(7) Sri Satyadas Chakraborty (former Registrar of PSV and eminent author)

Interview was taken from two leading officer of Rural Extension Centre, PSV, such as

(1) Programme Officer

(2) Project Officer.

In this chapter, I have analysed the data and the valuable information collected from the above sources and have tried to give a clear picture of the role of VDS in the light of present circumstances.

PSV affiliated thirty-two VDS under forty-six villages. Out of these villages only three villages are Muslim dominating. The collected data have been arranged in twelve tables.

In Table No. 6.1, an attempt has been made to record some of the general information of the twelve villages under my study area. The table shows that out of twelve villages, only one is Muslim dominating village and another is Santal village. Rest are Hindu dominating villages. Hindus and Muslims both live in three villages. These villages are Surul, Ruppur and Jadavpur. Santal village lies in between Sriniketan and Santiniketan and is composed of four hamlets named as Baganpara, Balipara, Pearsan Palli and Kaliganj. Only Baganpara hamlet is under Surul Mouza and under the Ruppur Gram Panchayat area. The rest three hamlets are under Sriniketan Santiniketan Development Authority (SSDA) Santal community lives in other five villages, Surul, Binuria, Ruppur, Nurpur and Khoskadambapur. Though various communities live in a single village, there is no conflict among various communities. Different people holding different political creeds are living in the village. At first Rabindranath started rural reconstruction programme in the nearest village at Sriniketan, named Surul and Mahidapur. These villages also belong to the selected twelve villages which are under my study.

It is seen from the table that all types of villages in respect of ethnicity and number of households, have been taken for the implementation of rural reconstruction programme. The distance of these villages from Sriniketan varies from 1/2 km to 12 Km.

Table No. 6.2 shows the occupational status of the households of these villages. The smallest village is Laldaha, which is nine kilometres away from Sriniketan and the number of household are forty-two. On the other hand, the village Ruppur which is about five kilometers away from Sriniketan has the highest number of households, 878. The next large sized village is Surul attached to Sriniketan where 752 household are living. The next higher Khoskhadambapur, Mahidapur, Jadavpur have households in between 500-640. Ballavpur, Santal village, Rajatpur and Nurpur have household above 150-303 and the rest are smaller in number, having household less than 100.

Surul, which is attached to Sriniketan, is a large size village but the percentage of land holding household is only about 31%. The rest 69% are land less households. The largest village. Ruppur has the highest land owning household 83.71% and the rest 143 (16.29%) are landless household. The Nurpur village, about six kilometres away from Sriniketan, has 279 household, out of which only 20.78% households have their own land and the rest 79.22% are landless. The inhabitants of this village are displaced persons from Bangladesh. The tribal village has also the highest number of landless households, 71.29%. Mahidapure,

Ballavpur, Binuria, Laldaha, Jadavpur, Rajatpur and Bagdowra are the villages where more than 70% of the household have their own land. In village Khoskadambapur about 50% of the household have their own land and rest are landless.

The twelve villages under my study have different ethnic groups and their socio-economic condition is also being influenced by the ownership of the main income earning asset land. However, in general literacy status of the people of these villages except Surul is not satisfactory. Health condition of the people of these villages is not satisfactory. However at present, there has been an improvement of the health status of the people of these villages, but due to the non implementation and non-extension of medical facilities till today the diseases like tuberculosis, leprosy, skin diseases and some water borne diseases are in existence in large scale in this area.

In these PSV adopted villages, under my study area, only a small number of persons are employed in service and a smaller number of persons as compared to service holders are engaged in small trade and cottage industry, while largest number of workers are daily labourers and most of them are casual agriculture workers, which is the main occupation of the villagers but the possibility of non-availability of alternative employment opportunity for the unemployed, underemployed man power in agriculture deprived them to suppliment their income. On the other hand, there are enough resources and manpower, which could be utilised to generate more income if these resources are properly invested in cottage industry. The load of unemployed persons is also very heavy.

Table No. 6.3 shows the different activities undertaken and are being pursued by the villages at present. The table shows that there are no health programmes in four villages like Santal village, Khoskadambapur, Laldaha and Bogdowra and the rest eight villages have their health programme. It may be noted that out of these first four villages Bogdowra is not under the PSV's rural reconstruction programme since 1965-66. But the elder people of this village told me that when the village was under PSV, different health programmes including health awareness camp was organised in this village. It is seen from the table that medical treatment is provided to the villagers of the rest eight villages mainly through private practitioners in their individual chambers. One health sub centre is functioning at Ruppur village, this centre is organised by the government of West Bengal. There are two health societies one at Surul and other at Binuria village. But these health societies are not active enough to provide medical facilities to all villagers. To prevent the water borne diseases safe and pure drinking water is essential for the people. The public works department (health) in collaboration with gram panchayat has provided some drinking water tube wells in these villages. Tap water facilities have been extended to Surul.

PSV introduce Jana-Siksha Nilaya Kendra (JSN Centre)* in seven villages, out of twelve villages in my study area which is functioning as an non-formal educational centre, to extent literacy status among the villagers. Library service has been extended to all PSV adopted villages. In each of the twelve villages there are primary school run by the government. But there is no other types of educational training centre in any one of the villages. However, literacy programme is being continued in these villages organised by Zilla Saksharata Samity. Functions and festivals, different cultural programmes and village fair, etc. are being organised in these villages by the joint effort of PSV and the villagers. But no village fair has been organised in two villages named Laldaha and Santal village.

Agriculture is the main source of income of the people in these villages. Irrigation facilities have been extended to eight villages only. On the other hand, there is no such facilities in four villages like Surul, Santal village, Nurpur and Khoskadambapur. Tractor is being used not only to cultivate land, but also to carry other goods. There are nine co-operative agricultural credit societies in nine villages to provide credit to the farmers. But these societies are not functioning well for lack of proper supervision. PSV workers

* Janasiksha Nilava Kendra is called in brief JSN centre.

and VDS are also not giving proper attention to revitalise these societies. However, there is no such agricultural credit society in the following three villages, named Ballavpur, Santal village and Nurpur. Neither the VDS nor the PSV workers have taken initiative to organise co-operative credit societies in these villages. In the era of advancement of agricultural technology efforts have been undertaken neither by the VDS nor by the PSV workers to organise agricultural training camp in these villages. However, there are some arrangements, to provide training to the rural youths through the project TRYSEM (Training of Rural Youth for Self-employment) by the government. Some may argue when there is some provisions for training of the rural youths under TRYSEM, what is the necessity of duplication in this regard? I am not insisting simply on training under TRYSEM scheme, but my point is that the quality of the training should be such that the rural youth could really be motivated to start project for their self-employment. After the completion of training necessary resources, including institutional finance and proper supervision by the technical experts, should be provided to these trainees for the successful implementation of self-employment programmes. PSV workers and the VDS should take more initiative towards this training scheme. No collective efforts are being made in this regard. The efforts undertaken by these development agencies are rather half-hearted.

Villagers keep domestic animals like bullocks, cows, goats, hens, etc. The villagers of Santal village keep bullocks only for cultivation purpose, but not cows for milk. It is unfortunate that no efforts have been made by the VDS and PSV to introduce hybrid animals in these villages. Fishery programme is done in every village. But no collective efforts is seen to improve fishery. Only in Santal village fishery is followed through the co-operative efforts of their locality. Fishery is also being followed in three villages through the VDS to enrich fund of the society. These villages are Jadavpur, Nurpur and Bogdowra.

The villagers have some cottage industries to earn money. Brati organisation is being continued in every village, except Bogdowra. However, in each village there is one VDS. Some of the rural youths are taking active part to run these development societies effectively. But for the lack of proper guidance, training and leadership, these societies are not in a position to improve the socio-economic condition of these villages in all its aspects. Mahila Samities are not in existence in four villages, named Surul, Mahidapur, Santal village and Bogdowra. It is known to all that once, during the lifetime of Tagore, a Mahila Samity was established in Surul. But unfortunately, for lack of proper supervision it faced a premature death. Eight Mahila Samities organised by VDS are under my study area. But, there is no separate identity of these Mahila Samity; these are functioning under VDS as an unit. So the different kinds of programmes are being implemented in the village through VDS. Naturally the members of Mahila Samity are also the members of the VDS and participate in all types of programme of VDS. Mahila Samity as an unit of VDS takes active part in protesting against atrocities against women. They participate in other developmental programme of women, but they failed to take any strong action against Dowry system.

One voluntary organisation named 'Rabindrapalli' has been organised by the people of six villages the centre of which is situated in the Binuria village. This organisation covers six villages named, Binuria, Islampur, Lohagarh, Bahadurpur, Binodpur, and Ruppur. Various programmes are carried through this organisation PSV provides library service to the villagers through this organisation. There is another voluntary organisation named 'Amarkutir Society' and a paper mill at Ballavpur, which have been established by private enterpreneurs. Some of the persons are employed in these units and earn money. It is unfortunate that PSV plays no role to establish cottage industry in any one of these villages. But we know that during Tagore's lifetime and also after his death some weaving centres were running in some of the villages under the guidance of PSV.

We have discussed earlier that, during Tagore's life time different programmes were implemented in the surrounding villages of Sriniketan through the united efforts of villagers. Health co-operatives societies, Night Schools and Girl's Schools were established. Different training programmes were organised for the villagers for rural reconstruction. According to an elderly man of 'Sarbanandapur village', Sriniketan inspired the villagers to earn money through animal husbandry and fishery. Poultry programme was also taken up in the villages and co-operative fishery development society was formed during the lifetime of Tagore. Another aged person at Ballavpur said that at that time the tank was re-excavated in the village for fishery programmes, rural industry was extended and villagers were trained up. Different welfare programmes were carried through the village development organisation. The Brati organisation participated in the developmental activities in the village. Mahila Samity was organised in the village and different training programmes were arranged by them.

Agricultural credit society, irrigation society, Dharmagola Samity and many other types of co-operative organisations were established through the co-operative efforts of the villagers. Dom society was formed to develop moral and economical upliftment of the Dom community. Santal Sahayak Samity and Santal Welfare Association etc. were organised to develop Santal community. One co-operative grocery was opened at the Santal village. One of the elderly person of Sarbanandapur told us that one cooperative cloth shop and grocery was set up at the village during that period.

It is known from the above discussion that various rural reconstruction programmes were implemented in the surrounding villages of Sriniketan in the Rabindra era, but now these programmes are not followed. The poet desired to reconstruct the village in all its aspects and to enrich the power of the villagers. Villagers also responded to this able much wanted leadership. He desired to make villages self-sufficient through co-operative efforts of the villagers, utilising village resources. At present different programmes are being formulated from the outside. Yet it is clear that villages are not self-reliant and cannot use its own resources. As we known Rabindranath disliked the outside charity to develop the village. He wanted to reconstruct the villages through the active participation of the villagers.

At present, there is no co-operative attitude among the villagers, they are not united to develop their socio-economic condition through their own efforts and, instead, they depend on outside help for their development. This is unfortunate because this type of attitude would not help the villagers to be self-reliant in near future.

Table No. 6.4 records the health programmes in the village. It shows that there is no health programmes in three villages: Laldaha, Khoskadambapur and Bogdowra. Medical treatment is provided to every village through private physicians. There is no private doctor in Santal village. Two health co-operative societies are somehow catering to the needs of the village Surul and Binuria. But these health societies are not active. This type of health society is not able to provide the medical facilities to the villagers. A government sponsored health sub-centre is present in Ruppur. But this centre is not so active to cater to the needs of the villagers. Homeopathic treatment is provided to the Santal villagers through 'Andrews health centre' of Visva-Bharati. It may be mentioned here that a noted physician, Dr. Sachindra Nath Mukherjee, former Chief Medical Officer of Visva-Bharati, and another Physician who lived at Sriniketan rendered free service to these Santals but after their death PSV and government have made arrangements to provide free treatment to the local people from Andrews Health Centre. But the local people, specially the Santals, are not at all satisfied with such arrangements, because the concerned physician are not serious to render service to these people. Therefore, that villagers around Sriniketan by and large are depended on government hospital and they are forced to go the government hospital at their last resort.

Every VDS of the village participates in the health and sanitation programmes of the village. But the VDS of Bogdowra village has not any such type of role to play as the other two villages, Laldaha and Khoskadambapur have also no health unit. The members of the other VDS including Laldaha and Khoskadambapur except Bogdowra, assist and look after the helpless patients. The VDS of Bogdowra is not active like the other VDS as at present, this villages is not an adopted village of PSV. PSV provides small amount of financial help to the indigent patients of these villages. VDS looks after the patients and participates in different health programmes to undertake preventive measures in the village through co-ordinating efforts of PSV, government and panchayat. In all the villages under study Child welfare programmes are implemented under I.C.D.S. However it is worth mentioning that PSV organised health education programme to make the villagers aware against infectious diseases in the village.

But, we know that during Tagore's lifetime the picture was quite different. We know that Malaria was spread out in an epidemic form in the surrounding villages of Sriniketan in the past. Different programmes regarding health and sanitation were taken to control Malaria. Co-operative health society and Co-operative dispensary etc. were established through united efforts of villagers. Besides villagers received medical facilities through Sriniketan dispensary and charitable dispensary.

One aged man of Mahidapur village who claims to have worked with Elmhirst told us that red kerosene was sprayed in the stagnant water to prevent Malaria. Ponds were re-cleaned. An old woman of Binuria village[1] informed us that Mr. Timber himself frequently used to go to the villages to prevent the spread Malaria. Another old man of Ballavpur told us that quinine and other medicines were distributed to the villagers. For nutrition, milk was distributed for the indigent child of the villages. In Ruppur village another old person said that one health centre was established in the village and noted social worker Kalimohan Ghosh inspired the villagers to prevent diseases and the villagers were encouraged to undertake sanitation work like jungle cleaning, pond cleaning, etc. In a group discussion at Sarbanandapur an old man told us that one health co-operative society was established at Laldaha, treatment was provided and medicines distributed to the malaria patients. Medicines were given free of cost. In Bogdowra village a person, aged about 70, said that one health cooperative society was organised by Visva-Bharati and that society had a doctor who frequently visited this village, provided medicines and treatment at free of cost.

So it is seen that various health programmes were undertaken in the villages to prevent the spread of diseases. But now villages are not self-dependent in respect to their health programmes. There are no health co-operative societies in all these villages except Surul and Binuria. But these two societies are two in a moribund condition. At present villagers are depending on government hospital services, which are not capable to meet needs of the rural people. Rabindranath instructed his workers and the villagers to take such programmes as to tackle and check the spread of epidemic form of malaria. He directed his followers to organise health co-operative society through the co-operative efforts of the villagers. At that time malaria disease was controlled through these health societies. But now due to lack of such programmes and schemes the village health problems are remaining unsolved.

Table No. 6.5 and 6.6 show the educational programmes and library service in the villages. At present in each of these villages there is a primary school which is founded by the government of West Bengal. A managing committee and local panchayat member render help to these schools from out side. PSV organised JSN Centre to extend education among the villagers. This type of educational centre is run in some of the villages through VDS such as Surul, Ballavpur, Ruppur, Santal village and Jadavpur. Two JSN Centres are being organised by villagers themselves in their respective villages under the supervision of the VDS without PSV's help. Mass literacy programme were conducted in all the villages and towns of Birbhum district through Zilla Saksharata Samity. (Refer to mass education schemes recently undertaken). All educated people and the members of VDS around Sriniketan participated in the programme. There are library services in every village, except Bogdowra.

Three VDS have their own library such as at Binuria, Ruppur and Santal village. One government sponsored rural library has been functioning at Mahidapur village. Besides this PSV sponsored rural libraries were been established at seven villages. A part of the fund comes from 'Raja Rammohan Roy Library Foundation'. Three libraries are continuing their activities through the efforts of VDS. The library service is provided to the six villages through the organisation established at "Rabindra Palli" which is situated at Binuria. Various types of books are in stock in rural library. VDS not only runs these libraries but also have contributed by arranging some fund to purchase books. Mobile library services are provided to two villages under my study area. Mahidapur and Binuria. Some rural youths have undergone short training to run the rural library organised by rural extension centre of PSV.

Though there is a primary school (Day school) in every village, but poor children do not get chance to study in this school. These poor children are busy in different work for earning their livelihood. On the other hand, the teaching in village primary school is totally neglected, though the various libraries are catering their services to the villages around Sriniketan, but some of the valuable books, including *Rabindra Rachanavali* (collected works) are not issued by the librarian. As a result of which the readers do not get any chance to study these serious books because there is no reading room facility. The other stock-cum-oflfice room is too small to study. Due to this reason literates, neo-literates and other educated villagers do not get chance to know about Rabindranath in spite of their interest. In these rural libraries, the number of readers is small. PSV could take initiative to encourage the readers so that they could form the habit of reading.

During Tagore's lifetime various educational programmes were implemented in these villages such as adult school, morning school for girls, night school and Loksiksha Samsad, etc. Tagore believed that proper education could only improve the quality of man and make him self-confident, which is the basic quality of a man in regard to his self-respect. Various information in respect of public health co-operative movement, education in science and technology were imparted through lantern lectures and other activities of Sriniketan during the life time of Tagore. We know that Rabindranath took education as the main motivating force of rural reconstruction. Different training programmes were conducted for the villagers for the successful implementation of rural reconstruction programmes in all its facets. He emphasised on the village workers for a self-reliance through enriching the power and united efforts of the villagers. An old man of Ruppur village told us that Kalimohan Ghosh tried to establish Night School in the village. Another old man of Sarbanandapur village informed that educational programmes upto primary school level education, adult education and library service, etc. were introduced in the villages.

But at present inspite of introduction of mass literacy programme by Zilla Saksharata Samity and extension of library services to the villagers about half of population remain illiterate. The percentage of literacy among female population and tribals are also very low. Thus wc see that the villagers around Sriniketan are not educated according to Tagore's aspiration. Rabindranath directed his followers to adopt various educational programmes to extend education for all villagers. At present it is seen that villagers are more interested to admit their children to the nearby schools of Visva-Bharati. Villagers think that teachings imparted by Visva-Bharati would be more valuable to their children. Tagore believed in such type of education which would not only extend the horizon of knowledge but would also have a close link with the reality and would help the people to earn their livelihood with honour and dignity. He introduced distance education 'Loksiksha Samsad' which has its relevance even today. The people think that they are being deprived of the education imparted by Visva-Bharati. But the reality is that the type of education which is being offered at present in Visva-Bharati is not at all comparable in quality to that of education offered during Tagore's lifetime. So to improve the quality of education library service should be more modified and more books on health, agriculture, science and cottage industry should be available in these rural libraries. Emphasis should be laid on JSN centre for the better participation of the villagers. Discussions on different topics should be held. Rabindranath's philosophy of education should be taken as essential part of Sriniketan's programmes on rural reconstruction. It is also essential for training suitable village workers and strengthening the VDS.

Table No. 6.7 shows the agricultural development programmes in the villages. In India till today more than two-third of the world population is dependent on agriculture. Indeed agriculture should be developed first to improve the rural economy.

Tagore, a pioneer in rural development movement, realised the truth and sent his only son Rathindranath Tagore, son-in-law Nagendranath Gongopadhyay and Santosh Mazumdar to USA to learn modern methods of agriculture and animal husbandry, when the India, specially the Indian villages, were plunged into darkness of ignorance and the villagers had no hope to improve their economy, to revitalise agriculture and cottage industry. Tagore with the help of his son, L.K. Elmhirst, Kalimohan Ghosh and some other social workers took the venture to improve all these areas and thus improve their economy specially the villages around Sriniketan. These activities are being continued till today in the adopted villages surrounding Sriniketan. It would be interesting to analyse the activities of agricultural development that is being practised in these villages which come under my study area. All this is done by the villagers themselves, VDS takes initiatives in collaboration with PSV. The people of villages around Sriniketan are basically dependent on agriculture. In the field of agriculture, irrigation is an essential input for its development. It is being provided through canal irrigation by the individual initiative of the farmers.

Some of the progressive farmers who could offer capital for installation of shallow tube well (STW) could cultivate their land through private shallow tube well. But due to the position of the under-ground water resources, the farmers of four of villages are not in a ppsition to install STW. Farmers of eight villages get chance to irrigate their land through river and canals. These villages are : Mahidapur, Ballavpur, Binuria, Ruppur, Laldaha, Jadavpur, Rajatpur, Bogdowra. Some farmers of Surul, Santal village, Nurpur,

Khoskadambapur irrigate their land through individual efforts with the help of tanks.

There are agricultural co-operative credit societies in nine villages. These villages are : Surul, Mahidapur, Binuraia, Ruppur, Laldaha, Jadavpur, Rajatpur, Khoskadambapur and Bogdowra. But these societies are not so active. A large number of the members have not repaid their loan and in three of the villages these societies are in a defunct condition.

In West Bengal, agricultural lands of the individual farmers are fragmented and scattered. It is necessary to protect the crop of these lands against theft and cattle menace. Some villagers tackle these problems collectively. and some other villagers entrust responsibility to some individuals against the payment a minor portion of fields crop. In my study area it is observed that only VDS of four villages participate to save their crop in the field. These villages are : Mahidapur, Ballavpur, Binuria and Rajatpur, etc. Rests of the villages have separate arrangements for these activities, the VDS of Jadavpur assist the village farmers to get loans from Regional Rural Bank. The VDS of Binuria gives loan to the village farmers form the own fund of the society and also from other sources. The village farmers use improved seeds and fertiliser for cultivation and some of progressive farmers use tractor. Tractors are also being used for non-agricultural purposes to carry goods. The village farmers get advice regarding the use of improved technology from the government agricultural development office, (ADO). Sriniketan Krishi College and Sriniketan Rathindra Krishi Vigyan Kendra implement different agricultural project experimentally in some of these villages. But village farmers are not self-reliant due to this routine oriented work.

Tagore repeatedly laid seriously emphasis on the role of co-operative societies in village development programme. In his lifetime he established a co-operative agricultural Bank to disburse credit for agricultural development. But it is unfortunate that out of these twelve adopted villages of PSV, four villages are not under any cooperative credit society. Of course they are taking loan from regional rural Banks (RRB) and Commercial Banks through their individual initiative. Not only that, it is unfortunate and painful to note that irrigation which is the most important input for agricultural development could not be extended to these villages all over agricultural land throughout the seasons. However, the unused potential water resources could be tapped if only the villagers could invest money for this purpose. But out of these twelve villages not a single village-has co-operative irrigation society and PSV has also not taken initiative in this regard. The PSV is trying to develop these villages keeping in mind the ideals of Gurudev. But the reality shows that Tagore's ideal, specially in relation to formation of co-operative society by the villagers with the help of PSV has not been realised.

Table 6.8 shows the cottage industry in the villages around Sriniketan. There are different kinds of rural industries in all the villages, under my study area. But a small number of artisans in some of the households of the village are persuing this occupation. There are industries like tannery, poultry, bamboo craft, weaving and woodwork, black smith, goldsmith in these villages. Artisans buy raw materials from outside the village and some of the raw materials are also available within the village.

A larger portion of the products of these industries are sold outside the village the rest are consumed by the villagers. It is not pleasant to note that not a single VDS takes interest in and plays active role for the development of rural industry. Some village youths are trained in rural industry by Silpa Sadana, PSV and also by TRYSEM. Yet the rural industries are not organised in proper way to generate self-employment opportunities for these trained-unemployed youths.. Neither by the VDS, nor by the villagers themselves take initiative positive steps in this direction. The PSV also does not take any initiaive in this regard. So these cottage industries are in a moribund condition inspite of having immense potentialities for development. Most of those who are receiving training in Silpa Sadana are not in a position to take initiative to start cottage industries. These rural artisans should not only be assisted by PSV and VDS to start their industry but also these organisation should provide them with raw materials, expertise knowledge and financial resource. They should make necessary arrangements for marketing their products at a fare price.

Under the present situation it seems that these agriculture based villagers are economically weak. Villagers are not being assisted by VDS to get agricultural credit from co-operative credit society. In the field of rural industry, trained artisans could not start cottage industries for lack of proper assistance from any organisation. So it would not be possible to make the villagers self-reliant unless the VDS takes interest in this regard.

Rabindranath emphasised on agriculture and rural industry for making economy of the village self-sufficient. While speaking about the significance of Visva-Bharati, he once said "এই বিদ্যালয় উৎকৃষ্ট আর্দশে চাষ করিবে, গো-পালন করিবে, কাপড় বুনিবে এবং নিজের আর্থিক সম্বললাভের জন্য সমবায় প্রণালী অবলম্বন করিয়া ছাত্র শিক্ষক ও চারিদিকের অধিবাসীদের সঙ্গে জাবিকার যোগে ঘনিষ্টভাবে যুক্ত হইবে। এই রূপ আর্দশ বিদ্যালয়কে আমি «বিশ্বভারতী» নাম দেবার প্রস্তাব করিয়াছি।"[3] (This school will arrange tilling in the best way, look after the cattle and weaving in ideal manner and by .adopting co-operative method will achieve financial self-sufficiency. They will have to associate with the students, teachers and neighbouring residents intimately. I have proposed to name this kind of institution as Visva-Bharati).

As Tagore desired, improved seeds and seedlings were distributed in the villages. Experts in agriculture supervised the agriculture and demonstrate on agricultural farms, and organised folk schools to provide knowledge on scientific method of cultivation to the villagers. Attempts were made by the VDS and PSV workers to provide raw materials and arrange marketing of the agricultural products at a fair price. Different training programmes were organised and rural youths were given training on agriculture and animal husbandry. Co-operative organisations were formed by the villagers themselves to solve the economic problems of the village. Agricultural co-operative credit society, irrigation society and Dharmagola Samity were organised during that period. Weaving training centre and adult literacy school were set up to train the villagers to improve their socio-economic conditions. Training was given on tannery to the village shoe makers. One old man of Ballavpur told us that various types of rural industries flourished during Tagore's life time apart from Dharmagola, fishery was practised. Another old man of Sarbanandapur said that Sriniketan workers guided the village farmers on agriculture. Seeds and seedlings were distributed among villagers. Agriculture credit society was organised. Rural industrial units were set up co-operative weaving society was organised. An aged person of Santal village informed that different kinds of training were given to some of the Santals of his village. An old teacher of Bogdowra said that in their village a weaving centre was formed by Visva-Bharati. Palmgur was made from the juice of palm tree on co-operative basis by the poor villagers.

It is noticed that villagers are still dependent on outside help. They have no interest to become self-sufficient through their own power. So it is necessary today to motivate the villagers to form various co-operative organisations for the development of village economy. Dharmagola Society is needed to save the village farmer from starvation, providing grain loan to them. At present Zilla Saksharata Samity under mass literacy programme tries to teach 3Rs to the illiterate villagers in a short period of time. But in post-literacy period some type of informal school is necessary for the villagers to provide knowledge on production and marketing of their products.

It is seen that VDS has no role to organise rural industry and to improve agriculture in the village. On the other hand, VDS takes up different types of programmes to enrich their own fund. VDS must take the responsibility to develop the village economy and employ the unemployed village youth by establishing suitable economic organisations. It is necessary today to organise various co-operative organisations on agricultural and rural industry through the united efforts of villagers. VDS must guide these co-operative society and reconstruct the village in all its aspects. PSV should take the initiative to motivate the villagers in such a manner, so that the members of VDS could organise Co-operative organisations for the self-reliance of the villagers. To make the villagers self-reliant, Tagore instructed his workers to help the villagers through Village development organisation, which should be organised, by villagers themselves.

Table no. 6.9 & 6.10 show the welfare activities of the VDS and activities undertaken by Brati Organisation, the tables show only two villages societies were established during Tagore's lifetime. These are Surul (1924) and Laldaha (1936), the other two societies are Ballavpur and Bogdowra which were formally established after the death of Tagore but before 1951, the year when central government declared Visva-Bharati as central university. Eight VDS under my study were established after 1951. Out of twelve only five societies were duly registered under the Societies Registration Act. However, at present all these VDS have been affiliated to PSV and working under the guidance of PSV, except the VDS of Bogdowra. Two different units (a) Brati Organisation and (b) Mahila Samities were organised under most of VDS.

Every VDS in my study area participates in the village development activities and cultural programmes. These VDS assist the indigent patient. PSV also provides a small amount of money to the helpless patients. VDS participates in health education programmes and takes preventive measures against different diseases in the village with the outside help. The VDS of Surul organises eye operation camp for the rural patients around Sriniketan at free of cost. As the VDS of Bogdowra are not so active like other VDS, some good-hearted villagers of Bogdowra assist the patients. No VDS has played any role to make necessary arrangements to supply pure drinking water. Arrangements for pure drinking water is made through Gram Panchayat (G.P.). But the G.P. is dependent on the government for this purpose. All VDS are participating in mass literacy programme, but the villagers of Bogdowra participate in the mass literacy programme through panchayat.

Every VDS organises cultural programmes throughout the year. Some of VDS organise religious festivals. The VDS of Surul organises three separate teaching units of dance, music and yogasana. The society of Santal village organises their own cultural programmes. Tagore's birthday is observed in every village except Santal gram and Bogdowra. The VDS organises such programmes. It happened during Tagore's lifetime two decades ago. Literacy activities like Sahitya Sabha were organised regularly in every village. But at present there is almost no touch with Tagore's idea on rural reconstruction and no Sahitya Sabha or other creative literacy activities are organised. Every VDS organises sports and the VDS of Surul organises teaching yogasana for the village children. It is worth mentioning to note that Tagore wanted the villagers through their own organisation should try to improve all their development activities in all its aspects. But at present, only cultural activities, functions and festivals are being organised by VDS, the VDS is not interested to undertake other development activities.

Eleven VDS under my study participate in the programme of communal harmony VDS of Santal village is not interested in solving the various problems of the Santals because external political pressure exerted upon the Santals. However, regarding their social disputes, they solve these problems through their traditional social system. The villagers of Bogdowra (though it is not under PSV at present), participate to solve the village conflicts with the help of panchayat. Other three PSV's affiliated to VDS assist the Panchayat to solve the village conflicts.

It is encouraging to note that most of the VDS takes active part in the movements against alcohol and harmful practices in the villages. But the VDS of Surul does not take any action in this regard. There is no such problem in Bogdowra village. Santal village has four hamlets, but the VDS of Santal Village is not interested to join in such movement.

Six VDS participate in road making programmes with the help of Panchayat. But none of the VDS is playing any role in clearing jungles and tanks. However, in some villages Panchayat takes initiative to clear jungles, if fiinds are available. It is very unfortunate that most of the VDS are dependent on outside help, specially on panchayat for fund to undertake village development activities, which Tagore disliked. It is also against the principles of self-reliance. The four VDS help the village farmers, these are, Ballavpur, Binuria, Jadavpur and Nurpur. The VDS of Jadavpur and Binuria assist the village farmers by providing loan to them. Three VDS organise fishery programmes to increase their fund. These villages are Jadavpur, Nurpur and Bogdowra.

Four VDS coordinate with other village development organisations within the village. The VDS of Surul coordinates with health society. The VDS of Mahidapur helps the government sponsor rural library. Binuria VDS works with Rabindrapalli Samity. VDS of Ruppur supports the programmes of health centre in the village. The VDS of Jadavpur coordinates with agricultural credit society. Four VDS do not participate in Sriniketan Maghmela (Krishi fair) on 6th February, but some of the members of these VDS come here to witness the fair. Rest of the VDS participate in the Magh mela through different programmes such as cultural programmes, sports, Brati organisation, voluntary work, agriculture and rural industry.

At present (1995-1996) Brati Organisation has been organised by four VDS out of eleven affiliated societies fall in my study area. In each of the Brati Organisation twenty boys and twenty girls are the members of the organisation, their age group is 9-14 years. They participate in different functions under the guidance of PSV. Boys and girls of Brati Organisation participate in sports and other activities which is directed by PSV, but they do not participate in health programmes in the village. We know that during Tagore's lifetime the members of Brati Organisation played an active role to eradicate Malaria through the clearing of jungles and tanks.

During Tagorean period, members of Brati organisation were trained up to enrich the quality of leadership among rural young boys and girls for making them worthy of a village worker. This organisation participates in the rural reconstruction, including health programmes actively. They help to organise Night Schools and demonstrate on handicrafts and agricultural products, Brati organisation set up cooperative stores. They participate in sports and drills. After sixteen years of age the members of Brati organisations are entitled to be member of youth organisation. The membership of these youths are shifted to youth organisations from Brati Organisation. Youth organisations participated in various welfare programmes in the village such as night schools, village schools, health programmes and folk culture. The youth organisations tried to solve the village problems through the guidance and help of Sriniketan. They participate in agriculture and rural industry of the villages. Mahila Samities were organised in the village. The women were trained in handicrafts, women and child welfare work, through Mahila Samity. An old lady of Binuria told us that Muslim women of Lohagarh village assembled and formed a Mahila Samity. They worked for the cause of women and children. An old man of Bogdowra village said that the former soical worker of Sriniketan named Sri Jnanendranath Ghosh organised a Mahila Samity in his village Laldaha. This organisation very actively participates in various welfare activities of the village, specially in health programmes. At present there are no Mahila Samities in four villages due to lack of proper leadership and initiative of VDS. These villages are Surul, Mahidapur, Santal village and Bogdowra. Mahila Samities are organised in rest of the eight villages. Mahila Samities participate in different kinds of developmental programmes with the VDS. But we are sorry to note that Surul and Mahidapur are the first two villages where village reconstruction programmes were under taken by PSV in 1922 under the instruction of Tagore. Training for women are also arranged during that period in these two villages.

Rabindranath desired to make suitable future leadership of the village and directed to establish Brati Organisation among rural young boys and girls so that in near future they could stand on their own feet. But at present, it is noticed that emphasis is not given on Brati organisation as it was given in the past. Now the Brati organisation is not organised by all VDS. Rabindranath instructed his followers to give training to the boys and girls of Brati organisation outside their school studies. But the ideology of Rabindranath is not being followed at present. It is noticed that even in these adopted villages there is no special quality among young boys and girls whether there is Brati organisation or not. The activities of Brati organisation are directed by PSV on the other hand, VDS have no interest to continue the activities of Brati organisation. PSV organises Brati organisation through VDS and give some financial help. But as soon as the financial and other support given by PSV are withdrawn the Brati organisation collapses. PSV has failed to inspire these VDS, and VDS are not interested in organising such programmes through its own efforts. PSV provides various programmes to VDS and the society accepts it. So it is clear to us that till now VDS are not able to organise the village programmes through the cooperative efforts of the villagers.

Villagers are not aware of the significant role of Brati organisation in rural reconstruction programmes. At the time of Rabindranath VDS took active part in rural reconstruction programme in all its aspects. Although VDS takes active part in the village programmes in collaboration with and active help from other outside agencies which was not the idea of Rabindranath. Till now villagers are dependent on the charity of outside agencies. It is seen that their are various diseases break out in the villages around Sriniketan, but VDS do not take active part to prevent these diseases through the establishment of cooperative health society. On the other hand, government hospital is not sufficient to provide treatment to the people due to lack of proper infrastructure. Although VDS participates in mass literacy programmes, the society does not look after the village school and has not allocated any funds on this head. VDS spend a large portion of fund in the cultural and religious functions, but the rural cultural traditions like yatra, baul, kirtan, kavigan, etc. are not being regularly organised. Santal village is still ridden with superstitions (with hunting and burning is still there). Neither PSV nor VDS has been able to fight against superstition. VDS is dependent on Panchayat regarding the solution of village conflict, but it is noticed that the activities of Panchayat are biased in favour of political cadres. VDS participates in the programme of communal harmony, but there are various political opinions among the members. At present some constructive work like jungle-cleaning, road-making, pond-cleaning, etc. are done by Panchayat and VDS helps from outside only. Actually, VDS does not participate in the socio-economic programmes of the village and youth members of the VDS do not take active part to solve village problems. Some of VDS organise fishery programmes to increase the fund of the society, but do not make a plan to develop the entire village economy. VDS can construct the village through the united efforts of the villagers. We note from the study that PSV affiliated VDS is more active than other VDS. So it is clear that the VDS are dependent on Sriniketan PSV's help.

We are informed from the interviews of the members of VDS that without the help of Sriniketan, it could not be possible to develop the villages. As villagers of Surul desire to get financial help from PSV. Villagers of Mahidapur also desire to get spray machine for cultivation from PSV. Residents of Ballavpur village desire to get health and education facilities from Sriniketan. Villagers of Laldaha asked Sriniketan authority to arrange irrigation facilities free of cost. Villagers of Santal village said that their village is not under Panchayat areas, except 'Baganpara' locality. For this reason they do not get any help from outside. They said that Sriniketan promised to provide a project on piggery and poultry free of cost. But Sriniketan had not the unlimited resource to provide all these facilities. Rabindranath desired to reconstruct the village in all its aspects through the active participation of the villagers and the utilisation of the local resources. But it is known that the villagers are not aware of the ideals of Rabindranath.

At the present moment VDS is facing multiple problems regarding the village development activities such as:

(a) Political problems : Villagers are not united, conflicts among the different groups of people, having different political ideologies are destroying the unity among the villagers. On the other hand, villagers are self-centric due to social change influenced by western culture. So it could not be possible to develop the village through the united efforts of the villagers, if VDS and the workers of PSV do not pay attention to this direction.

(b) Economical problem: At present maximum number of youth of the village are unemployed in spite of having some education and training. These village youths are frustrated, they are not interested in organising self-employment activities. They want handy jobs.

(c) Communication problem: Lack of communication with Sriniketan workers is responsible for not getting counselling.

The members of VDS suggested some solution to implement Tagore's ideas on rural reconstruction such as:

(1) Discussions, formal, informal should be held in the villages by eminent experts or personalities on rural reconstruction.

(2) Different training should be provided to rural youths to make economy self-reliant.

(3) Guidance is required to the rural artisans to run and improve their rural industry.

(4) To create suitable leadership in VDS and make them conscious of Tagore's ideals on rural reconstruction.

VDS is the key organisation that can organise rural potentials. So it is possible to reconstruct the village in all its facets through the organised strength of societies. VDS could be and can inspire and give proper guidance to the villagers and try to form various cooperative organisations to solve the rural problems. Panchayat and rural development department has been taking different plans and programmes for the upliftment of rural people since long ago. But it is seen that majority of people still belong to below poverty line (BPL). So it is clear that there are many difficulties towards planning and implementation of these programmes. People primarily plan passive role not an active role. Panchayat Act has been amended in several times to achieve the target. 73rd Constitutional Amendment has emphasised development as empowerment. Gram Sabha and Gram Sansad were formed to enrich people's participation in villages. West Bengal Panchayat system emphasised an active participation of villagers and through correction of panchayat laws (2003). West Bengal was directed to form Village Development Society (Palli Unnayan Samity) in every Gram Sansad area in the year 2005 (January) for the development of the Sansad area through united efforts of the villagers. But it is noticed this type of village development society is not the common platform for all people of the village. It is controlled by a few person and also under influential political parties. So in these circumstances development process could not be smooth running due to political intervention and power politics.

Table No. 6.11 shows allocation of funds to different development programmes taken up by the VDS and enrich their source of finance. All the VDS require funds along with man power and other resources for effective implementation of the rural development programmes. In this table, data regarding the allocation of funds on different development programmes and the allocation of these funds have been depicted in all the twelve villages under my study.

It is seen from the table that in all these villages VDS allocated funds for cultural programmes. In four villages under VDS there are either a theatre unit or yatra (a kind of rural opera) party. These units (2.3) organise dramatic performances in or outside the villages. Besides performing drama, other cultural programmes comprising Rabindrasangeet and other songs, dance and other types of traditional programmes like Kathakatha, kavigan, leto, kirtan, etc. are being organised in all the villages by this VDS. But these traditional cultural programmes which had importance to the villagers in the past had lost their appeal now. It has little significance to present younger generation of the villagers. As a result, such types of traditional cultural programme are being held casually and the songs, specially Hindi cinema and western style dance, have been introduced almost in all functions and festivals organised by this VDS.

Tagore wanted to revive our unique Indian traditional culture, which would help the villagers to know their glorious past. But western culture, which is being spread through various mass media, has distorted our cultural taste. It is high time that the VDS should revived this traditional culture and thereby focused on the Indian past glorious history.

Sports are a favourite activity to all members of VDS. Naturally in all villages, except Laldaha, VDS allocates their funds for various sports programmes like football, cricket and indoor games like carom, cards, etc. It may be noted that most of the VDS have created Brati organisation for rural boys and girls and have contributed part of their requirements.

Out of twelve VDS only eight VDS have allocated small part of their funds towards medical programmes. It is unfortunate that no fund has been allocated either to any of the educational programmes or training programme. However, in Nurpur, VDS has allocated small amount of fund on educational programmes for distribution of books and reading material for rural poor children at free of cost. The logic behind this non-allocation of funds for these programmes, according to the members of VDS, is that the government, specially Zilla Sakshrata Samity and District Resource Unit spend lot of money and takes initiative to literate the illiterate persons under Mass literacy programme (MLP). Regarding the logic of the training programme the arrangement made by this unit is that DRDA. (District Rural Development Agency) under Panchayat has been implementing various training to the rural youth under TRYSEM.

So there is no justification to divert the fund towards these programmes. It is unfortunate that none of VDS except two, in Binuria and Jadavpur have allocated their fund to other programmes, specially for productive purposes. These two VDS have provided agricultural loan to the farmers.

Source of finance: One should be happy to know that in all VDS members contribute regularly to their society. Out of twelve VDS eight collect funds from the villagers by giving services to the village, e.g. protection of field crops etc. Some times, this society collects donations from the villagers and individual members and various functions e.g., marriage ceremony and other merry-making festivals. Besides this, all the VDS except Bogdowra, which is not under PSV at present, received regular assistance from PSV. Only the VDS of Ruppur get financial assistance in the form of rent of a room giving to the health department for Anganwari activities. Almost all VDS under my study except Laldaha, collect funds through various ways from outside agencies or people.

It is interesting to note that most of the members of VDS take active part in fund collection for sports and cultural programmes, but at the same time these societies are less interested in paying attention to education and training and in economic programmes which would ultimately benefit the villagers to increase their economic earning and there by make them self-reliant which will ultimately lead to improving their quality of life, the ultimate goal of rural development.

Table No. 6.12 shows the role of PSV to implement Tagore's idea on rural reconstruction in the surrounding villages of Sriniketan. Village workers of PSV supervise the affiliated VDS according to necessity and advise them on different aspects. PSV provides financial help to the VDS for various types of work such as repairing the house of the VDS, financial help to the indigent patients and cultural programmes, etc. PSV also provides books to rural library, sports goods to the VDS. But PSV does not provide any medicine to the village patients but campaigns against infectious diseases. Workers of PSV participate in the cultural programme of the VDS. PSV implements various programmes through affiliated VDS. As the VDS of Bogdowra is not at present affiliated to PSV, no programmes are being implemented there by PSV.

Some officials of PSV gave their comment regarding the role of PSV. The Principal of PSV said, that PSV is trying to make the villagers aware of the necessity to solve various village problems and organises training camps, seminar, etc for this purpose. Another worker of Rural Extension Centre, PSV (project officer) said, that different types of training for rural development are given to the villagers and Programme Officer informed us, that the need of the villagers has differed according to social change. Yet, it is necessary to inspire villagers to participate in VDS and instill their scientific attitude. But they cannot do such work due to financial crisis.

It was Rabindranath's desire to implement different rural reconstruction programmes in the surrounding villages of Sriniketan through the cooperative efforts of villagers. Health cooperative society was organised to develop the village health. Various types of educational units were established in the village. Mahila Samity was organised to improve the socio-economic condition of the rural women. He desired to make economy self-sufficient and directed rural people to organise such cooperative organisation so that the economical problems of the villages could be solved through cooperative efforts. In the past, different programmes were implemented at Bogdowra village through Srinikean. But PSV has not been implementing any developmental programmes in these villages. One old man of Bogdowra informed that previously welfare activities were undertaken by PSV in the village. Different activities were taken up by Sriniketan such as improving the village health through health cooperative society and there was a doctor in the village and Visva-Bharati provided medicine and money to the village health cooperative societies. Rural library, Dharamagola society, etc. were established and cooperative efforts were made to make 'gur' from sugarcane. The villagers participated in the Sriniketan fair on 6th February. One weaving centre was established and Mahila Samity was organised. Villagers assembled every morning and various aspects of village development programmes were discussed there. We came to know that at that time Bogdowra village was so improved that their activities and achievements were got wide publicity through newspapers. We came to know further that no discussion on Rabindranath's ideals for rural upliftment takes place in the villages. The VDS named Tarun Samity is not so active in these days. As of now village development programmes are carried on by Panchayat. On the other hand, villagers are not united and they put emphasis on their individual prosperity instead of looking after the interest of the entire village. The old man reminded us that when the villagers have the dire need to improve the socio-economic and cultural conditions. At that crucial moment they are helpless. Sriniketan withdraw its affiliation from Tarun Samity. At this moment they do not need money but wanted that suitable PSV workers should visit this village, specially dedicated workers like Dhirananda Roy, Gour Gopal Ghosh, Jnanendranath Ghosh to encourage and motivate them, so that the villagers could revitalize their sinking socio-economic position.

The discussion above shows that the present societies of Sriniketan do not reflect Tagore's ideology. Once it was recognised and Viswa Bharati was undertaken by Central Government to follow and implement the Philosophy of Tagore. At present, near about forty three villages are adopted by Sriniketan. Only twelve villages are selected for the study which have already been under our discussion. Aged villagers have been interviewed, along with some PSV personnel. It was shockingly discovered that Tagore's aspirations were not fulfilled. Rabindranath emphasised to collect data from all levels for the improvement of villages. This mission he had started at his zamindari estate and later at Sriniketan. But it is unfortunate that Sriniketan is not interested to collect all types of data to achieve the ultimate goal as Tagore dreamt. Rabindranath desired to make Sriniketan a model village-development centre before the country. But now Sriniketan is deviated from its objectives. "The path breaking experiments that Rabindranath and L.K. Elmhirst started in Sriniketan in 1921 has inspired many other similar experiments in other parts of the world. Unfortunately Sriniketan has now lagged behind and is no longer the pioneer"[4] The Principal of PSV has also admitted the deviation of Sriniketan. He regretted that the village youth are not interested in taking up village welfare activities due to unemployment. Besides this, community development programmes of the government are being implemented in the village from the top administrative level and these programmes are not being formulated through the cooperative efforts of the villagers. The principal further said that the village youtns want immediate solution of their problems and that village youths go to the Block for training, but they do not come to Sriniketan because Blocks provide stipends to the trainees. In his opinion, Sriniketan is also neglected by the Visva-Bharati authority, "The perpetual neglect of Sriniketan on the other hand had a viral effect on the teachers, students and official of Visva-Bharati who looked down upon Sriniketan as an useless area of activities and service area of punishment"[5].

Smt. Amita Sen ('Ashram Kanya' and mother of Nobel laureate Amartya Sen) narrated her experience through an interview: Once she had gone to different villages around Sriniketan during Tagore's lifetime. At that time Mahila Samity, named 'Alaponi', was functioning. Twenty five members participated in the Mahila Samity programmes. Baby show was organised and one muslim lady won a prize. Excursion was organised for seven days in the village around Sriniketan to do rural reconstruction work. Silpa Sadana of Sriniketan had been so long functioning well. But at present the programmes of Silpa Sadana have deteriorated due to their internal conflicts. She further said that village workers of Sriniketan did not go to the village. At present they do desk work only. But it is noticed that Tagore's idea on rural reconstruction is being implemented at different places. She expressed her disappointment on the functioning of PSV. The idea of Tagore on rural reconstruction programme was deep rooted. But at present the original root and stock are dried up. Yet Tagore's original idea, like the roots of an old and banian tree, is struggling to keep the idea alive.

The daughter of Kalimohan Ghosh an ex-worker of PSV, Mrs. Sujata Mitra told us in an interview that her father organised different developmental programmes in the village through the cooperative spirit of the villagers. He tried to solve various village disputes through discussion. Different trainnings were given to the rural women by establishing Mahila Samity and after training they could earn some money. She said that they stayed at the village in tents.

Different programmes were organised even among the rural women of Muslims and Santal community. At that time Visva-Bharati had not enough financial resources, yet the village workers worked in the village whole-heartedly. At present the village workers do their routine work. Various government programmes are being implemented in the village. They think that the role of Sriniketan has become limited. But many experienced persons think that Sriniketan has the vital role to play in the village. Panchayat always puts emphasis on political side in the village developmental programmes. So it is necessary to do welfare work in the village in an impartial manner. Sriniketan must take the responsibility to do work on the basic problems of the village through the collective efforts of the villagers.

Now Ashramic Shantidev Ghosh (son of Kalimohan Ghosh) told us in an interview that along with other developmental activities folk culture was cultivated at the time of Rabindranath. But now only Rabindra Sangeet is being taught to the villagers. So it is necessary to give proper attention to improve the dying village culture. He gave an instance that the Kenduli fair is organised without government help every year and village culture is followed. He further informed that Rabindranath was influenced by 'Lanan Snai' but now nobody of Visva-Bharati accepts Tagore's ideology whole-heartedly. He said that financial condition of Visva-Bharati is not bad but the function of Visva-Bharati is not satisfactory. Now Sriniketan organises various seminars with this money but the work is not done in the village. He made some observation through a Bengali book named *Jivaner Dhrubatara*. He said that government is implementing different welfare programmes in the village but these programmes are not sufficient according to the Tagore's idea. So Sriniketan has the duty to do some welfare work in the village. Enough money and also chance is available to Sriniketan. He said that Sriniketan does not work for the poor villagers but work for the son of middle class service holders. He advised the VDS of Ballavpur through an annual journal of the society to evaluate and compare the rural reconstruction work with present and past activities and make a future plan out of this evaluation.

An eminent social worker Pannalal Dasgupta says that though famous persons like Gandhiji, Rabindranath, Vinova Bhave and many others emphasised on village welfare, the ideal of village centric India is not followed even the villagers uprooted themselves turned to urban habitats. At present nobody want to live in village though Rabindranath sang : "ফিরে চল মাটির টানে" (Let us respond to the call of the rural soil).

Employment could be provided to the youth in their own village through utilisation of village resources. There are potential resources and these resources could be utilised for the improvement of village economy. In the past there was a stable economy in the village and it was destroyed by the British government. So today it is necessary to select one village and plan for it which was Rabindranath's objectives. Unfortunately a large portion of Sriniketan workers are not even aware of Rabindranath's concept and village workers do not like to go to the village.

A former village worker of Sriniketan, Jnanendranath Ghosh informed us that they visited to the village regularly and organised different constructive projects through united efforts of the villagers, such as clearing-drain, filling up the pits, ponds-cleaning etc. In the past the PSV also gave emphasis on the improvement of animal husbandry. L.K. Elmhirst sometimes visited the village and supervised the cattle and cattle-shed. The old Sriniketan workers said that different programmes were carried out by Silpa Sadana of Sriniketan but at present the workers of Sriniketan do not work whole-heartedly for this purpose. Thus the dream of Sriniketan has not been successful.

Another ex-worker of PSV, Sundar Gopal Debangshi told us that they worked in the surrounding villages of Sriniketan. At that time economic problems were faced but different types of work have been done only through the labour of the villagers. Different cooperative organisations were established in the village but now such type of organisation are abandoned due to negligence of Sriniketan. Regrettably the Sriniketan-staff misbehave with villagers. They forget that the main force of Sriniketan is the inhabitants of the villages.

Another village worker of Sriniketan (ex-BDO), Sunil Sarkar told us that when Sriniketan was not undertaken by the government of India the Sriniketan people worked unitedly and the villagers had taken up different developmental programmes. Emphasis was laid on to enrich the power of the villagers. Rural reconstruction programmes, including health were implemented through the united efforts of villagers. As he said, Sriniketan is more interested in paper work only At that time villagers gave money to labourers for continuing the Sriniketan programmes, but now villagers depend on government programmes.

The former Assistant Registrar, PSV and eminent Author, Satyadas Chakraborty, observed that the basic ideal theme of Rabindranath has more importance today. He advised all to follow the ideology of Rabindranath such as :

a. To work through the power of self confident villagers,

b. To work through united efforts of the villagers,

c. To develop the village economy based on cooperative principle,

d. To make united efforts to solve the various village problems like poverty, illiteracy, diseases, etc.

e. To cultivate aesthetic aspects of life.

So it is known from the discussion with different eminent persons and their opinions that rural reconstruction programmes were implemented in an effective way in the villages around Sriniketan to make them self-reliant. Such programmes are not carried out now. Today it would be possible to implement Tagore's ideals of rural upliftment in the villages only if dedicated workers take up the job sincerely. Although socio-economic condition of the village is changed now, there is no reason for frustration Tagore hoped that ""বর্তমান কালের মধ্যে যে ব্যাধি আছে বর্তমানের কালের ক্ষেত্রেই তার ঔষধ বেরোবে"[6] (The remedy to cure diseases of the times will be found out by the modern social missionaries).

In the concluding chapter attempt has been made to summarize the salient features of my study and suggest some ways through which the VDS with the help of PSV could play an effective role for successful implementation of Tagore's ideals for rural development.

REFERENCES

1. Rabindranath Tagore : A letter to Rathindranath Tagore 31st October 1930, Chithipatra. 2 Russiar Chithi, Visva-Bharati Granthan Vibhąga, Calcutta, Vaisakh 1338B.S., p. 156.
2. Rabindranath Tagore : *Sriniketaner Itihas O Adarsha* (Sriniketaner Karmider Sabhai Kathito) 1346 B.S., *Palliprakriti,* Visva-Bharati Gramthan Vibhaga, Calcutta, Magh 1368B.S., p. 104.
3. Rabindranath Tagore : Visva-Bharati (essay), Vaisakh 1326 B.S., Rabindra Rachanavoli (Vol. 14), (collected works) Visva-Bharati Granthan Vibhaga, Calcutta, Aswin 1398 B.S., p.244.
4. S.R. Sen : "Leonard Knight Elmhirst", A tribute to Leonard Knight Elmhirst (A Friend of India), Birth Centenary celebration (1893-1993). Elmbirst Institute of Community studies Santiniketan, West Bengal, India, 1994, p. 15
5. Arun Mukhopadhyay : Tagore's Sriniketan Experiment Past and Present. An Assessment, Reprinted from *IASSI Quarterly,* Vol. 4, April-June 1995, Indian Association of Social Science Institutions (IASSI), SAMAJ VIDYA, New Delhi, p. 11.
6. Prabir Dasgupta : *Rahindranather Pallichinta Abong Siksha Bhavnai Silpa Tar Punarujibane Sriniketaner Bhumika,* Amarkutir Society for Rural Development, Calcutta, p. 29.

TABLE 6.1
GENERAL INFORMATION OF THE VILLAGES

Sl. No.	Name of the village	Mauza	J.L. No.	Block	Gram Panchayat	Distance from Sriniketan		No. of house holds				
						Puccka	Kancha	Scheduled Caste (SC)	Scheduled Tribe (ST)	General Muslim	General Hindu	Total No. of House holds
1	2	3	4	5	6	7	8	9	10	11	12	13
1	Surul	Surul	104	Bolpur Sriniketan Block	Ruppur Gram Panchayat	$\frac{1}{2}$ k.m.	-	286	7	46	413	752
2	Mahidapur	Mahidapur	105	Bolpur Sriniketan Block	Raipur Supur Gram Panchayat	$2\frac{1}{2}$ k.m.	$\frac{1}{2}$ k.m.	40	-	485	-	525
3	Ballavpur	Ballavpur	63	Bolpur Sriniketan Block	Ruppur Gram Panchayat	$1\frac{1}{2}$ k.m.	$\frac{1}{2}$ k.m.	78	-	-	81	159
4.	Binuria	Binuria	54	Bolpur Sriniketan Block	Ruppur Gram Panchayat	2 k.m	-	35	16	-	25	76
5.	Ruppur	Ruppur	52	Bolpur Sriniketan Block	Ruppur Gram Panchayat	4 k.m.	1 k.m.	225	258	110	285	878
6	Laldaha	Laldaha	31	Bolpur Sriniketan Block	Albandha Sarpalehana Gram Panchayat	9 k.m.	2 k.m.	20	-	-	22	42

Contd ...

Sl. No.	Name of the village	Mauza	J.L. No.	Block	Gram Panchayat	Distance from Sriniketan		No. of house holds				
						Puccka	Kancha	Scheduled Caste (SC)	Scheduled Tribe (ST)	General Muslim	General Hindu	Total No. of House holds
1	2	3	4	5	6	7	8	9	10	11	12	13
7.	Santal Village (near Sriniketan)	Surul	104	Bolpur Sriniketan Block	Ruppur Gram Panchayat	1 k.m.	-	303	-	-	-	303
8	Jadavpur	Jadavpur	42	Bolpur Sriniketan Block	Sattore Gram Panchayat	5 k.m.	2 k.m.	65	-	263	290	618
9	Rajatpur	Rajatpur	117	Bolpur Sriniketan Block	Raipur Supur Gram Panchayat	5 k.m.	1 k.m	135	-	-	60	195
10	Nurpur	Nurpur	117	Bolpur Sriniketan Block	Raipur Supur Gram Panchayat	6 k.m.	2 k.m.	230	20	-	29	279
11	Khoskadambapur	Khoska-dambapur	95	Bolpur Sriniketan Block	Kankali Gram Panchayat	5 k.m.	1 k.m.	160	300	-	75	535
12	Bogdowra	Bogdowra	75	Bolpur Sriniketan Block	Kankali Gram Panchayat	12 k.m.	1 k.m.	35	-	-	40	75

TABLE 6.2

OCCUPATIONAL STATUS OF THE HOUSEHOLDS OF THE VILLAGES

Sl. No.	Name of the village	Total no. of house holds	No. of land owner's house holds	Type of Farmer				No. of Barga farmer house holds	No. of land-less house holds	House holds involved in other occupations				Unemployment persons		Has their any training	Whether any chronic disease.
				Marginal	Small	Medium	Big			Daily labour	Service man	Cottage industry	Business	Male	Female		
1	2	3	4	5	6	7	8	9	10	11	12	13	14	15	16	17	18
1.	Surul	752 (100.00)	233 (30.98)	135	67	23	8	58	519 (69.02)	281	277 (36.83)	12	109	125	30	Yes	Yes
2.	Mahidapur	525 (100.00)	438 (83.42)	205	132	80	11	30	87 (16.58)	268	20	1	52	8	-	Yes	Yes
3.	Ballavpur	159 (100.00)	131 (82.38)	48	33	44	6	6	28 (17.62)	18	35 (26.71)	3	29	25	12	Yes	No
4.	Bınuria	76 (100.00)	57 (75%)	32	15	7	3	3	19 (25)	42	5	2	2	30	5	Yes	Yes
5	Ruppur	878 (100.00)	735 (83.71)	325	347	38	25	120	143 (16.29)	435	20	8	15	145	25	Yes	Yes
6	Laldaha	42 (100.00)	38 (90.47)	12	8	13	5	3	4 (9.53)	19	4	3	1	12	4	Yes	Yes
7.	Santal Village (near Sriniketan)	303 (100.00)	87 (28.71)	26	34	24	3	37	216 (71.39)	186	42 (13.86)	-	21	5	2	Yes	Yes
8.	Jadavpur	618 (100.00)	442 (71.52)	235	90	70	47	5	176 (28.48)	185	25	5	36	40	15	Yes	Yes
9	Rajatpur	195 (100.00)	177 (90.76)	125	44	5	3	14	18 (9.24)	130	6	5	14	17	5	Yes	No
10.	Nurpur	279 (100.00)	58 (20.78)	45	6	5	2	-	221 (79.22)	235	14	2	41	115	40	Yes	No
11.	Khoskadambapur	535 (100.00)	270 (50.46)	175	65	22	8	125	265 (49.54)	285	7	3	5	120	25	Yes	Yes
12.	Bogdowra	75 (100.00)	71 (94.66)	9	15	35	12	4	4 (5.34)	12	20 (26.66)	2	3	17	-	Yes	Yes

(Figures within bracket indicate percentage)

TABLE 6.3
DIFFERENT ACTIVITIES UNDERTAKEN AND ARE BEING PURSUED BY THE VILLAGES AT PRESENT

Sl. No.	Name of the village	Whether any health programmes	Education			Whether any cultural Programme	Economic Programme							Village Development Society		Cooperative Society		Any other society
			Adult education	Library	Other types of education and training		Agriculture		Animal Husbandry				Whether any cottage industry					
							Development Programme	Training Programme	Dairy	Poultry	Fishery	Others		Brati organisation	Mahila Samity	Health Society	Credit Society	
1	2	3	4	5	6	7	8	9	10	11	12	13	14	15	16	17	18	19
1.	Surul	Yes	Yes	Yes	Yes	Yes	No	No	Yes	Yes	Yes	Yes	Yes	Yes	No	Yes	Yes	Yes
2.	Mahidapur	Yes	No	Yes	Yes	Yes	Yes	No	Yes	Yes	Yes	Yes	Yes	No	No	No	Yes	No
3.	Ballavpur	Yes	Yes	Yes	Yes	Yes	Yes	No	Yes	Yes	Yes	Yes	Yes	Yes	Yes	No	No	Yes
4.	Binuria	Yes	Yes	Yes	Yes	Yes	Yes	No	Yes	Yes	Yes	Yes	Yes	Yes	Yes	Yes	Yes	Yes
5.	Ruppur	yes	Yes	Yes	Yes	Yes	Yes	No	Yes	Yes	Yes	Yes	Yes	No	Yes	No	Yes	Yes
6.	Laldaba	No	No	Yes	Yes	Yes	Yes	No	Yes	Yes	Yes	Yes	Yes	No	Yes	No	Yes	Yes
7	Santal Village (near Sriniketan)	No	Yes	Yes	Yes	Yes	No	No	No	Yes	Yes	Yes	Yes	No	No	No	No	No
8	Jadavpur	Yes	Yes	Yes	Yes	Yes	Yes	No	Yes	Yes	Yes	Yes	Yes	No	Yes	No	Yes	Yes
9.	Rajatpur	Yes	No	Yes	Yes	Yes	Yes	No	Yes	Yes	Yes	Yes	Yes	No	Yes	No	Yes	No
10.	Nurpur	Yes	No	Yes	Yes	Yes	No	No	Yes	Yes	Yes	Yes	Yes	Yes	Yes	No	No	Yes
11.	Khoskadambapur	No	Yes	Yes	Yes	Yes	No	No	Yes	Yes	Yes	Yes	Yes	No	Yes	No	Yes	Yes
12.	Bogdowra	No	No	No	Yes	Yes	Yes	No	Yes	Yes	Yes	Yes	Yes	No	No	No	Yes	Yes

TABLE 6.4
HEALTH PROGRAMMES IN THE VILLAGES

Sl. No.	Name of the village	Whether any health unit	Type of Health Unit			Whether VDS has a role	Whether any role of PSV
			Individual	Cooperative	Government		
1	2	3	4	5	6	7	8
1.	Surul	Yes	Yes	Yes	No	Yes	Yes
2.	Mahidapur	Yes	Yes	No	No	Yes	Yes
3.	Ballavpur	Yes	Yes	No	No	Yes	Yes
4.	Binuria	Yes	Yes	Yes	No	Yes	Yes
5.	Ruppur	Yes	Yes	No	Yes	Yes	Yes
6.	Laldaha	No	Yes	No	No	Yes	Yes
7.	Santal Village (near Sriniketan)	Yes	No	No	Yes	Yes	Yes
8.	Jadavpur	Yes	Yes	No	No	Yes	Yes
9.	Rajatpur	Yes,	Yes	No	No	Yes	Yes
10.	Nurpur	Yes	Yes	No	No	Yes	Yes
11.	Khoskadambapur	No	No	No	No	Yes	Yes
12.	Bogdowra	No	No	No	No	No	No

TABLE 6.5
EDUCATIONAL PROGRAMMES IN THE VILLAGES

Sl. No.	Name of the Village	School Service in the village (Primary)	Sponsored by	Whether any adult education Programme	Sponsored by	Whether any mass literacy Programme in the village	Organised by	Role of VDS		Whether any library service	Sponsored by
								Teaching	Help from out side		
1	2	3	4	5	6	7	8	9	10	11	12
1	Surul	Yes	Govt	JSN	PSV	Yes	BZSS and DRU	Yes	Yes	Yes	PSV
2.	Mahidapur	Yes	Govt	-	-	Yes	BZSS & DRU	Yes	Yes	Yes	Govt
3.	Ballavpur	Yes	Govt	JSN	PSV	Yes	BZSS & DRU	Yes	Yes	Yes	PSV
4.	Binuria	Yes	Govt	JSN	Own	Yes	BZSS & DRU	Yes	Yes	Yes	Own
5.	Ruppur	Yes	Govt	JSN	PSV	Yes	BZSS & DRU	Yes	Yes	Yes	Own
6.	Laldaha	Yes	Govt	-	-	Yes	BZSS & DRU	Yes	Yes	Yes	PSV
7.	Santal Village (near Sriniketan)	Yes	Govt	JSN	PSV	Yes	BZSS & DRU	Yes	Yes	Yes	Own
8	Jadavpur	Yes	Govt	JSN	PSV	Yes	BZSS & DRU	Yes	Yes	Yes	PSV

Contd. ....

Sl. No.	Name of the Village	School Service in the village (Primary)	Sponsored by	Whether any adult education Programme	Sponsored by	Whether any mass literacy Programme in the village	Organised by	Role of VDS		Whether any library service	Sponsored by
								Teaching	Help from out side		
1	2	3	4	5	6	7	8	9	10	11	12
9.	Rajatpur	Yes	Govt	-	-	Yes	BZSS & DRU	Yes	Yes	Yes	PSV
10.	Nurpur	Yes	Govt	-	-	Yes	BZSS & DRU	Yes	Yes	Yes	PSV
11.	Khoskadambapur	Yes	Govt	JSN	Own	Yes	BZSS & DRU	Yes	Yes	Yes	PSV
12.	Bogdowra	Yes	Govt	-	-	Yes	BZSS & DRU	Yes	Yes	No	-

* PSV Palli Samgathan Vibhaga
* JSN Jana Siksha Nilaya.
* BZSS Birbhum Zilla Sakshrata Samity
* DRU District Resource Unit

TABLE 6.6
LIBRARY SERVICE IN THE VILLAGES

Sl. No.	Name of the village	Name of the VDS	Name of the library	Year of establishment	Types of Books				No. of Books Provided by			Total no of books	No. of Readers		Involvement of Youth		Mobile Library		
					Science	Novel	Books of Children	Books of Rabindra-nath	VDS	PSV	Govt		Male	Female	Male	Female	Total no. of Readers		Total no of books
1	2	3	4	5	6	7	8	9	10	11	12	13	14	15	16	17	18	19	20
1	Surul	Surul Ananda Mayee Samity	Surul Ananda Mayee Pathagar	1975	√	√	√	√	340	1216	-	1556	478	470	20	15	-	-	-
2	Mahidapur	Mahidapur Samaj Kalyan Samity	Mahidapur Sadharan Pathagar	1978	√	√	√	√	120	-	2609	2729	60	15	15	-	21	99	120
3	Ballavpur	Ballavpur Jyoti Sangha	Ballavpur Jyoti Sangha Pathagar	1975	√	√	√	√	1235	1265	-	2500	206	104	18	8	-	-	-
4.	Bonura	Bonura Jagrit Sangha	-	-	√	√	√	√	530	-	-	530	40	10	5	2	117	128	292
5	Ruppur	Ruppur Palli Unayan Samity	-	-	√	√	√	√	525	-	-	525	90	30	4	1	-	-	-
6	Lakdaha	Lakdaha Saraswati Club	Lakdaha Rammohan Library	1975	√	√	√	√	118	1255	-	1373	212	106	12	3	-	-	-
7	Santal Village (near Sriniketan)	Santumkalan Adibasi Kalyan Samity		-	√	√	√	√	487	-	-	487	3	2	12	-	-	-	-

Contd. ...

Sl. No.	Name of the village	Name of the VDS.	Name of the library	Year of establish-ment	Types of Books				No of Books Provided by			Total no of books	No. of Readers		Involvement of Youth		Mobile Library		
					Science	Novel	Books of Children	Books of Rabindra-nath	VDS	PSV	Govt		Male	Female	Male	Female	Total no. of Readers		Total no of books
1	2	3	4	5	6	7	8	9	10	11	12	13	14	15	16	17	18	19	20
8	Jadavpur	Jadavpur Palli Unnayan Samity	Jadav-pur Ram-mohan Patha-gar	1980	√	√	√	√	250	892	-	1142	460	121	7	1	-	-	-
9	Rajatpur	Rajatpur Kishoremohon Smriti Sangha	Rajat-pur Kisho-remo-hon Smriti Sangha Patha-gar	1983	√	√	√	√	90	617	-	707	259	171	10	-	-	-	-
10.	Nurpur	Nurpur Ambagan Gram Unnayan Samity	Nurpur Netaji Library	1975	√	√	√	√	101	1264	-	1365	305	205	12	5	-	-	-
11	Khoskadambapur	Khoska-damba-pur Palli Seva Sangha	Kho-ska-damba-pur Palli Seva Patha-gar	1993	√	√	√	√	5	430	-	435	133	3	15	-	-	-	-
12	Bogdewra	Bogdewra Tarun Samity	-	-	-	-	-	-	-	-	-	-	-	-	-	-	-	-	-

TABLE 6.7

AGRICULTURAL DEVELOPMENT PROGRAMMES IN THE VILLAGES

Sl. No.	Name of the Village	Irrigation Programme			Cooperative Credit Society	Whether any other Organisation	Adopt Scientific Method if any	Whether any role of VDS	Whether any help from PSV
		Individual	Cooperative	Govt.					
1	2	3	4	5	6	7	8	9	10
1	Surul	No	No	No	Yes	Yes	Yes	No	No
2.	Mahidapur	Yes	No	No	Yes	No	Yes	Yes	Yes
3.	Ballavpur	Yes	No	Yes	No	No	Yes	Yes	Yes
4.	Binuria	Yes	No	Yes	Yes	No.	Yes	Yes	Yes
5.	Ruppur	Yes	No	Yes	Yes	Yes	Yes	No	No
6.	Laldaha	Yes	No	Yes	Yes	Yes	Yes	No	No
7.	Santal Village (near Sriniketan)	No	No	No	No	No	Yes	No	No
8.	Jadavpur	Yes	No	Yes	Yes	Yes	Yes	Yes	Yes
9.	Rajatpur	Yes	No	Yes	Yes	No	Yes	Yes	No
10.	Nurpur	No	No	No	No	Yes	Yes	Yes	No
11.	Khoskadambapur	No	No	No	Yes	Yes	Yes	No	No
12.	Bogdowra	Yes	No	No	Yes	Yes	Yes	No	No

TABLE 6.8

COTTAGE INDUSTRIES IN THE VILLAGES

Sl. No.	Name of the Village	Whether any cottage industry	Types of organisation		Source of finance	Place of marketing		Average monthly income per artisans	Role of VDS	Whether any help from PSV
			Individual	Cooperative		Village	Out side of the village			
1	2	3	4	5	6	7	8	9	10	11
1	Surul	Yes	Yes	No	Own	Yes	Yes	1200	No	Yes
2.	Mahidapur	Yes	Yes	No	Own	Yes	Yes	1000	No	Yes
3.	Ballavpur	Yes	Yes	No	Own	Yes	Yes	750	No	Yes
4.	Binuria	Yes	Yes	No	Own	Yes	Yes	1100	No	Yes
5.	Ruppur	Yes	Yes	No	Own	Yes	Yes	500	No	Yes
6.	Laldaha	Yes	Yes	No	Own	Yes	Yes	650	No	Yes
7.	Santal Village(near Sriniketan)	Yes	Yes	No	Own	Yes	No	200	No	No
8.	Jadavpur	Yes	Yes	No	Own	Yes	Yes	500	No	Yes
9.	Rajatpur	Yes	Yes	No	Own	Yes	Yes	700	No	Yes
10.	Nurpur	Yes	Yes	No	Own	Yes	Yes	450	No	Yes
11.	Khoskadambapur	Yes	Yes	No	Own	Yes	Yes	1000	No	Yes
12.	Bogdowra.	Yes	Yes	No	Own	Yes	No	1200	No	No

TABLE 6.9
WELFARE ACTIVITIES OF THE VDS

Sl. No	Name of the Village	Name of the VDS	Year of establishment and Regd. No.	No. of members of the VDS	Service to the helpless patient	Any activities against infectious disease	Supplying drinking water	Participated in mass literacy programme	Participated against superstition	Tagore's birth day observation	Cultural Activities of the VDS	Participated in sports and games
1	2	3	4	5	6	7	8	9	10	11	12	13
1	Surul	Surul Anandamayee Samity	Estb-1924 S/4190	170	Yes	Yes	No	Yes	Yes	Yes	Yes	Yes
2.	Mahidapur	Mahidapur Samaj Kalyan Samity	Estb-1978 S/44382	130	Yes	Yes	No	Yes	Yes	Yes	Yes	Yes
3.	Ballavpur	Ballavpur Jyoti Sangha	Estb-1947 S/39105	250	Yes	Yes	No	Yes	Yes	Yes	Yes	Yes
4.	Binuria	Binuria Jagriti Sangha	Estb-1969	200	Yes	Yes	No	Yes	Yes	Yes	Yes	Yes
5.	Ruppur	Ruppur Palli Unnayan Samity	Estb-1979	60	Yes	Yes	No	Yes	Yes	Yes	Yes	Yes
6.	Laldaha	Laldaha Saraswati Club	Estb-1936	150	Yes	Yes	No	Yes	Yes	Yes	Yes	Yes
7.	Santal Village (near Sriniketan)	Santiniketan Adibasi Kalyan Samity	Estb-1975	21	Yes	Yes	No	Yes	Yes	No	Yes	Yes
8.	Jadavpur	Jadavpur Palli Unayan Samity	Estb-1977	54	Yes	Yes	No	Yes	Yes	Yes	Yes	Yes
9.	Rajatpur	Rajatpur Kishorimohan Smriti Sangha	Estb-1955	103	Yes	Yes	No	Yes	Yes	Yes	Yes	Yes
10.	Nurpur	Nurpur Ambagan Gram Unnayan Samity	Estb-1968 S/16535	165	Yes	Yes	No	Yes	Yes	Yes	Yes	Yes
11.	Khoskadambapur	Khaskadambapur Palli Seva Samity	Estb-1975 S/46594	110	Yes	Yes	No	Yes	Yes	Yes	Yes	Yes
12.	Bogdowra	Bogdowra Tarun Samiti	Estb-1949	35	No	No	No	No	No	No	Yes	Yes

Contd. ...

Sl. No.	Name of the village	Name of the VDS	Whether take part to solve village conflict	Activities against alcohol and mal practices	Whether Participate road reconstruction	Excavation of tanks	Whether participate in jungle cleaning	Whether any help to the farmer	Participate economical programme in the village	Whether any role of Mahila Samity	Whether coordination with other organisation	Whether participate in Magh mela	Participate in communal harmony
1	2	3	14	15	16	17	18	19	20	21	22	23	24
1	Surul	Surul Anandamayee Samity	No	No	No	No	No	No	No	No	Yes	Yes	Yes
2.	Mahidapur	Mahidapur Samaj Kalyan Samity	No	Yes	Yes	No	No	No	Yes	No	Yes	Yes	Yes
3	Ballavpur	Ballavpur Jyoti Sangha	Yes	Yes	Yes	No	No	Yes	Yes	Yes	No	Yes	Yes
4	Binuria	Binuria Jagriti Sangha	No	Yes	No	No	No	Yes	Yes	Yes	Yes	Yes	Yes
5	Ruppur	Ruppur Palli Unnayan Samity	No	Yes	Yes	No	No	No	No	Yes	Yes	No	Yes
6	Laldaha	Laldaha Saraswati Club	No	Yes	Yes	No	No	No	No	Yes	No	No	Yes

Contd. ...

Sl. No.	Name of the village	Name of the VDS	Whether take part to solve village conflict	Activities against alcohol and mal practices	Whether Partici-pate road recon-struction	Exca-vation of tanks	Whether partici-pate in jungle cleaning	Whether any help to the farmer	Partici-pate economi-cal program me in the village	Whether any role of Mahila Samity	Whether coordinati on with other organi-sation	Whether parti-cipate in Magh mela	Partici-pate in commu-nal harmony
1	2	3	14	15	16	17	18	19	20	21	22	23	24
7.	Santal Village (near Sriniketan)	Santi-niketan Adibasi Kalyan Samity	No	Yes	No	No	No	No	No	No	No	Yes	Yes
8.	Jadavpur	Jadavpur Palli Unnayan Samity	Yes	Yes	Yes	No	No	Yes	Yes	Yes	Yes	No	Yes
9.	Rajatpur	Rajatpur Kishori-mohan Smriti Sangha	No	Yes	No	No	No	No	Yes	Yes	No	Yes	Yes
10.	Nurpur	Nurpur Ambagan Gram Unnayan Samity	No	Yes	No	No	No	Yes	Yes	Yes	No	Yes	Yes
11.	Khoskadambapur	Khaska-dambapur Palli Seva Samity	Yes	Yes	Yes	No	No	No	No	Yes	No	Yes	Yes
12.	Bogdowra	Bogdowra Tarun Samity	No	--	No	No	No	No	Yes	No	No	No	No

TABLE 6.10
ACTIVITIES UNDERTAKEN BY BRATI ORGANISATION

Sl. No.	Name of the Village	Name of the VDS of the village	No. of Brati Balaka/ Balika		Whether Participated in Sports	Whether construction work undertaken	Whether medical help by Brati Organisation	Educational help by Brati Organisation	Other activities of Brati Organisation	Whether organised by PSV
			Boys	Girls						
1	2	3	4	5	6	7	8	9	10	11
1.	Surul	Surul Anandamayee Samity	20	20	Yes	No	No	No	Yes	Yes
2.	Mahidapur	Mahidapur Samaj Kalyan Samity	-	-	-	-	-	-	-	-
3.	Ballavpur	Ballavpur Jyoti Sangha	20	20	Yes	No	No	No	Yes	Yes
4.	Binuria	Binuria Jagriti Sangha	20	20	Yes	No	No	No	Yes	Yes
5.	Ruppur	Ruppur Palli Unayan Samity	-	-	-	-	-	-	-	-
6.	Laldaha	Laldaha Saraswati Club	-	-	-	-	-	-	-	-
7.	Santal Village near Sriniketan	Sriniketan Adibasi Kalyan Samity	-	-	-	-	-	-	-	-
8.	Jadavpur	Jadavpur Palli Unayan Samity	-	-	-		-	-	-	-
9.	Rajatpur	Rajatpur Kishorimohan Smriti Sangha	-	-	-	-	-	-	-	-
10.	Nurpur	Nurpur Ambagan Gram Unayan Samity	20	20	Yes	No	No	No	Yes	Yes
11.	Khoskhadambapur	Khoskhadambapur Palli Seva Samity	-	-	-	-	-	-	-	-
12.	Bogdowra	Bogdowra Tarun Samity	-	-	-	-	-	-	-	-

TABLE 6.11

EXPENDITURE OF THE VDS IN DIFFERENT ACTIVITIES

Sl. No.	Name of the village	Name of the VDS	Allocation of fund Programme wise						Source of finance						
			Cultural Progra-mme	Sports Progra-mme	Medical Progra-mme	Educa-tional Progra-mme	Training Progra-mme	Others Progra-mme	Contribute by members	Collection from villagers	Outside Assistants	Donation from individual member	PSV.Assis-tance	Govt. Assistance	Other sources
1	2	3	4	5	6	7	8	9	10	11	12	13	14	15	16
1	Surul	Surul Ananda-mayee Samity	Yes	Yes	Yes	No	No	No	Yes	No	Yes	Yes	Yes	No	Yes
2.	Mahidapur	Mahida-pur Samaj Kalyan Samity	Yes	Yes	Yes	No	No	No	Yes	No	No	Yes	Yes	No	Yes
3.	Ballavpur	Ballavpur Jyoti Sangha	Yes	Yes	Yes	No	No	No	Yes	No	No	No	Yes	No	Yes
4.	Binuria	Binuria Jagriti Sangha	Yes	Yes	Yes	No	No	Yes	Yes	Yes	No	No	Yes	No	Yes
5.	Ruppur	Ruppur Palli Unnayan Samity	Yes	Yes	No	No	No	No	Yes	Yes	No	No	Yes	Yes	Yes
6.	Laldaha	Laldaha Saraswati Club	Yes	No	No	NO	NO	No	Yes	Yes	No	Yes	Yes	No	No

Contd. ...

Sl. No.	Name of the village	Name of the VDS	Alloocation of fund Programme wise						Source of finance						
			Cultural Progra-mme	Sports Progra-mme	Medical Progra-mme	Educa-tional Progra-mme	Training Progra-mme	Others Progra-mme	Contribute by members	Collection from villagers	Outside Assistanta	Donation from individual member	PSV Assistance	Govt. Assistance	Other sources
1	2	3	4	5	6	7	8	9	10	11	12	13	14	15	16
7	Santal Village (near Sriniketan)	Santi-niketan Adibasi Kalyan Samity	Yes	Yes	Yes	No	No	No	Yes	Yes	No	Yes	Yes	No	Yes
8	Jadavpur	Jadavpur Palli Unavan Samity	Yes	Yes	Yes	No	No	Yes	Yes	No	No	Yes	Yes	No	Yes
9.	Rajatpur	Rajatpur Kishori-mohan Smriti Sangha	Yes	Yes	Yes	No	No	No	Yes	Yes	No	Yes	Yes	No	Yes
10	Nurpur	Nurpur Ambagan Gram Unnayan Samity	Yes	Yes	Yes	Yes	No	No	Yes	Yes	No	Yes	Yes	No	Yes
11.	Khoskadampur	Khoska-dambapur Palli Seva Sangha	Yes	Yes	No	No	No	No	Yes	Yes	No	Yes	Yes	No	Yes
12	Bogdowra	Bogdowra Tarun Samity	Yes	Yes	No	No	No	No	Yes	Yes	No	No	No	No	Yes

TABLE 6.12

ROLE OF PSV

Sl. No.	Name of the village	Name of the VDS	Frequency of visit by PSV				Type of activities done by PSV							To organise cultural activities	Whether any enterprise under taken by PSV and VDS
			Daily	Weekly	Monthly	Yearly	Expertise knowledge	Money	Books	Sports goods	Medicine	Instrument of rural industry	Instrument of Agriculture		
1	2	3	4	5	6	7	8	9	10	11	12	13	14	15	16
1.	Surul	Surul Ananda-mayee Samity	-	-	-	-	Yes	Yes	Yes	Yes	No	No	No	No	No
2.	Mahidapur	Mahida-pur Samaj Kalyan Samity	-	-	-	-	Yes	Yes	Yes	Yes	No	No	No	No	No
3.	Ballavpur	Ballavpur Jyoti Sangha	-	-	-	-	Yes	Yes	Yes	Yes	No	No	No	No	No
4.	Binuria	Binuria Jagriti Sangha	-	-	-	-	Yes	Yes	Yes	Yes	No	No	No	No	No
5.	Ruppur	Ruppur Palli Unnayan Samity	-	-	-	-	Yes	Yes	Yes	Yes	No	No	No	No	No
6.	Laldaha	Laldaha Saraswati Club	-	-	-	-	Yes	Yes	Yes	Yes	No	No	No	No	No
7.	Santal Village (near Sriniketan)	Santi-niketan Adibasi Kalyan Samity	-	-	-	-	Yes	Yes	Yes	Yes	No	No	No	No	No
8.	Jadavpur	Jadavpur Palli Unayan Samity	-	-	-	-	Yes	Yes	Yes	Yes	No	No	No	No	No
9.	Rajatpur	Rajatpur Kishorimohan Smriti Sangha	-	-	-	-	Yes	Yes	Yes	Yes	No	No	No	No	No
10.	Nurpur	Nurpur Ambagan Gram Unnayan Samity	-	-	-	-	Yes	Yes	Yes	Yes	No	No	No	No	No
11.	Khoskadampur	Khoskadamba-pur Palli Seva Sangha	-	-	-	-	Yes	Yes	Yes	Yes	No	No	No	No	No
12.	Bogdowra	Bogdowra Tarun Samity	x	x	x	x	x	x	x	x	x	x	x	x	x

According to the need, PSV workers visit the village.

7

Summary and Conclusion

The first chapter is an introduction of this study in which I have discussed Tagore's views on rural reconstruction programmes, in which he emphasises the fact that cooperative efforts and united force of the villagers are the guiding force for rural reconstruction programme. Our discussion shows that during Tagore's lifetime villages under study had taken the responsibility unitedly to rebuild their areas in all aspects. For this reason, they established various cooperative organisations along with VDS through which many of the-village problems had been solved. Tagore wanted proper utilisation of village resources including human resources. Rabindranath desired to reconstruct the village only through its own efforts and unutilised resources to bring relief to the suffering villagers in such a manner that villagers would be able to help themselves. Social workers would provide them only with expertise knowledge and appropriate technology. Tagore directed those social workers to organise village level organisations so that the members of this village organisation could play an effective role in rural reconstruction programme. We have seen that since the establishment of PSV, different types of VDS were organised in the surrounding villages of Sriniketan. The village welfare department (PSV, Sriniketan) has given affiliation to such type of development society of the village.

PSV has been implementing various rural development programmes through this development society.

I have made an attempt to give an idea about the role of VDS according to Tagore's idea to reconstruct the village through the utilisation of village resources with the help of cooperative efforts of rural people. For this purpose, I have collected various data from different sources, and analysed them in the present socio-economic context of the village. I have tried to give a clear idea about the role of VDS in the welfare programmes in the present situation of problematic village. I have tried to bring home the significance of Tagore's idea on rural reconstruction in the context of changing rural society.

The object of my study is as follows:

(1) To show in what way the VDS takes part in rural reconstruction programme in the present circumstances.

(2) What are the problems faced by VDS in implementing Tagore's thought to solve the present evil of rural area.

(3) How Tagore's idea can be effective to enrich the. quality of life in the rural society, socially and economically.

I followed a particular method to get useful data for my study. Twelve VDS were selected in the surrounding villages of Sriniketan, where various types of caste, community, socio-economical characters were taken into account. One of these villages is selected where Sriniketan had undertaken to implement various types of welfare programmes in the past but at present PSV has withdrawn affiliation from this village. Rests of the villages are selected from the PSV's, present adopted villages where different development programmes are being continued through their PSV affiliated village Development societies.

Elderly villagers have been interviewed and leading members of the VDS have been consulted regarding the different welfare activities and the problems and also about the implementation of Tagore's thought on rural reconstruction. I have given thought as to how Tagore's idea on rural reconstruction can be implemented to solve the present social problem. Interviews were also granted by some well-known persons who are interested in implementing the Rabindranath's dream of Sriniketan.

In the second chapter, I have reviewed many publications on Tagore's thought on rural reconstruction, but it is seen that nobody had considered the role of village development organisations or VDS in the field of rural reconstruction in the present changed situation, which Tagore once had emphasised to enrich the villager's inner strength and to reconstruct their villages through utilisation of local resources. Although they have highlighted Tagore's ideas on rural reconstruction in various aspects only. I have tried to discuss in detail about the role of VDS in my study through analysis of the collected data.

In the third chapter, I have discussed Tagore's experiment and his ideas on rural reconstruction to relieve the villagers from the sufferings and sorrows of the helpless villagers in his Zamindari Estate. My discussion focused on the fact that Gurudev had implemented various welfare programmes with the help of the villagers' joint effort. The great poet desired to relieve the distress of our village-based country.

Due to this, Tagore desired to make a model village as a pioneer for the development of the whole country. With appropriate quotations Tagore's dream of an ideal village have been visualised.

In the fourth chapter, a brief discussion has been made about Santiniketan and dealt in details about Sriniketan activities. It may be clear from the discussion that Rabindranath always emphasised on cooperative principle and village wealth to restructure the village life. At that time many cooperative organisations were formed by the rural people and cooperative organisations and village development organisations played vital role on rural reconstruction programmes.

In the fifth chapter, I have tried to discuss through tables the village extension activities of Sriniketan from the beginning and upto the year 1995-96. Various welfare activities were implemented in the village around Sriniketan. The discussion is made from three premises.

(1) During Tagore's life time (1922-1941)

(2) Post-Tagorean period (1942-50)

(3) From the period 1951, when Visva-Bharati was recognised as a central university by the government of India upto the period 1995-96. These three phases are comparatively analysed.

In the sixth chapter, on the basis of the collected data, 1 have discussed and analysed the activities of VDS and PSV in regard to the rural development programmes. Data and other information have also been collected from villagers and leading members of VDS, some elderly persons of these villages and also from some eminent persons also who are interested in Rabindranath's Sriniketan experiment. In this context I have tried to highlight the role of VDS and PSV in the various types of activities. This analysis has been made with the help of collected data and other information from villages. This data have been presented in tables.

In the last chapter, I have concluded with some modest suggestions regarding the role of VDS in the present socio-economic conditions. Further I have tried to bring home the significance of Tagore's idea on rural reconstruction in the present changed social circumstances. It has been pointed out how Tagore's idea can be effective and relevant in modern times for the sustained development and solutions of present village problems in spite of vast social changes and complex problems.

It is observed from this study that the villages around Sriniketan are basically agriculture-based like the other villages of the country. Although Indian villages are economically poor and socially depressed. Various welfare programmes are being formulated from outside agencies - government and non-government for the development of the villages. Various infrastructural facilities have also been extended to the rural areas, but it is a matter of regret that till now the Indian villages are not self-reliant due to the inadequate utilisation of village material and human resources. Tagore's desire to establish Sriniketan as a model for the whole country has rather failed. At present it is realised that villagers around Sriniketan are not aware about the idea that self-reliance with the help of village resources are the only way out, not only to improve their Socio-economic condition but also to improve their own power. At present villagers of Sriniketan are dependent on outside agencies. A large number of problems are facing the surrounding villages of Sriniketan. There are no active village organisations, nor any cooperative attitude among the villagers. No doubt this is the main cause for these village problems. Villagers do not participate unitedly to solve their problems. A question may be raised why should villagers pray for help from the outside agencies for their development. In fact, they should not if they can exploit their own resources. But in stead of uniting themselves, the villagers are politically divided and faction ridden.

Rabindranath desired to tap the resources of the villagers and directed his followers to guide the rural people around Sriniketan to enrich their inner strength, so that through the united efforts, they could be able to solve their own problems. Villagers also responded to Rabindranath's call and participated unitedly to reconstruct the village. Rural people around Sriniketan formed different types of village organisations with their cooperative efforts. At that time villagers realised the importance of Tagore's mission and understood how to make a village self-sufficient. Village organisation was an important common platform for all types of villagers and they assembled and tried to solve the various common problems. Sriniketan workers guided them only from outside. This way, all rural reconstruction activities were conducted by the suitable leadership of rural people. Already we know that epidemic form of malaria was tackled by the joint venture of villagers and health cooperative societies, which were established for the improvement of health and sanitation condition.

My observation and analysis shows that at present villagers around Sriniketan are not self sufficient in matters of health. They are fully dependent on government hospital or private doctors. Poor village patients have to go to medical practitioners (mostly quacks) by paying huge fees. All we know is that government hospital is not able to provide treatment sufficiently according to the need of the villagers due to many problems of the government including not functioning and mis-management. On the other hand, it is unfortunate that poor patients were not able to continue treatment by private medical practitioners. So it is a matter of shame and regret that health problems are destroying the vitals of every village. These problems cannot be eradicated by the efforts of outside agency unless villagers put in their collective effort.

Though there are VDS in every village around Sriniketan, the organisation is not active to solve the health problems. PSV, provides only a little fund (Aruna Amita fund) to the local patients for treatment. It is insufficient. As a result, due to this dependence on outside direct financial help, the villagers are at the mercy of the direct continuous help from Sriniketan agency, which Tagore disliked. It will be better if the money could be utilised for the health programmes of the village concerned. Some preventive measures are taken in the village around Sriniketan by PSV, Panchayat and government effort, some rural people and VDS assist to implement these programmes. But they do not play any effective role to improve their health conditions through the utilisation of their village resources which was Tagore's aspiration. So it is obvious that present village health and sanitation conditions are not being solved for the lack of proper implementation of Tagore's ideology of rural reconstruction.

Thus it is absolutely necessary that more and more village people should take initiative to solve the village health problems through their collective efforts. Again, cooperative health society should be established in a modified form and PSV provides to the villagers only guidance. This cooperative health society should function under the control of VDS. This common platform of the village should take the responsibility to make the villagers aware regarding the utility of health cooperative society, which would be run by the minimum subscription, contributed by the villagers. Poor local patients may derive benefit from this society. VDS should coordinate with the government hospital and other outside health agencies. VDS should take active part through health cooperative society for an all round health programmes in the village, such as, preventive measures, health and sanitation programme in the village, etc. Tagorean ideals practised during the poet's lifetime at Sriniketan should be the guiding principles. Tagore's idea for self-reliant in the field of health and sanitation could only be re-introduced if the villagers could be motivated in this aspect through health education programme, PSV should organise such kinds of programmes to motivate and aware the villagers about health and sanitation.

Rabindranath put emphasis on the vital role of education to enrich the power of self-motivation of the villagers in rural reconstruction programme. He desired to remove ignorance of villagers and superstitions from their life. Tagore thought that only at least basic education and literacy could develop their living standard. This is the view of the economist Amartya Sen also, among others. So according to Tagore's noble idea a number of educational units were formed in the village around Sriniketan, including Night schools, Day schools, Girl's night schools, Rural Library Service and Lok Siksha Samsad (distance education). Side by side, awareness programmes were arranged to enrich the daily life of villagers. Rural people were also involved in all these programmes whole-heartedly by the proper guidance of Sriniketan organisations.

But it is unfortunate that, although literacy rate is higher than before (Tagorean period), it is not sufficient according to Tagore's aspirations. The poet-philosopher wanted to establish Sriniketan as a model before the country and for illustration, some villages around Sriniketan were taken up. But it is a matter of regret that till today no villages around Sriniketan is free from illiteracy problem. PSV could take a leading role to remove illiteracy in its adopted villages. It is unfortunate that the project 'District Resource Unit' (Sriniketan, V-B.) in its traditional way has taken a role to eradicate illiteracy from the district through providing technopadegogic support to Zilla Sakshrata Samity. This unit is performing the duty like the other districts in our country. PSV is only helping them as and when the unit feels it. As a result of this, post-literacy programme and continuing education programmes are not functioning according to Tagore's ideal.

It is observed to day that village primary schools are in a deplorable condition. So villagers around Sriniketan are naturally interested to get their children admitted in the schools of Visva-Bharati. Again the villagers do not take up any plan or programmes to mobilise the village primary schools through their collective efforts. Tagore always tried to provide education to all sections of people and flagged off a unique educational programme at Sriniketan named 'Lok Siksha Samsad'. Thus mass education programme was launched through correspondence. These programmes continued for long years. But it is unfortunate that such type of programme is discontinued now and people are deprived of the advantages. Today all we know is that distance education is in great demand and a number of courses are provided to the masses. If the Lok Siksha Samsad programme is run properly, people who have no opportunity to have regular education will be benefited. Needless to say that illiteracy is the root cause of economic deprivation of our country. Nobel laureate Amartya Sen and other eminent economists agree about this burning issue. Recently Government has taken steps to overcome this problem. PSV should take the initiative in this aspect to extend the education facility at the doors step of every rural households and VDS should take the responsibility and leadership in this aspect.

To extend education in the village around Sriniketan PSV organise a Rural library service through the affiliated VDS. But there are many problems connected with the library service in the countryside. Rural people do not get the opportunity to study in library room due to lack of proper infrastructure. Library room is too small to study. There is no reading room. On the other hand, some special books in demand are not issued like *Rabindra-Rachanavali.* As a result villagers are deprived of knowledge and information in this special areas in spite of their great interest.

In the field of educational extension or literacy programme only VDS could improve the situation by the collective support of villagers. Active role should be taken by VDS, which should supervise the educational unit in the village. The villagers unitedly should cooperate with the VDS to implement the plan. VDS should take the leadership and initiative to create conducive environment for providing education to the village adult and children through village primary schools or literacy centres. Rural library service should also be modified by the constructive action of the VDS. Side by side, VDS should try to provide not only education but also folk culture to provide healthy recreation to the villagers.

Tagore wanted to develop a self-reliant village economy. He laid emphasis on agriculture. As our country is agriculture based, he sent his son, son-in-law and his friend's son to study agriculture and allied aspects in USA. He desired to improve the agricultural system of India through advanced technology and modern science. Tagore established an agricultural faculty first time in our country at Sriniketan. During Tagore era village farmers around Sriniketan took various useful training to make them self-dependent. Besides this, a number of agricultural cooperative organisations were set up by the villagers. Many agricultural problems had been tackled by their cooperative organisations. Fishery and Animal husbandry and other programmes were introduced among villagers only make the Village economy self-sufficient. Rural people around Sriniketan participated in the programme guided by the valuable suggestions and gained knowledge from experimental field.

Now it is noted from the study that agriculture, fishery and animal husbandry etc. are developed comparatively in a better way than before but not a single village around Sriniketan has got self-reliant economy. Till now much resources remain unutilised due to lack of proper plan or follow-up action. At present rural people are dependent on outside economical help for their own prosperity. Though many subsidised loans and agricultural equipments are provided to the villages, villagers are not turning enough self-sufficient by this outside help. The poet realised that outside charity could not relieve the villagers from their poverty and wants, unless they jointly utilise the abundant resources inherent in the villages. Today it is regrettable that still many educated or trained village youth are jobless. They want only service but are not interested in creating any self-employment programme, which Tagore wanted to implement in the village. Rabindranath wished to reconstruct two or three villages as models. But Tagore's aspiration is not fulfilled, not a single adopted village around Sriniketan can be called a model for the country. We know from our investigation of a PSV adopted village that there are still some outstanding economic problems in the village. Rabindranath directed his devoted social workers to establish cooperative organisations among villagers. Now there is also no such society functioning which is able to tackle the economical problems menacing the villages. Due to lack of joint efforts of villagers, they are not economically self-dependent.

To improve the economic condition of the villages, agriculture should be developed by adopting proper plan and action in the light of Tagore's ideas of rural reconstruction. Villagers should utilise local resources to improve cultivation. So now only the existing organisation, VDS should take active role to make the villagers strong enough to stand on their feet through creating awareness among villagers on cooperative method. VDS could excavate tank for the solution of irrigation problems, defunct Agricultural credit society and Dharmagola society should be re-vitalised by the active plan of VDS. Today the village farmers are facing many problems which could be solved by introducing the above mentioned programmes which had been implemented in the Tagorean period. So, VDS should implement these programmes in the village through friendly discussions with entire villagers. Side by side, it is necessary to apply knowledge of science and technology to develop agricultural system, animal husbandry and fishery programmes. Today only Tagorean rural reconstruction can make the village self-reliant based on agriculture.

During Tagore's time rural industry was also emphasised to make the economy self-reliant along with agriculture. Sriniketan provided various training on rural industries to the rural pecple. Village youth was also trained up and they also participated in the economical programme of the village. Rabindranath realised that only agriculture was not sufficient to make the economy self-reliant in the village. So he triggered various kinds of village industry in the rural area of Sriniketan. Tagore desired that he would be able to remove the sufferings of the rural folk through following Sriniketan model. Infact, the poet wanted to free the village people from the misrule of the British rulers. (Refer to his scathing letter to Miss Rathbone, British M.P.).

At present some rural industries are found in the villages around Sriniketan. These rural industries are not well organised and villagers cannot earn money in spite of their having resources. At present handicraft goods are so much in demand that villagers fail to cope with the demand and cannot supply them to the market. As a result, village youth are jobless. Some of educated village youths were trained on rural handicraft but they are not interested in improving the village industry due to lack of proper guidance and financial crisis. Tagore wanted to provide job through self- employment programmes. But now Tagore's ideals have not been followed. VDS have not any role to improve the existing sick rural industries through utilisation of village resources and human power.

So it is felt in the present circumstances, that VDS should take active role to standardize the rural industries. VDS should take the valuable guidance from PSV experts regarding this. PSV should take care and create suitable environment through campaign and try to arrange employment facilities among village youth.

Rabindranath called the youth force to take the responsibility to remove the sufferings of the villages. So he tried to develop the quality of leadership among rural youth and establish a special common platform named 'Brati organisation'. Tagore wanted that the young boys and girls of the village would be the future leaders of the village. So they must acquire suitable training and adequate knowledge regarding the problem of the village and find out the remedy. The boys and girls would participate also in rural upliftment programmes with suitable guidance of Sriniketan. Mahila samity was also founded in the village to upgrade the status of women at all levels. Brati organisations and Mahila samities were popular active-youth-organisation in Tagorean period.

It is observed that at present Brati organisation is not being formed spontaneously by the villagers themselves or VDS. These are being organised according to the direction of PSV. At present Brati organisation is only a routine oriented work but not so effective for the implementation of village development programmes. The organisation does not involve itself in the welfare programmes of the village. Only PSV is instructing the affiliated VDS from outside and the members of VDS follow this instruction and implement it. Most of the Mahila samities are functioning under VDS and these Mahila Samities are branches of VDS. Today Mahila samity does not take steps properly to tackle the various problems of rural women in the present changed Society. My feelings is that Mahila Samity should have its autonomy, which would empower them to solve the various problems of rural women including the social injustice, if any against them.

So, VDS should take initiative to utilise the potentials of Brati organisation and Mahila samity in the development work in the village. It is necessary today also that more resources are required to establish Brati organisation and Mahila samity. VDS should take action to establish these organisations in the village with the help of PSV of Sriniketan. VDS and PSV both should take proper action plan in such a manner that the villagers could be motivated and every sections of village community could be involved the development programmes, which would be helpful to build a self-reliant economy. It is known to all that our government is not able to meet all requirements of the village. So villagers should unitedly stands on their .own feet. VDS is the only common platform for the rural people by which village resources could be properly mobilised and utilised to meet the villager's need.

At present, PSV affiliated VDS should take a plan according to Tagore's vision of Sriniketan. Once again rural young boys and girls should be trained on different aspects of rural development so that they could take up the leadership. VDS and Sriniketan should together put effort to enrich the leadership capabilities of the members of Brati organisation.

Further, VDS should organise Mahila samity in the village. Environment should be created by which rural women can tackle their current problems through this unit. In our society, women are weaker sections and that was realised by Tagore very long ago. So he advised his followers to set up Mahila samity so that rural women would be self-dependent socially and economically. But it is a matter of regret to note that there is no active role of Mahila samity or Mahila organisation to relieve the rural women from their sufferings.

At present Gram panchayat and other outside development agencies are taking leading role to improve the village economy and society. The VDS have a passive role in this regard. But Tagore expected that development society should take the active role to improve the villagers life. He wanted that all problems of the village would be solved through the utilisation of village resources based on cooperative principles. In today's circumstances, all types of village evils should be solved by the villager's joint effort. In this regard Panchayat should only help the villagers to implement development programmes without its political intervention.

Rabindranath believed in united human power to rebuild the rural folk. He experimented it in his zamindari estate and at Sriniketan. The result was good. His noble objective was to relieve the country from servitude. So he wrote a letter in 1930 regarding the experiment at Sriniketan, "এটা খুব করে বুঝেছি, আমাদের সব চেয়ে বড়ো কাজ শ্রীনিকেতনে। সমস্ত দেশকে কী করে বাঁচাতে হবে ঐখানে ছোটো আকারে তারই নিষ্পত্তি করা আমাদের ব্রত"[1] (I have realised very well that our great objective has to be implemented at Sriniketan. It is our mission to demonstrate how through these efforts even if in a small way, the entire country can be saved). In fact villagers progressed through the able guidance of Sriniketan during Tagorean period.

The ideology of Rabindranath was highlighted in the village and villagers thought that this was the only way to give relief to the sufferers. A suitable environment was created in the village for the implementation of rural reconstruction programmes. But after the death of Tagore and Visva-Bharati's control was taken up by central government, the workers of Sriniketan did not or could not exploit properly the previous Tagorean environment for these purposes. Now, a large number of villagers are not even aware of the actual motto of Rabindranath. At present various VDS around Sriniketan are affiliated to Sriniketan (PSV) and a number of programmes are implemented in the village by this society under the direction of Sriniketan PSV. Now PSV do not undertake any practical programme by which village around Sriniketan will be self-reliant which was the basic aspiration of Rabindranath. Village people also depend on outside help due to the formulation of different programme from outside. Government and PSV both do not discuss apolitically with the villagers regarding the developmental schemes of the village. So villagers are not perhaps interested in utilising village resources and their human resources for their improvement.

It is studied from the villages around Sriniketan that there are many problems in the way of implementing Tagore's idea of rural reconstruction. The following problems are generally faced by the VDS in the village.

(1) Villagers are not aware of Rabindranath's thoughts on rural reconstruction.

(2) Due to changing conditions of the country the villagers have become rather self-centered who try to safeguard their personal interest.

(3) The influences of different political parties are creating obstructions in the way of cooperation among villagers with one another for their own development.

(4) Villagers are not being taken into confidence by the various outside development agencies. This is contradictory to Tagore's idea. The agencies impose their development blueprints on the villagers often unwarrantedly.
(5) Proper attention and emphasis has not been focused on development of the villagers to make them socio-economically solvent.
(6) Developmental programmes are being formulated at the top of the administration • and then administrators are intervening too much.
(7) Power politics of panchayat is one of the hurdles for implementation of developmental programmes in the villages.
(8) The villagers are hardly being consulted regarding the development of the concerned villages but a large portion of fund is provided by the government. As a result, the people are wholly dependent on outside agency for their own development, which Tagore absolutely disliked.

Only PSV could take proper action to implement Tagore's idea in the village with the full participation of the villagers. We think the above problems should be overcome through creating a suitable environment. PSV better take the initiative to mobilise the affiliated VDS and guide the villagers to build a suitable infrastructure in their own interest.

We suggest that PSV should take policies to make the leading members of VDS aware about the significance of Tagore's idea on rural reconstruction and past activities of Sriniketan, because the present rural problems could be solved only through the proper implementation of Tagore's thoughts. Today it will be more useful to encourage the villagers to utilise their human power on cooperative principles and villagers would solve all the village problems by their mass involvement. Training should be provided to the villagers according to the need of the present society. Side by side, PSV should also try to implement many developmental programmes through the cooperation of the village people.

It may be noted that there is no way for sustained rural development and to implement Tagore's idea to solve various present problems, if the VDS fail to take up the responsibility. So we must try to overcome these obstacles and follow the past Sriniketan experiments to develop our whole country in the changed situation. It is realised that outside agencies cannot develop the villages unless the villagers unitedly take proper action and utilise their local resources. It is not desirable that outside agency implements the development programme in the village without involving the villagers. Arun Kumar Mukhopadhya has discussed in his book in Bengali on "Rabindranath: Village reconstruction" with regard to the significance of Tagore's thought and the present problem of Indian villages : "এখনো ভারতে অনেক গ্রাম আছে যেখানে বিজলি বাতি, পাকা পায়খানা, বিশুদ্ধ পানীয় জল, প্রাথমিক বিদ্যালয় ও প্রাথমিক চিকিৎসা ব্যবস্থার অভাব আছে।"[2] (Still there are wants of electrification, latrine, pure drinking water, primary school and first aid arrangements in many villages of India). He has also criticised the present character of the villagers. "স্বাধীন ভারতে যত গ্রামোন্নয়নের কাজ চলছে তাতে গ্রামবাসীর সরকারি দাক্ষিণ্যের জন্য হাহাকার নিজেদের আত্মশক্তির প্রতি বিশ্বাস কমিয়েছে"[3] (Rural development programmes are being carried on rapidly in free India. Due to this the villagers cry for government help, thus they have reduced their faith in their own power). It is observed from my study also that the comment of the author is very true. It is experienced by all that the government subsidy which is being provided for the welfare of the village is not enough to implement various welfare programmes. Today we are observing different strategies used for rural development, but to some extent, these policies belong on outside charity. We see, in the Budget of 2008, Government made farmers debt-free. Government planned to provide direct financial help through NREGA (Scheme). This scheme is also deviated from self-help activities and villagers chronologically depend on outside help. Rural people are not interested to utilise the defunct village resources to make the village self-reliant. Gandhiji and Rabindranath both believed in self-help which is the best help, but the government planning has been derived from making villages self-reliant.

Though rural development process is dynamic, we should proceed on right path. Some persons perhaps may believe that these government planning and strategies are experimental to achieve the ultimate goal, but I think that these strategies are being derived from Tagore and Gandhiji's rural concept. It creates dependency on outside help or charity instead of self-dependency of villagers. Mahatma Gandhi implemented his `Gram Swaraj' movement in such way that the people must be helped through self-help to help themselves. Gurudev also implemented the same process at Sriniketan as a model for the whole country.

So it is my conclusion that the vision of Rabindranath and Gandhiji is the best way to make the villages self-reliant in all respects. Now we must emphasise on Rural Reconstruction instead of rural development. We may utilise the abandoned village resources through the active participation of village people. Village development society (VDS) or village club, which is the common platform of all villagers should play active role for planning and improvement of the village which Tagore desired at Sriniketan.

At present, at some of the places, various non-government development agencies have taken the villagers into confidence and they are formulating and implementing different development programmes meant for the concerned villages through the village organisation to make them self-reliant as Tagore desired. The writer who was former Principal of PSV felt also about the utility of Tagore's idea on rural reconstruction in the present society. He wrote in his article published in the magazine *College Street* : "গ্রামবাসীদের চিন্তাভাবনা, আশা চাহিদা অনেক পাল্টে গিয়েছে। বিশেষতঃ মূল্যবোধেরও পরিবর্তন হয়েছে অনেকটা এতদ সত্বেও রবীন্দ্রনাথের পল্লীভাবনার মধ্যে এমন কতগুলি মৌলিক বিষয় ছিলো যেগুলি আজও অভ্রান্ত ও প্রাসঙ্গিক।"[4] (The demands and hopes of the villagers have changed a lot, especially the values have changed. In spite of these changes, Tagore's ideas gave its originality and are still actually relevant).

Today we must recall the idea of Tagore to relieve the villagers of their sufferings. Rabindranath instructed his followers to eradicate village problems through active people's participation. Tagorean thoughts on rural reconstruction are also very relevant today and Sriniketan has the important role to solve the village problems. So we should try again to follow Tagore's Sriniketan experiments and make a model for India.

Only VDS is the common platform of all villagers from where all village people should take major decision to develop the village and Sriniketan should guide the VDS from outside. In the present situation VDS and the NGO can reconstruct the village through utilising human power and village resources. This way the whole country will be developed which had been visualised by the great visionary.

PSV affiliated VDS are functioning in the village around Sriniketan. But all villagers do not participate in the activities of VDS and no self-reliant programmes of the village are undertaken. VDS are functioning by the direction of PSV from outside. But PSV does not create the suitable environment to make a self-sufficient village.

On the other hand, VDS do not take the responsibility to develop the whole village without narrow self-interest VDS collect the fund from different sources and spend the large portion of the fund for sports and cultural programmes. At present side VDS does not try to revive the folk-culture. Rather the members of VDS try to perform modern cultural programmes in their villages. These youths do not have any knowledge about our past glorious culture. This should be well acquainted with our Indian culture, tradition and heritage. The villagers are not well aware about the global message of Tagore and its significance in the context of rural development, which will ultimately make them self-reliant. Tagore wanted the Sriniketan should have a pioneering role regarding rural upliftment in India. Tagore planned to form a Sriniketan as a Model centre through which villages would be self-dependent. He always disliked outside charity or help without properly using the local resources. For this reason, the author repeatedly hammered on Sriniketan's present role in rural reconstruction strategies. Gurudev wanted Sriniketan to be a model in the country. So it is clear that Sriniketan has an important role to guide rural development policy of the Government. In the present complex social situation, Sriniketan should further organise the VDS (sister organisation of PSV) and implement various types of rural development projects through utilising resources in scientific way (all types of village data should be gathered and compiled). Though the problems and demands of villages are far changed, but villagers' life style has not been changed and problems are not eradicated which the author already has discussed so it may be concluded that Tagore's rural concept is relevant today in all senses of the term. At present, we notice that self-help groups (SHGs), SC/ST, Micro Credit Programme etc. Grameen Bank of Mohd. Yunus (Bangladesh) have enlightened the village people and also villagers are getting new dimension in the framework of their own welfare.

However, if these institutions (PSV and VDS) imbibes Tagore's idea there is no reason to be pessimistic PSV is capable of implementing the developmental programmes in such a manner that the adopted villages of Sriniketan could be made self-reliant in near future. Here we must remember the Tagore's word to the followers:

"যে কাজে তোমরা প্রবৃত্ত হচ্চ সেটা তোমাদেরই যথার্থ সৃষ্টিকার্য হয় এই আমার ইচ্ছা, তোমরা তার মধ্যে নিজের স্বাধীনতা এবং নিজের দায়িত্ব সমপূর্ণ পরিমানে অনুভব করবে — যখন মূর্তিটি গড়া হয়ে যাবে তখন তোমরা তার ভিতর নিজের জীবনের সাধনার প্রতিমূর্তি দেখতে পাবে। আমি কেবল তোমাদের ক্ষেত্র দিয়েছি এই পর্যন্ত — এবং যদি কখনো তোমরা আমাকে কোনো বিষয়ে তোমাদের সহযোগী করতে চাও তা হলে আমাকে পাবে।

হবে জয়, হবে জয়, হবে জয় হে--
ওহে বীর, হে নির্ভয়"[5]

(My desire is that the mission you have embarked upon may turn into a worthy creative work. You people will feel in it entirely your sense of freedom and responsibility. When the structure is built up, you will find the reflection of your own mission in it. I have only provided you with an area to work with. You will get me as a co-worker if you want my assistance in some subjects.

O hero! O, the dauntless! Victory
Will be Yours
Yours and yours only.)

It is happy to say, Recently, there has been a trend to revitalise the activities of PSV and some of the institutions like CAREER (Centre for Applied Rural Education, Extension and Research), CSV (Centre for Science in Villages) have been established to help and train up the villagers so that they could apply scientific technology to improve their village economy by themselves.

At present, all the institutions of Sriniketan like Siksha Satra, PSV and Institute of Agriculture (PSB) are being recognised in such a manner that the man power resource of this institution can immeasurable help the villagers with their expert knowledge. Only then the villagers would be self-reliant in all aspects as Tagore dreamt.

REFERENCES

1. Rabindranath Tagore : A letter to Rathindranath Tagore, Chithi patra-2, 31st October 1930. *Russiar Chithi,* Visva-Bharati Granthan Vibhaga, Calcutta, Vaisakh 1338 B.S., p. 156.
2. Arun Kumar Mukhopadhyay : *Rabindranath : Palli punargathan,* Dey's Publishing, Calcutta, 1403 B.S., p. 27.
3. *Ibid.*, p. 67.
4. Arun Mukhopadhyay, "A Yuge Rabindra Palli bhabnar prasangikata", Nababarsha O Rabindra Sankhya, *College Street,* Calcutta, April, May 1996, p. 17.
5. Rabindranath Tagore : A letter to Atul Sen, *Palliprakrili,* Visva-Bharati Granthan Vibhaga, Calcutta, Magh 1368 B.S., p. 259.

Select Bibliography

Relevant books in Bengali by Rabindranath Tagore

Gora (Novel), Visva-Bharati Granthan Vibhaga, Calcutta, 1910.

Chhinna Patra (letters), Visva-Bharati Granthalaya, Calcutta, 1319 B.S.

Jivansmriti (Reminiscences), Visva-Bharati Granthan Vibhaga, Calcutta, 1319 B.S.

Falguni (Drama), Visva-Bharati Granthan Vibhaga, Calcutta, 1916.

Balaka (Collection of poems), Visva-Bharati Granthan Vibhaga, Calcutta, 1916.

Sankalan (essay, letter, Diary and talk), Visva-Bharati Granthan Vibhaga, Calcutta, 1332 B.S.

Sanchayita (Collection of poems), Visva-Bharati Granthan Vibhaga, Calcutta, 1338 B.S., 10th edition 1389 B.S.

Russiar Chithi (Letters from Russia), Visva-Bharati Granthan Vibhaga, Calcutta, Vaisakh, 1338 B.S.

Kaler Yatra (Drama), Visva-Bharati Granthan Vibhaga. Calcutta, Bhadra 1339 B.S.

Kalantar (essays), Visva-Bharati Granthan Vibhaga, Calcutta, Vaisakh 1344 B.S. Revised Edition 1367 B.S.

Ashramer Rup O Bikash (Essay), Visva-Bharati Granthan Vibhaga, Calcutta, Ashara, 1348 B.S.

Rabindra Rachanavali (Collected works), Vol.14, Visva-Bharati Granthan Vibhaga. Calcutta, Aswin 1398 B.S.

Sanchayan (Collection of poems), Visva-Bharati Granthan Vibhaga, Calcutta, Vaisakh 1354.

Visva Bharati (Essay), Visva-Bharati Granthan Vibhaga, Calcutta, Pous 1358 B.S.

Satnabay Neeti (Essay), Visva-Bharati Granthan Vibhaga, Calcutta, 1360 B.S.

Palliprakriti (Essays, lectures and letters regarding the objectives of Sriniketan), Visva-Bharati Granthan Vibhaga, Calcutta, Magh 1368 B.S,

Swadeshi Sanmj (Essay), Visva-Bharati, Calcutta, Pous 1369 B.S.

Relevant Books and Pamphlets on Tagore and Other Concerned Books

Adhikary, Sachindranath, *Sahaj manush Rabindranalh,* Brindabon Dhar and Sons limited, Calcutta, 1349 BS.

Adhikary, Sachindranath, *Pallir Manush Rabindranath,* Brindaban Dhar and Sons Limited, Calcutta, 1352 B.S.

Adhikary, Sachindranath, *Rabindra manaser utso sandhane,* Ananda Publishers Private Limited, Calcutta, Vaisakh, 1366 B.S.

Adhikary, Sachindranath, *Silaidạh O Rabindranath,* Jijnasa, Calcutta, January 1974.

Ali, Hashim Amir, Indian Statistical Series No.9, *The Environs of Tagore,* A Preliminary Assessment for a pilot project in Regional Survey and planning around the Visva-Bharati. Asia Publishing House Statistical Publishing Society, Calcutta, Indian Statistical Institute 1960.

Ali, Hashim Amir, Indian Statistical Series No. 10, *Then and Now (1933-1950), A Study of Socio-economic Structure and Change in some Villages near Viswa-Bharati University,* Asia Publishing House.

Bandopadhyay, Charuchandra, *Ravirasmi* (Vol.2), College Street Publication Private Limited, Calcutta, 1st College Street Edition 1396 B.S., 2nd College Street edition, 1401 B.S.

Banerjee, Hiranmay, *Experiments in Rural Reconstruction,* Visva-Bharati, Calcutta, 1966.

Basu, Nimai Sadhan, *Bhagnaneer Visva-Bharati,* Ananda Publishers limited, Calcutta, 1991.

Basu, Bishnu, and Bandopadhyay, Binay, (Edited by) *Rabindranather Siksha Bhabna,* Pratibhash, Calcutta, 1989.

Bose, Manjula, *Centenary Volume LK. Elmhirst* (1893-1993), Tagore Research Institute, Calcutta, 1994.

Chakraborty, Satish Chandra, (Edited) *Maharshi Devendranath Thakurer Atmajibani,* Visva-Bharati Granthalaya, Calcutta, 1927, 4th edition 1962.

Chakraborty, Satyadas, *Sriniketaner Godar Katha,* Subarna Rekha, Calcutta, 1985, (2nd edition 1399 B.S.).

Chakraborty, Satyadas, *Gramer Kaje Rabindranath,* Sahitya Samaj, Sriniketan, 1985.

Das, Sajanikanta, *Rabindranath Jiban O Sahitya,* Satabdi Grantha Bhavan, Calcutta, Rathayatra 1367 B.S.

Das, Kshudiram, *Samaj: Pragati: Rabindranath,* Karuna Prakashani, Calcutta, 1990.

Dasgupta, Sugata, *Poet and a plan,* Thacker Spink & Co. (1933) Private Limited, 3 Esplanade east Calcutta-1.

Dasgupta, Prabir, *Rabindranather Palli Chinta Abong Siksha Bhabnai Silpa abong tar punarjjibane Sriniketaner Bhumika,* Amar Kutir Society for Rural Development, Calcutta.

Dasgupta, Uma, *Santinketan and Sriniketan,* Visva-Bharati, Calcutta, 1983.

Dasgupta, Pannalal, *Bitarka, Bikalpa O Biplab,* Mitra O Ghosh Publishers Private Limited, Calcutta, Bhadra 1398 B.S.

Elmhirst, L.K., *Poet and Ploughman,* Visva-Bharati, Calcutta 1975.

Elmhirst, L.K., *Rabindranath Tagore, Pioneer in Education,* (Essays and Exchange between Rabindranath Tagore and L.K. Elmhirst) distributed by JOHN MURRAY : 50 Albemarle Street, London, W.I., Visva-Bharati, Calcutta 1961.

Ghosal, Shachinandan, *Palli Unnayne Rabindranath,* Ratna Book Agency, Calcutta, 1390 B.S.

Ghosh, Santidev, *Jibaner Dhrubatara,* Ananda Publishers Private Limited, Calcutta, Sravan 1403, B.S.

Kar, Sudhir Chandra, *Santiniketaner Siksha O Sadhana,* Orient Book Company, Calcutta, 1360 B.S.. Third edition, 1370 B.S.

Kausal, G., *Economic histo: .j of India* (1957-1966), Kalyani Publishers, New Delhi 1996.

Kripalani, Krishna, *Tagore, A life,* National Book Trust, India 1961, third edition, 1986.

Kuryenson, *Rural Reconstruction,* Principles and method, Printed at the Good Pastor, Press 5 Armenian street, Madras-1, 1950.

Lal, Prem Chand, *Reconstruction and Education in Rural India,* London, George Allen and Unwin Ltd., Museum Street, 1932.

Mallick, Sukumar, *Rabindranather Pallichinta,* Nabapatra Prakashan, Calcutta, 1989.

Mukherjee, Naba, (editor), *A Tribute to Leonard Knight Elnihirst,* (A friend of India), 1893-1993, Birth Centenary Celebration (commemorative volume), Elmhirst Institute of Community studies, Santiniketan, West Bengal, India, 1994.

Mukherjee, Neela, *Participatory Rural Appraisal: Methodology and Applications,* Concept Publishing Company, New Delhi 1993.

Mukhopadhyay, Bina, *Chithipatre Rabindranath,* Navana, Calcutta, Agrahayan 1372 B.S.

Mukhopadhyay, Prabhat Kumar, *Rabindra jibani O Rabindra Sahitya -Prabeshak,* Volume-1, Visva-Bharati Granthan Vibhaga; Calcutta, 1340 B.S., Forth edition Vaisakh 1377 B.S.

Mukhopadhyay, Prabhat Kumar, *Rabindra jibani O Rabindra Sahitya Prabeshak,* Volume-2, Visva-Bharati Granthan Vibhaga; Calcutta, 1343 B.S., Forth edition, Chaitra H83 B.S.

Mukhopadhyay, Prabhat Kumar, *Rabindra jihani O Rahindra Sahitya Prabeshak,* Volume-3, Visva-Bharati Granthan Vibhaga; Calcutta, 1359 B.S., Second edition, Agrahayan 1368 B.S.

Mukhopadhyay, Prabhat Kumar, *Rabindra jibani O Rabindra Sahitya Prabeshak*, Volume-4, Visva-Bharati Granthan Vibhaga; Calcutta, 1363 B.S., Third edition, Ashara 1401 B.S.

Mukhopadhyay, Prabhat Kumar, *Visva-Bharati*, Volume-1, Book Land Private Limited, Calcutta, 1369 B.S.

Mukhopadhyay, Arun Kumar, *Rabindranath : Pallipunargathan*, Dey's Publishing, Calcutta, 1403 B.S.

Mukhopadhyay, A.K., *The Panchayat Administration in West Bengal*. The World Press Private Limited, Calcutta, First edition, January 1977, Second and enlarged edition, April 1980.

Pramanik, Subodh Chandra, *Rabindranather Samaj Chinta*, Satabdi Grantha Bhavan, Calcutta, Falgun 1368 B.S.

Roy, Satyendranath, (editor) *Rabindranather Chinta Jagat, Siksha Chinta, Rabindra Rachana Sankalan*, financed by Rabindra Bhavan, Visva-Bharati, Granthalaya Private Limited, Calcutta, Sravan 1389 B.S.

Ray, Satyendranath (editor), *Rabindranather Chinta Jagat, Samaj Chinta Rabindra Rachana Sankalan* financed by Rabindra Bhavan, Visva-Bharati, Granthalaya Private Limited, Calcutta, Agrahayan 1392 B.S.

Sen, Sudhir, *Rabindranath Tagore on Rural Reconstruction and Community Development in India*, Visva-Bharati, Calcutta 1943, Revised and enlarged edition 1991.

Sinha, Sasadhar, *Social thinking of Rabindranath Tagore*, Bombay (etc) Asia Publishing House, 1962.

Sinha, Sasadhar, *Tagore's Approach to Social Problems*, Modern Books Ltd., Calcutta 1947.

Sykes, Marjorick, *Rabindranath Tagore*, The Longmans Green & Co. Ltd., Bombay, 1943.

Tagore, Rathindranath, *Pitrismriti*, Jijnasa, Calcutta, Agrahayan, 1378 B.S.

Relevant Articles and Reports Published in Journal

Chakraborty, Satya Das, "Rabindranath O Surul Kuthi"; *Smritisudha* (Hundreds Years of Pousmela). Santiniketan Express, Santiniketan, West Bengal.

Das, Sudhi Ranjan, 'Tagore's Welfare Society', *Rabindranath Tagore Birth Centenary Celebration. Proceedings of conferences'*, Indian Philosophical congress, thirty-six session, Volume 111, Editor - Kalidas Bhattacharya, Santiniketan, 1961.

Dasgupta, Pannalal, "Gramke Shudhu Bhanglai Gorlo Na", *Desh,* editor - Amitava Chowdhuri, Calcutta, 7th February, 1998.

Datta, Amlan, "Aspects of Gandhian Economic thought", *The Visva-Bharati Quarterly,* Gandhi number Edited by Sisir Kumar Ghosh, Volume 35 (Numbers 1, 2, 3 & 4), Santiniketan West Bengal, 1971.

Ghose, Tanayendranath, "Rabindranath's contribution to education in India" *The Visva-Bharati Quarterly,* Education number, Signet Press, Elgin Road, Calcutta, May-October, 1947.

Ghosh, Santidev, "Ballavpur", *Smaranika-Nabajagaran,* Ballavpur Jyoti Songha (a village development society) Sriniketan, Birbhum, W.B., India, 15th August 1996.

Mandal, G.C., "Three village : A view of the Impact of Sriniketan" : *Rabindranath birth centenary celebrations, proceedings of conferences,* Seminar on human factor in the growth of Rural Economy, Volume-VIII, Editor, Gobinda Chandra Mandal, Visva-Bharati, Calcutta, 1961-62.

Mukhopadhyay, Arun, "A yuge Rabindra Palli Bhabnar Prasangikata", Nababarsha O Rabindra Sankhya; *College street,* Calcutta, April-May 1996.

Mukhopadhyay, Arun, *Tagore's Sriniketan Experiment - Past and Present, An Assessment.* IASS1 occasional paper no.4 reprinted from lASSI Quarterly (Vol.4; April-June 1995), Indian Association of Social Science Institutions (IASSI), SAMAJVIDYA, New Delhi.

Tagore, Rathindranath, "Father as I knew him", *A Centenary Volume, Rabindranath Tagore,* (1861-1961). Aspects of Indian Culture, Edited by Mahendra Kulasrestha, Sahitya Akademi, New Delhi, November 1961.

Timber, Harri G., "A Village Health Programme", *Visva-Bharati news,* July, 1932 (Volume I, number 1).

Visva-Bharati Bulletin No.6, "The Institute of Rural Reconstruction", (Prospects of Apprentice and Training Camp), November, 1925.

Visva-Bharati Bulletin No. 11, "Sriniketan, The Institute of Rural Reconstruction", December 1928.

Visva-Bharati Bulletin No. 15, "Rabindranath Tagore in Russia", Edited by P.C. Mahalanobis, November, 1930.

Visva-Bharati Bulletin No. 25, "Health Cooperatives, The Institute of Rural Reconstaiction" Edited by Rathindranath Tagore, July, 1938.

Annual Report December 1996, Rathindra Krishi Vigyan Kendra, Palli, Siksha Bhavana, (Institute of Agriculture), Visva-Bharati, Sriniketan, West Bengal, 731236.

Annual Report (1995-96), Rathindra Krishi Vigyan Kendra, Palli Siksha Bhavana, (Institute of Agriculture), Visva-Bharati, Sriniketan, West Bengal, 731236.

Visva-Bharati Annual Reports and Audited Accounts

During Tagore's lifetime (1922-1941) 1922, 1923, 1925, 1926, 1927, 1928, 1929, 1930, 1931, 1932, 1933, 1934, 1935, 1936, 1937, 1938, 1939, 1940, 1941.

After the death of Tagore (1942-50) 1942, 1943, 1944, 1945, 1946, 1950.

After taking over of Visva-Bharati by Central Government (1951-1995-96) 1952-53, 1953-54, 1954-55, 1955-56, 1956-57, 1957-58, 1958-59, 1959-60, 1960-61, 1961-62, 1963-64, 1964-65, 1965-66, 1966-67, 1967-68, 1968-69, 1970-71, 1971-72, 1972-73, 1978-79, 1979-80, 1980-81, 1981-82, 1982-83, 1984-85, 1987-88, 1988-89, 1989-90, 1990-91, 1991-92, 1992-93, 1993-94, 1995-96.